THE
CIVILIZATION
OF THE
RENAISSANCE
IN ITALY

VOLUME II

*the text of this book is printed
on 100% recycled paper*

THREE WOMEN FROM THE PICTURE OF SAINT CHRYSOSTOM
By Sebastiano del Piombo
S. Giovanni e Crisostomo, Venice

THE CIVILIZATION OF THE RENAISSANCE IN ITALY

VOLUME II

JACOB BURCKHARDT

HARPER COLOPHON BOOKS
Harper & Row, Publishers
New York, Hagerstown, San Francisco, London

THE CIVILIZATION OF THE RENAISSANCE IN ITALY

Introduction copyright © 1958 by Harper & Row, Publishers, Incorporated
Printed in the United States of America

This edition of *The Civilization of the Renaissance* was
first published in the United States by Harper & Row,
Publishers, Incorporated in 1929.

First HARPER COLOPHON edition published 1975.

ISBN: 0-06-090460-7

Translator's Note

This translation is made from the fifteenth edition of the German original,
with slight additions to the text and large additions to the notes by Dr. Ludwig
Geiger and Professor Walther Götz.

In a few cases where Dr. Geiger's and Professor Götz's views differ from
those taken by Dr. Burckhardt I have called attention to the fact by bracket-
ing their opinions and adding their initials.

The illustrations in the present edition appear for the first time in an
English translation of this work. Previous English editions have not been
illustrated. It is hoped that the illustrations will be found to be a valuable
adjunct to the text.

S. G. C. MIDDLEMORE

Library of Congress catalog card number: 58-10149 - Vol. II

78 79 80   20 19 18

CONTENTS

ILLUSTRATIONS

PLATES

ILLUSTRATIONS

ILLUSTRATIONS

PART IV

THE DISCOVERY OF THE WORLD
AND OF MAN

CHAPTER I

JOURNEYS OF THE ITALIANS

FREED from the countless bonds which elsewhere in Europe checked progress, having reached a high degree of individual development and been schooled by the teachings of antiquity, the Italian mind now turned to the discovery of the outward universe, and to the representation of it in speech and in form.

On the journeys of the Italians to distant parts of the world we can here make but a few general observations. The Crusades had opened unknown distances to the European mind, and awakened in all the passion for travel and adventure. It may be hard to indicate precisely the point where this passion allied itself with, or became the servant of, the thirst for knowledge; but it was in Italy that this was first and most completely the case. Even in the Crusades the interest of the Italians was wider than that of other nations, since they already were a naval Power and had commercial relations with the East. From time immemorial the Mediterranean Sea had given to the nations that dwelt on its shores mental impulses different from those which governed the peoples of the North; and never, from the very structure of their character, could the Italians be adventurers in the sense which the word bore among the Teutons. After they were once at home in all the eastern harbours of the Mediterranean it was natural that the most enterprising among them should be led to join that vast international movement of the Mohammedans which there found its outlet. A new half of the world lay, as it were, freshly discovered before them. Or, like Polo of Venice, they were caught in the current of the Mongolian peoples, and carried on to the steps of the throne of the Great Khan. At an early period we find Italians sharing in the discoveries made in the Atlantic Ocean; it was the Genoese who in the thirteenth century found the Canary Islands.[1] In the same year, 1291, when Ptolemais, the last remnant of the Christian East, was lost, it was again the Genoese who made the first known attempt to find

[1] Luigi Bossi, *Vita di Cristoforo Colombo*, in which there is a sketch of earlier Italian journeys and discoveries, pp. 91 *sqq.* For a printed collection of letters and passages from contemporary chronicles referring to the discovery of the New World see the *Raccolta di Documenti e Studi pubblicati dalla R. Commissione Colombiana pel Quarto Centenario della Scoperta dell' America*, iii, 2, 1893 (15 folio vols., Rome, 1892–96).

a sea-passage to the East Indies.[1] Columbus himself is but the greatest of a long list of Italians who, in the service of the Western nations, sailed into distant seas. The true discoverer, however, is not the man who first chances to stumble upon anything, but the man who finds what he has sought. Such a one alone stands in a link with the thoughts and interests of his predecessors, and this relationship will also determine the account he gives of his search. For which reason the Italians, although their claim to be the first comers on this

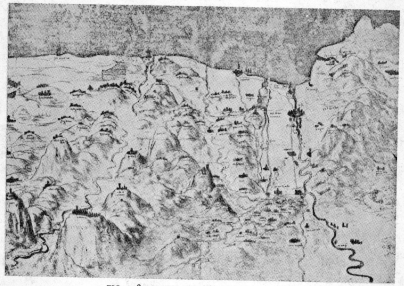

FIG. 128. RELIEF MAP OF PART OF TUSCANY
By Leonardo da Vinci

or that shore may be disputed, will yet retain their title to be pre-eminently the nation of discoverers for the whole latter part of the Middle Ages. The fuller proof of this assertion belongs to the special history of discoveries.[2] Yet ever and again we turn with admiration to the august figure of the great Genoese, by whom a new continent beyond the ocean was demanded, sought, and found; and who was the first to be able to say *il mondo è poco*—the world is not so large as men have thought. At the time when Spain gave Alexander VI to the Italians Italy gave Columbus to the Spaniards. Only a few weeks before the death of that Pope (July 7, 1503) Columbus wrote from Jamaica his noble letter to the thankless Catholic kings, which the ages to come can never read without

[1] See on this subject a treatise by Pertz, *Der älteste Versuch zur Entdeckung des Seewegs nach Ostindien*. An inadequate account is to be found in Æneas Sylvius, *Europæ Status sub Frederico III Imp.*, cap. 44 (in Freher's *Scriptores*, ii, 87, ed. 1624). On Æneas Sylvius see Peschel, *op. cit.*, pp. 217 *sqq.*

[2] *Cf.* O. Peschel, *Geschichte der Erdkunde*, 2nd ed., by Sophus Ruge, pp. 209 *sqq., et passim* (Munich, 1877).

profound emotion.[1]   In a codicil to his will,[2] dated Valladolid, May 4, 1506, he bequeathed to his " beloved home, the Republic of Genoa, the prayer-book which Pope Alexander had given him, and which in prison, in conflict, and in every kind of adversity had been to him the greatest of comforts."   It seems as if these words cast upon the abhorred name of Borgia one last gleam of grace and mercy.

The development of geographical and the allied sciences among the Italians must, like the history of their voyages, be touched upon but very briefly.   A superficial comparison of their achievements with those of other nations shows

FIG. 129. THE ARTIST
From the *View of Florence.   Cf.* plate facing p. 84
Photo Hiersemann, Leipzig

an early and striking superiority on their part.   Where in the middle of the fifteenth century could be found anywhere but in Italy such a union of geographical, statistical, and historical knowledge as was found in Æneas Sylvius? Not only in his great geographical work, but in his letters and commentaries he describes with equal mastery landscapes, cities, manners, industries and products, political conditions and constitutions, wherever he can use his own observation or the evidence of eye-witnesses.   What he takes from books is naturally of less moment.   Even the short sketch [3] of that valley in the Tyrolese Alps where Frederick III had given him a benefice, and still more his description of Scotland, leaves untouched none of the relations of human life, and displays a power and method of unbiased observation and comparison impossible in any but a

[1] Published in the *Scritti di C. Colombo*, ii, 205 (Rome, 1894).

[2] Its authenticity, however, is questioned.—W. G.]

[3] *Pii II Comment.*, lib. i, p. 14.   That he did not always observe correctly, and sometimes filled up the picture from his fancy, is clearly shown, for example, by his description of Basel.   Yet his merit on the whole is nevertheless great.   On the description of Basel see G. Voigt, *Enea Silvio*, i, 228; on Æneas Sylvius as geographer, ii, 302-309.   *Cf.* i, 91 *sqq.*

countryman of Columbus, trained in the school of the ancients. Thousands saw and, in part, knew what he did, but they felt no impulse to draw a picture of it, and were unconscious that the world desired such pictures.

In geography,[1] as in other matters, it is vain to attempt to distinguish how much is to be attributed to the study of the ancients, and how much to the special genius of the Italians. They saw and treated the things of this world from an objective point of view, even before they were familiar with ancient literature, partly because they were themselves a half-ancient people, and partly because their political circumstances predisposed them to it; but they would not have attained to such perfection so rapidly had not the old geographers showed them the way. The influence of the existing Italian geographies on the spirit and tendencies of the travellers and discoverers was also inestimable. Even the simple *dilettante* of a science—if in the present case we should assign to Æneas Sylvius so low a rank—can diffuse just that sort of general interest in the subject which prepares for new pioneers the indispensable groundwork of a favourable predisposition in the public mind. True discoverers in any science know well what they owe to such mediation.

[1] In the sixteenth century Italy continued to be the home of geographical literature, at a time when the discoverers themselves belonged almost exclusively to the countries on the shores of the Atlantic. Native geography produced in the middle of the century the great and remarkable work of Leandro Alberti, *Descrizione di Tutta l' Italia* (1582). In the first half of the sixteenth century the maps in Italy were in advance of those of other countries. See Wieser, *Der Portulan des Infanten Philipp II von Spanien* in *Sitzungsberichte der Wien. Acad. Phil. Hist. Kl.*, Bd. 82, pp. 541 *sqq.* (1876). For the different Italian maps and voyages of discovery see the excellent work of Oscar Peschel, *Abhandl. zur Erd- und Völkerkunde* (Leipzig, 1878). *Cf.* also, *inter alia*, Berchet, *Il Planisfero di Giovanni Leandro del' Anno 1452 fa-simil nella Grandezza del' Original Nota Illustrativa*, 16 S. 4⁰. (Venezia, 1879). *Cf.* Voigt, ii, 516, and G. B. de Rossi, *Piante Iconografiche di Roma Anteriori al Secolo XVI* (Rome, 1879). For Petrarch's attempt to draw out a map of Italy *cf.* Flavio Biondo, *Italia Illustrata*, ed. Basil., pp. 352 *sqq.*, also *Petr. Epist. var. LXI*, ed. Fracassetti, iii, 476. A remarkable attempt at a map of Europe, Asia, and Africa is to be found on the obverse of a medal of Charles IV of Anjou, executed by Francesco da Laurana in 1462.

CHAPTER II

Natural Science in Italy

FOR the position of the Italians in the sphere of the natural sciences we must refer the reader to the special treatises on the subject, of which the only one with which we are familiar is the superficial and depreciatory work of Libri.[1] The dispute as to the priority of particular discoveries concerns us all the less since we hold that, at any time, and among any civilized people, a man may appear who, starting with very scanty preparation, is driven by an irresistible impulse into the path of scientific investigation, and through his native gifts achieves the most astonishing success. Such men were Gerbert of Reims and Roger Bacon. That they were masters of the whole knowledge of the age in their several departments was a natural consequence of the spirit in which they worked. When once the veil of illusion was torn asunder, when once the dread of nature and the slavery to books and tradition were overcome, countless problems lay before them for solution. It is another matter when a whole people takes a natural delight in the study and investigation of nature, at a time when other nations are indifferent—that is to say, when the discoverer is not threatened or wholly ignored, but can count on the friendly support of congenial spirits. That this was the case in Italy is unquestionable.[2] The Italian students of nature trace with pride in the *Divine Comedy* the hints and proofs of Dante's scientific interest in nature.[3] On his claim to priority in this or that discovery or reference we must leave the men of science to decide; but every layman must be struck by the wealth of his observations on the external world, shown merely in his pictures and comparisons. He more than any other modern poet takes them from reality, whether in nature or human life, and uses them, never as mere ornament, but in order to give the reader the fullest and most adequate sense of his meaning. It is in astronomy that he appears chiefly as a scientific specialist, though it must not be forgotten that many astronomical allusions in his great poem, which now appear to us learned, must then have been intelligible to the general reader. Dante, learning apart, appeals to a popular knowledge of the heavens, which the Italians of his day,

[1] Libri, *Histoire des Sciences Mathématiques en Italie* (4 vols., Paris, 1838).

[2] To pronounce a conclusive judgment on this point the growth of the habit of collecting observations, in other than the mathematical sciences, would need to be illustrated in detail. But this lies outside the limits of our task.

[3] Libri, *op. cit.*, ii, pp. 174 *sqq.* See also Dante's treatise *De Aqua et Terra*, and W. Schmidt, *Dantes Stellung in der Geschichte der Kosmographie* (Graz, 1876). The passages bearing on geography and natural science from the *Tesoro* of Brunetto Latini are published separately, *Il Trattato della Sfera di S. Br. L.*, by Bart. Sorio (Milan, 1858), who has added Brunetto Latini's system of historical chronology.

from the mere fact that they were a nautical people, had in common with the ancients. This knowledge of the rising and setting of the constellations has been rendered superfluous to the modern world by calendars and clocks, and with it gone whatever interest in astronomy the people may once have had. Nowadays, with our schools and text-books, every child knows—what Dante

FIG. 130. LUCA PACCIOLI
By Jacopo de' Barbari
Naples, Museo Nazionale

did not know—that the earth moves round the sun; but the interest once taken in the subject itself has given place, except in the case of astronomical specialists, to the most absolute indifference.

The pseudo-science, which also dealt with the stars, proves nothing against the inductive spirit of the Italians of that day. That spirit was but crossed, and at times overcome, by the passionate desire to penetrate the future. We shall recur to the subject of astrology when we come to speak of the moral and religious character of the people.

The Church treated this and other pseudo-sciences nearly always with toleration, and showed itself actually hostile even to genuine science only when a charge of heresy or necromancy was also in question—which certainly was often the case. A point which it would be interesting to decide is this: whether, and in what cases, the Dominican (and also the Franciscan) Inquisitors in Italy were conscious of the false-hood of the charges, and yet condemned the accused, either to oblige some enemy of the prisoner or from hatred to natural science, and particularly to experiments. The latter doubtless occurred, but it is not easy to prove the fact. What helped to cause such persecutions in the North—namely, the opposition made to the innovators by the upholders of the received official, scholastic system of nature—was of little or no weight in Italy. Pietro of Albano at the beginning of the fourteenth century is well known to have fallen a victim to the envy of another physician, who accused him before the Inquisition of heresy and magic; [1] and something of the same kind may have happened in the case of his Paduan contemporary, Giovannino Sanguinnacci, who was known as an innovator in medical practice. He escaped, however, with banishment. Nor must it be forgotten that the inquisitorial power of the Dominicans was exercised less uniformly in Italy than in the North. Tyrants and free cities in the fourteenth

FIG. 131. FLOWER-STUDY
From the sketch-book of Jacopo Bellini
Paris, Louvre

century treated the clergy at times with such sovereign contempt that very different matters from natural science went unpunished. [2] But when, with

[1] Scardeonius, *De Urb. Patav. Antiq.*, in Græv., *Thesaur. Ant. Ital.*, tom. vi, Pars III, col. 227. Albano died in 1312 during the investigation; his statue was burnt. On Giovannino Sanguinnacci see *op. cit.*, col. 228 *sqq.* *Cf.* on him Fabricius, *Bibl. Lat.*, *s.v.* Petrus de Apono. Sprenger in *Esch. u. Gruber*, i, 33. He translated (1292–93) astrological works of Abraham ibn Esra, printed 1506. [2] See below, Part VI, Chapter II.

the fifteenth century, antiquity became the leading power in Italy the breach it made in the old system was turned to account by every branch of secular science. Humanism, nevertheless, attracted to itself the best strength of the nation, and thereby, no doubt, did injury to the inductive investigation of nature.[1] Here and there the Inquisition suddenly started into life, and punished or burned physicians as blasphemers or magicians. In such cases it is hard to discover what was the true motive underlying the condemnation. And after all, at the close of the fifteenth century Italy, with Paolo Toscanelli, Luca

FIG. 132. STUDY OF A LION
From the sketch-book of Jacopo Bellini
Paris, Louvre

Paccioli, and Leonardo da Vinci, held incomparably the highest place among European nations in mathematics and the natural sciences, and the learned men of every country, even Regiomontanus and Copernicus, confessed themselves its pupils.[2]

A significant proof of the widespread interest in natural history is found in the zeal which showed itself at an early period for the collection and comparative study of plants and animals. Italy claims to be the first creator of botanical gardens, though possibly they may have served a chiefly practical end, and the claim to priority may be itself disputed.[3] It is of far greater importance that princes and wealthy men in laying out their pleasure-gardens instinctively made a point of collecting the greatest possible number of different plants in all their species and varieties. Thus in the fifteenth century the noble grounds of the

---

[1] See the exaggerated complaints of Libri, *op. cit.*, ii, pp. 258 *sqq.* Regrettable as it may be that a people so highly gifted did not devote more of its strength to the natural sciences, we nevertheless believe that it pursued, and in part attained, still more important ends.

[2] On the studies of the latter in Italy *cf.* the thorough investigation by C. Malagola in his work on Codrus Urceus (cap. vii, 360–366, Bologna, 1878).

[3] Italians also laid out botanical gardens in foreign countries—for example, Angelo of Florence, a contemporary of Petrarch, in Prague (Friedjung, *Carl IV*, p. 311, note 4).

Medicean Villa Careggi appear from the descriptions we have of them to have been almost a botanical garden,[1] with countless specimens of different trees and shrubs. Of the same kind was a villa of Cardinal Trivulzio, at the beginning of the sixteenth century, in the Roman Campagna toward Tivoli,[2] with hedges made up of various species of roses, with trees of every description—the fruit-trees especially showing an astonishing variety—with twenty different sorts of vines and a large kitchen-garden. This is evidently something very different from the score or two of familiar medicinal plants which were to be found

FIG. 133. CHEETAHS
From the sketch-book of Jacopo Bellini
Paris, Louvre

in the garden of any castle or monastery in Western Europe. Along with a careful cultivation of fruit for the purposes of the table we find an interest in the plant for its own sake, on account of the pleasure it gives to the eye. We learn from the history of art at how late a period this passion for botanical collections was laid aside, and gave place to what was considered the picturesque style of landscape-gardening.

The collections of foreign animals too not only gratified curiosity, but served also the higher purposes of observation. The facility of transport from the southern and eastern harbours of the Mediterranean and the mildness of the Italian climate made it practicable to buy the largest animals of the South, or to accept them as presents from the Sultans.[3] The cities and princes were especially anxious to keep live lions, even when the lion was not, as in Florence,

---

[1] *Alexandri Bracii Descriptio Horti Laurentii Med.*, printed as Appendix No. 58 to Roscoe's *Lorenzo de' Medici*. Also to be found in the appendices to Fabroni's *Laurentius*.

[2] *Mondanarii Villa*, printed in the *Poemata Aliqua Insignia Illustr. Poetar. Recent.*

[3] On the zoological garden at Palermo under Henry VI see Otto de S. Blasio, for the year 1194 (Böhmer, *Fontes*, iii, p. 623); that of Henry I of England in the park of Woodstock (William of Malmesbury, p. 638) contained lions, leopards, camels, and a porcupine, all gifts of foreign princes.

the emblem of the State.[1] The lions' den was generally in or near the Government palace, as in Perugia and Florence; in Rome it lay on the slope of the Capitol. The beasts sometimes served as executioners of political judgments,[2] and no doubt, apart from this, they kept alive a certain terror in the popular

FIG. 134. SIGISMONDO MALATESTA WITH HIS DOGS
By Piero della Francesca
Rimini, Cathedral

mind. Their condition was also held to be ominous of good or evil. Their fertility especially was considered a sign of public prosperity, and no less a man than Giovanni Villani thought it worth recording that he was present at the delivery of a lioness.[3] The cubs were often given to allied states and princes,

[1] As such he was called, whether painted or carved in stone, "Marzocco." At Pisa eagles were kept. See the commentators on Dante, *Inferno*, xxxiii, 22. The falcon in Boccaccio, *Decamerone*, v, 9. See for the whole subject *Due Trattati del Governo e delle Infermità degli Uccelli, Testi di Lingua Inediti* (Rome, 1864). They are works of the fourteenth century, possibly translated from the Persian.

[2] See the extract from Ægid. Viterb., in Papencordt, *Gesch. der Stadt Rom im Mittelalter*, p. 367, note, with an incident of the year 1328. Combats of wild animals among themselves and with dogs served to amuse the people on great occasions. At the reception of Pius II and of Galeazzo Maria Sforza at Florence in 1459, in an enclosed space on the Piazza della Signoria, bulls, horses, boars, dogs, lions, and a giraffe were turned out together, but the lions lay down and refused to attack the other animals. Cf. *Ricordi di Firenze, Rer. Ital. Script. ex Florent. Codd.*, tom. ii, col. 741. A different account in *Vita Pii II*, in Murat., iii, ii, col. 977. Voigt, *Enea Silvio*, iii, pp. 40 *sqq.* A second giraffe was presented to Lorenzo the Magnificent by the Mameluke Sultan Kaytbey. Cf. Paul. Jovius, *Vita Leonis X*, lib. i. In Lorenzo's menagerie one magnificent lion was especially famous, and his destruction by the other lions was reckoned a presage of the death of his owner.

[3] Gio. Villani, x, 185; xi, 66. Matteo Villani, iii, 90; v, 68. It was a bad omen if the lions fought, and worse still if they killed one another. Cf. Varchi, *Stor. Fiorent.*, iii, p. 143. Matteo Villani devotes the first of the two chapters quoted to prove (1) that lions were born in Italy, and (2) that they came into the world alive.

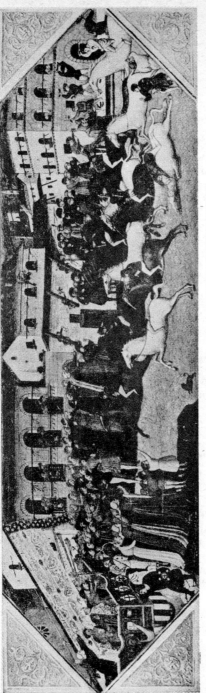

FIG. 135. HORSERACING IN THE FIRST HALF OF THE FIFTEENTH CENTURY

By a Florentine artist

Cleveland Museum

or to *condottieri* as a reward of valour.[1] In addition to the lions the Florentines began very early to keep leopards, for which a special keeper was appointed.[2] Borso[3] of Ferrara used to set his lions to fight with bulls, bears, and wild boars.

By the end of the fifteenth century, however, true menageries (*serragli*), now reckoned part of the suitable appointments of a Court, were kept by many of the princes. "It belongs to the position of the great," says Matarazzo,[4] "to keep horses, dogs, mules, falcons and other birds, Court jesters, singers, and foreign animals." The menagerie at Naples in the time of Ferrante and others contained a giraffe and a zebra, presented, it seems, by the ruler of Bagdad.[5] Filippo Maria Visconti possessed not only horses which cost him five hundred or a thousand pieces of gold each, and valuable English dogs, but a number of leopards brought from all parts of the East; the expense of his hunting-birds, which were collected from the countries of Northern Europe, amounted to three thousand pieces of gold a month.[6] "The Cremonese say that the Emperor Frederick II brought an elephant into their city, sent him from India by Prester John," we read in Brunetto Latini; Petrarch records the dying out of the elephants in Italy.[7] King Emanuel the Great of Portugal knew well what he was about when he presented Leo X with an elephant and a rhinoceros.[8] It was under such circumstances that the foundations of a scientific zoology and botany were laid.

A practical fruit of these zoological studies was the establishment of studs, of which the Mantuan, under Francesco Gonzaga, was esteemed the first in

[1] *Cron. di Perugia, Archiv. Stor.*, xvii, ii, p. 77, year 1497. A pair of lions once escaped from Perugia; *ibid.*, xvi, i, p. 382, year 1434. Florence, for example, sent to King Wladislaw of Poland (May 1406) a pair of lions "ut utriusque sexus animalia ad procreandos catulos haberetis." The accompanying statement is amusing in a diplomatic document: "Sunt equidem hi leones Florentini, et satis quantum natura promittere potuit mansueti deposita feritate, quam insitam habent, hique in Gætulorum regionibus nascuntur et Indorum, in quibus multitudo dictorum animalium evalescit, sicuti prohibent naturales. Et cum leonum complexio sit frigoribus inimica, quod natura sagax ostendit, natura in regionibus æstu ferventibus generantur, necessarium est, quod vostra serenitas, si dictorum animalium vitam et sobolis propagationem, ut remur, desiderat, faciat provideri, quod in locis calidis educentur et maneant. Conveniunt nempe cum regia majestate leones quoniam leo græce latine rex dicitur. Sicut enim rex dignitate potentia, magnanimitate ceteros homines antecellit, sic leonis generositas et vigor imperterritus animalia cuncta præsit. Et sicut rex, sic leo adversus imbecilles et timidos clementissimum se ostendit, et adversus inquietos et tumidos terribilem se offert animadversione justissima"— *Cod. Epistolaris Sæculi. Mon. Med. Ævi Hist. Res Gestas Poloniæ Illustr.*, p. 25 (Krakau, 1876).

[2] Gaye, *Carteggio*, i, p. 422, year 1291. The Visconti used trained leopards for hunting hares, which were started by little dogs. See Kobel, *Wildanger*, p. 247, where later instances of hunting with leopards are mentioned.

[3] *Strozzii Poetæ*, p. 146, *De Leone Borsii Ducis*. The lion spares the hare and the small dog, imitating, so says the poet, his master. *Cf.* fol. 188, the words, "et inclusis condita septa feris," and fol. 193, an epigram of fourteen lines, "in leporarii ingressu quam maximi"; see *ibid.* for the hunting-park.

[4] *Cron. di Perugia, loc. cit.*, xvi, ii, p. 199. Something of the same kind is to be found in Petrarch, *De Remed. utriusque Fortunæ*, i, 61, but less clearly expressed. Here Gaudium, in the conversation with Ratio, boasts of owning monkeys and *ludicra animalia*.

[5] Jov. Pontan., *De Magnificentia*. In the zoological garden of the Cardinal of Aquileia, at Albano, there were, in 1463, peacocks and Indian fowls and Syrian goats with long ears. *Pii II Comment.*, lib. xi, pp. 562 *sqq.*

[6] *Decembrio*, in Murat., xx, col. 1012.

[7] Brunetti Latini, *Tesoro*, lib. i (ed. Chabaille, Paris, 1863). In Petrarch's time there were no elephants in Italy. "Itaque et in Italia avorum memoria unum Frederico Romanorum principi fuisse et nunc Egyptio tyranno nonnisi unicum esse fama est" (*De Rem. utr. Fort.*, i, 58).

[8] The details which are most amusing are in Paul. Jovius, *Elogia*, on Tristanus Acunius. On the porcupines and ostriches in the Pallazzo Strozzi see Rabelais, *Pantagruel*, iv, chapter 11. Lorenzo the Magnificent received a giraffe from Egypt through some merchants, Baluz., *Miscell.*, iv, 416. The elephant sent to Leo was greatly bewailed by the people when it died, its portrait was painted, and verses on it were written by the younger Beroaldus.

Europe.[1] All interest in and knowledge of the different breeds of horses is as old, no doubt, as riding itself, and the crossing of the European with the Asiatic must have been common from the time of the Crusades. In Italy a special inducement to perfect the breed was offered by the prizes at the horse-races held in every considerable town in the peninsula. In the Mantuan stables were found the infallible winners in these contests, as well as the best military chargers, and the horses best suited by their stately appearance for

FIG. 136. THE EQUESTRIAN HALL IN THE PALAZZO DEL TE, MANTUA

presents to great people. Gonzaga kept stallions and mares from Spain, Ireland, Africa, Thrace, and Cilicia, and for the sake of the last he cultivated the friendship of the Sultan. All possible experiments were here tried in order to produce the most perfect animals.

Even human menageries were not wanting. The famous Cardinal Ippolito de' Medici,[2] bastard of Giuliano, Duke of Nemours, kept at his strange Court a troop of barbarians who talked no fewer than twenty different languages, and who were all of them perfect specimens of their races. Among them were incomparable *voltigeurs* of the best blood of the North African Moors, Tartar bowmen, Negro wrestlers, Indian divers, and Turks, who generally accompanied the Cardinal on his hunting expeditions. When he was overtaken by an early death (1535) this motley band carried the corpse on their shoulders

---

[1] *Cf.* Paul. Jovius, *Elogia*, p. 234, speaking of Francesco Gonzaga. For the luxury at Milan in this respect see Bandello, ii, *Nov.* 3 and 8. In the narrative poems we also sometimes hear the opinion of a judge of horses. *Cf.* Pulci, *Morgante*, xv, 105 *sqq.*   [2] Paul. Jovius, *Elogia*, speaking of Hipp. Medices, pp. 307 *sqq.*

from Itri to Rome, and mingled with the general mourning for the open-handed Cardinal their medley of tongues and violent gesticulations.[1]

These scattered notices of the relations of the Italians to natural science, and their interest in the wealth and variety of the products of nature, are only fragments of a great subject. No one is more conscious than the author of the defects in his knowledge on this point. Of the multitude of special works in which the subject is adequately treated even the names are but imperfectly known to him.

FIG. 137. DRAWING OF A BEETLE
By Leonardo da Vinci

[1] At this point a few notices on slavery in Italy at the time of the Renaissance will not be out of place. A short but important passage in Jov. Pontan., *De Obedientia*, lib. iii, cap. i: "An homo, cum liber natura sit, domino parere debeat?" In North Italy there were no slaves. Elsewhere even Christians, as well as Circassians and Bulgarians, were bought from the Turks and made to serve till they had earned their ransom. The negroes, on the contrary, remained slaves; but it was not permitted, at least in the kingdom of Naples, to emasculate them. The word *moro* signifies any dark-skinned man; the negro was called *moro nero*. Fabroni, *Cosmos*, Adnot. 110, document on the sale of a female Circassian slave (1427); Adnot. 141, list of the female slaves of Cosimo.—Nantiporto, in Murat., iii, ii, col. 1106. Innocent VIII received a hundred Moors as a present from Ferdinand the Catholic, and gave them to cardinals and other great men (1488).—Marsuccio, *Novelle*, 14, sale of slaves; 24 and 25, negro slaves who also (for the benefit of their owner ?) work as *facchini*, and gain the love of the women; 48, Moors from Tunis caught by Catalans and sold at Pisa.—Gaye, *Carteggio*, i, 360, manumission and reward of a negro slave in a Florentine will (1490).—Paul. Jovius, *Elogia*, *sub*. Franc. Sfortia; Porzio, *Congiura*, iii, 194; and Comines, *Charles VIII*, Chapter 17, negroes as gaolers and executioners of the house of Aragon in Naples.—Paul. Jovius, *Elogia*, *sub* Galeatio, negroes as followers of the prince on his excursions.—Æneæ Sylvii, *Opera*, p. 456, a negro slave as a musician.—Paul. Jovius, *De Piscibus*, cap. 3, a (free?) negro as diver and swimming-master at Genoa.—Alex. Benedictus, *De Carolo VIII*, in Eccard, *Scriptores*, ii, col. 1608, a negro (Æthiops) as superior officer at Venice, according to which we are justified in thinking of Othello as a negro.—Bandello, iii, *Nov.* 21, when a slave at Genoa deserved punishment he was sold away to Iviza, one of the Balearic isles, to carry salt.

The foregoing remarks, although they make no claim to completeness, may be allowed to stand as they are on account of the excellent selection of instances they contain, and because they have not met with sufficient notice in the works upon the subject. A good deal has been written on the slave-trade in Italy. The very curious book of Filippo Zamboni, *Gli Ezzelini, Dante e gli Schiavi, ossia Roma e la Schiavitù Personale Domestica. Con Documenti Inediti. Seconda Edizione Aumentata* (Vienna, 1870), does not contain what the title promises, but gives, pp. 241 *sqq.*, valuable information on the slave-trade; p. 270, a remarkable document on the buying and selling of a female slave; p. 282, a list of various slaves (with the place where they were bought and sold, their home, age, and price) in the thirteenth and three following centuries. A treatise by Wattenbach, *Sklavenhandel im Mittelalter* (*Anzeiger für Kunde der deutschen Vorzeit*, pp. 37-40, 1874), refers only in part to Italy: Clement V decides in 1309 that the Venetian prisoners should be made slaves; in 1501, after the capture of Capua, many Capuan women were sold at Rome for a low price. In the *Monum. Historica Slavorum Meridionalium*, ed. Vinc. Macusceo, tom. i (Warsaw, 1874), we read at p. 199 a decision (Ancona, 1458) that the "Greci, Turci, Tartari, Sarraceni, Bossinenses, Burgari vel Albanenses," should be and always remain slaves, unless their masters freed them by a legal document. Egnatius, *Exempl. Ill. Vir.*, Ven., fol. 246a, praises Venice on the ground that "servorum Venetis ipsis nullum unquam usum extitisse"; but, on the other hand, *cf.* Zamboni, p. 223, and especially Vincenzo Lazari, "Del traffico e delle condizioni degli schiavi, in Venezia nel tempo di mezzo," in *Miscellanea di Stor. Ital.*, i, 463-501 (Torino, 1862).

CHAPTER III

The Discovery of Natural Beauty

BUT. outside the sphere of scientific investigation there is another way to draw near to nature. The Italians are the first among modern peoples by whom the outward world was seen and felt as something beautiful.[1]

The power to do so is always the result of a long and complicated development, and its origin is not easily detected, since a dim feeling of this kind may exist long before it shows itself in poetry and painting, and thereby becomes conscious of itself. Among the ancients, for example, art and poetry had gone through the whole circle of human interests before they turned to the representation of nature, and even then the latter filled always a limited and subordinate place. And yet from the time of Homer downward the powerful impression made by nature upon man is shown by countless verses and chance expressions. The Germanic races, which founded their states on the ruins of the Roman Empire, were thoroughly and specially fitted to understand the spirit of natural scenery; and though Christianity compelled them for a while to see in the springs and mountains, in the lakes and woods, which they had till then revered, the working of evil demons, yet this transitional conception was soon outgrown. By the year 1200, at the height of the Middle Ages, a genuine, hearty enjoyment of the external world was again in existence, and found lively expression in the minstrelsy of different nations,[2] which gives evidence of the sympathy felt with all the simple phenomena of nature—spring with its flowers, the green fields, and the woods. But these pictures are all foreground without perspective. Even the Crusaders, who travelled so far and saw so much, are not recognizable as such in these poems. The epic poetry, which describes armour and costumes so fully, does not attempt more than a sketch of outward nature; and even the great Wolfram von Eschenbach scarcely anywhere gives us an adequate picture of the scene on which his heroes move. From these poems it would never be guessed that their noble authors in all countries inhabited or visited lofty castles commanding distant prospects. Even in the Latin poems of the wandering clerks (p. 180) we find no traces of a distant view—of landscape properly so called—but what lies near is sometimes described with a glow and splendour which none of the knightly minstrels can surpass. What picture of the Grove of

---

[1] It is hardly necessary to refer the reader to the famous chapters on this subject in Humboldt's *Kosmos.*

[2] See on this subject the observations of Wilhelm Grimm, quoted by Humboldt in the work referred to.

Love can equal that of the Italian poet—for such we take him to be—of the twelfth century?

> Immortalis fieret
> Ibi manens homo;
> Arbor ibi quælibet
> Suo gaudet pomo;
> Viæ myrrha, cinnamo
> Fragrant, et amomo—
> Conjectari poterat
> Dominus ex domo,[1] etc.

To the Italian mind, at all events, nature had by this time lost its taint of sin, and had shaken off all trace of demoniacal powers. St Francis of Assisi, in his *Hymn to the Sun*, frankly praises the Lord for creating the heavenly bodies and the four elements.

But the unmistakable proofs of a deepening effect of nature on the human

FIG. 138. PART OF THE FRAME OF GHIBERTI'S "GATE OF PARADISE" IN THE BAPTISTERY, FLORENCE

spirit begin with Dante. Not only does he awaken in us by a few vigorous lines the sense of the morning airs and the trembling light on the distant ocean, or of the grandeur of the storm-beaten forest, but he makes the ascent of lofty peaks, with the only possible object of enjoying the view [2]—the first man, perhaps, since the days of antiquity who did so. In Boccaccio we can do little more than infer how country scenery affected him; [3] yet his pastoral romances show his imagination to have been filled with it. But the significance of nature for a receptive spirit is fully and clearly displayed by Petrarch—one of the first truly modern men. That clear soul—who first collected from the literature of all countries evidence of the origin and progress of the sense of natural beauty, and himself, in his *Ansichten der Natur*, achieved the noblest masterpiece of

---

[1] *Carmina Burana*, p. 162, *De Phyllide et Flora*, str. 66.

[2] It would be hard to say what else he had to do at the top of the Bismantova, in the province of Reggio, *Purgatorio*, iv, 26. [Renier (*Giorn. Stor.*, 37, 415) questions whether Dante ever did climb high mountains.— W. G.] The precision with which he brings before us all the parts of his supernatural world shows a remarkable sense of form and space. That there was a belief in the existence of hidden treasures on the tops of mountains, and that such spots were regarded with superstitious terror, may be clearly inferred from the *Chron. Novaliciense*, ii, 5, in Pertz, *Scriptores*, vii, and *Monum. Hist. Patriæ, Scriptores*, iii.

[3] Besides the description of Baiæ in the *Fiammetta*, of the grove in the *Ameto*, etc., a passage in the *De Genealogia Deorum*, xv, 11, is of importance, where he enumerates a number of rural beauties—trees, meadows, brooks, flocks and herds, cottages, etc.—and adds that these things " animum mulcent "; their effect is " mentem in se colligere."

description—Alexander von Humboldt, has not done full justice to Petrarch; and, following in the steps of the great reaper, we may still hope to glean a few ears of interest and value.

Petrarch was not only a distinguished geographer—the first map of Italy

FIG. 139. THE MIRACLE OF THE SPRING
School of Giotto. *Assisi, Upper Church of S. Francesco*
Photo Deutsche Verlagsanstalt, Stuttgart

is said to have been drawn by his direction [1]—and not only a reproducer of the sayings of the ancients,[2] but felt himself the influence of natural beauty.   The

[1] Flavio Biondo, *Italia Illustrata* (ed. Basil.), pp. 352 *sqq.*. Cf. *Epist. Var.*, ed. Fracassetti (Lat.), iii, 476. On Petrarch's plan of writing a great geographical work see the proofs given by Attilio Hortis, *Accenni alle Scienze Naturali nelle Opere di G. Boccacci*, pp. 45 *sqq.* (Trieste, 1877).   Libri, *Hist. des Sciences Math.*, ii, p. 249.

[2] Although he is fond of referring to them—for example, *De Vita Solitaria* (*Opera*, ed. Basil., 1581), especially p. 241, where he quotes the description of a vine-arbour from St Augustine.

enjoyment of nature is, for him, the favourite accompaniment of intellectual pursuits; it was to combine the two that he lived in learned retirement at Vaucluse and elsewhere, that he at times fled from the world and from his age.[1] We should do him wrong by inferring from his weak and undeveloped power of describing natural scenery that he did not feel it deeply. His picture, for instance, of the lovely Gulf of Spezzia and Porto Venere, which he inserts at the end of the sixth book of the *Africa*, for the reason that none of the ancients or moderns had sung of it,[2] is no more than a simple enumeration, but the descriptions in letters to his friends of Rome, Naples, and other Italian cities in which he willingly lingered are picturesque and worthy of the subject. Petrarch is also conscious of the beauty of rock scenery, and is perfectly able to distinguish the picturesqueness from the utility of nature.[3] During his stay among the woods of Reggio the sudden sight of an impressive landscape so affected him that he resumed a poem which he had long laid aside.[4] But the deepest impression of all was made upon him by the ascent of Mont Ventoux, near Avignon.[5] An indefinable longing for a distant panorama grew stronger and stronger in him, till at length the accidental sight of a passage in Livy, where King Philip, the enemy of Rome, ascends the Hæmus, decided him. He thought that what was not blamed in a grey-headed monarch might be well *excused* in a young man of private station. The ascent of a mountain for its own sake was unheard of, and there could be no thought of the companionship of friends or acquaintances. Petrarch took with him only his younger brother and two country people from the last place where he halted. At the foot of the mountain an old herdsman besought him to turn back, saying that he himself had attempted to climb it fifty years before, and had brought home nothing but repentance, broken bones, and torn clothes, and that neither before nor after had anyone ventured to do the same. Nevertheless, they struggled forward and upward, till the clouds lay beneath their feet, and at last they reached the top. A description of the view from the summit would be looked for in vain not because the poet was insensible to it, but, on the contrary, because the impression was too overwhelming. His whole past life, with all its follies, rose before his mind; he remembered that ten years ago that day he had quitted Bologna a young man, and turned a longing gaze toward his native country; he opened a book which then was his constant companion, the *Confessions of St Augustine*, and his eye fell on the passage in the tenth chapter, " and men go forth, and admire lofty mountains and broad seas, and roaring torrents, and the ocean, and the course of the stars, and forget their own selves while doing so."

[1] *Epist. Fam.*, vii, 4, ed. Fracassetti, i, 367. "Interea utinam scire posses, quanta cum voluptate solivagus ac liber, inter montes et nemora, inter fontes et flumina, inter libros et maximorum hominum ingenia respiro, quamque me in ea, quæ ante sunt, cum Apostolo extendens et præterita oblivisci nitor et præsentia non videre." Cf. vi, 3, *op. cit.*, 316 *sqq.*, especially 334 *sqq.* Cf. L. Geiger, *Petrarca*, p. 75, note 5, and p. 269.

[2] " Jacuit sine carmine sacro." Cf. *Itinerar. Syriacum, Opp.*, p. 558.

[3] He distinguishes in the *Itinerar. Syr.*, p. 557, on the Riviera di Levante: "colles asperitate gratissima et mira fertilitate conspicuos." On the port of Gaeta see his *De Remediis utriusque Fortunæ*, i, 54.

[4] *Letter to Posterity*: " Subito loci specie percussus." Descriptions of great natural events: a storm at Naples, 1343, *Epist. Fam.*, i, 263 *sqq.*; an earthquake at Basel, 1355, *Epist. Seniles*, lib. x, 2, and *De Rem utr. Fort.*, ii, 91.

[5] *Epist. Fam.*, ed. Fracassetti, i, 193 *sqq.*

His brother, to whom he read these words, could not understand why he closed the book and said no more.

Some decades later, about 1360, Fazio degli Uberti describes in his rhyming geography [1] (p. 183), the wide panorama from the mountains of Auvergne, with the interest, it is true, of the geographer and antiquarian only, but still

FIG. 140. MADONNA IN THE WOOD
By Filippo Lippi
Berlin, Kaiser-Friedrich Museum

showing clearly that he himself had seen it. He must, however, have ascended far higher peaks, since he is familiar with facts which occur only at a height of 10,000 feet or more above the sea—mountain-sickness and its accompaniments —of which his imaginary comrade Solinus tries to cure him with a sponge dipped in an essence. The ascents of Parnassus and Olympus,[2] of which he speaks, are perhaps only fictions.

[1] *Dittamondo*, iii, cap. 9.
[2] *Dittamondo*, iii, cap. 21; iv, cap. 4. Papencordt, *Gesch. der Stadt Rom*, says that the Emperor Charles IV had a strong taste for beautiful scenery, and quotes on this point Pelzel, *Carl IV*, p. 456. (The two other

In the fifteenth century the great masters of the Flemish school, Hubert and Johann van Eyck, suddenly lifted the veil from nature. Their landscapes are not merely the fruit of an endeavour to reflect the real world in art, but have, even if expressed conventionally, a certain poetical meaning—in short, a soul. Their influence on the whole art of the West is undeniable, and extended to the landscape-painting of the Italians, but without preventing the characteristic interest of the Italian eye for nature from finding its own expression.

On this point, as in the scientific description of nature, Æneas Sylvius is again one of the most weighty voices of his time. Even if we grant the justice of all that has been said against his character, we must nevertheless admit that in few other men was the picture of the age and its culture so fully reflected, and that few came nearer to the normal type of the men of the early Renaissance. It may be added parenthetically that even in respect to his moral character he will not be fairly judged if we listen solely to the complaints of the German Church, which his fickleness helped to baulk of the council it so ardently desired.[1]

He here claims our attention as the first who not only enjoyed the magnificence of the Italian landscape, but described it with enthusiasm down to its minutest details. The ecclesiastical state and the South of Tuscany—his native home—he knew thoroughly, and after he became Pope he spent his leisure during the favourable season chiefly in excursions to the country. Then at last the gouty man was rich enough to have himself carried in a litter through the mountains and valleys; and when we compare his enjoyments with those of the Popes who succeeded him Pius, whose chief delight was in nature, antiquity, and simple but noble architecture, appears almost a saint. In the elegant and flowing Latin of his *Commentaries* he freely tells us of his happiness.[2]

His eye seems as keen and practised as that of any modern observer. He enjoys with rapture the panoramic splendour of the view from the summit of the Alban Hills—from Monte Cavo—whence he could see the shores of St Peter from Terracina and the promontory of Circe as far as Monte Argentaro, and the wide expanse of country round about, with the ruined cities of the past, and with the mountain chains of Central Italy beyond; and then his eye would turn to the green woods in the hollows beneath and the mountain-lakes among them. He feels the beauty of the position of Todi, crowning the vineyards and olive-clad slopes, looking down upon distant woods and upon the valley of the Tiber, where towns and castles rise above the winding river. The lovely hills about Siena, with villas and monasteries on every height, are his own

passages which he quotes do not say the same.) It is possible that the Emperor took this fancy from intercourse with the humanists (see above, p. 154). For the interest taken by Charles in natural science see H. Friedjung, *op. cit.*, p. 224, note 1.

[1] We may also compare Platina, *Vitæ Pontiff.*, p. 310: " Homo fuit [Pius II] verus, integer, apertus; nil habuit ficti, nil simulati "—an enemy of hypocrisy and superstition, courageous and consistent. See Voigt, ii, 261 *sqq.*, and iii, 724. He does not, however, give an analysis of the character of Pius.

[2] The most important passages are the following: *Pii II, P. M. Comment.*, lib. iv, p. 183, spring in his native country; lib. v, p. 251, summer residence at Tivoli; lib. vi, p. 306, the meal at the spring of Vicovaro; lib. viii, p. 378, the neighbourhood of Viterbo; p. 387, the mountain monastery of St Martin; p. 388, the Lake of Bolsena; lib. ix, p. 396, a splendid description of Monte Amiata; lib. x, p. 483, the situation of Monte Oliveto; p. 497, the view from Todi; lib. xi, p. 554, Ostia and Porto; p. 562, description of the Alban Hills; lib. xii, p. 609, Frascati and Grottaferrata; *cf.* pp. 568–571.

home, and his descriptions of them are touched with a peculiar feeling. Single picturesque glimpses charm him too, like the little promontory of Capo di Monte that stretches out into the Lake of Bolsena. "Rocky steps," we read, "shaded by vines, descend to the water's edge, where the evergreen oaks stand between the cliffs, alive with the song of thrushes." On the path round the Lake of Nemi, beneath the chestnuts and fruit-trees, he feels that here, if anywhere, a poet's soul must awake—here in the hiding-place of Diana! He often held

FIG. 141. LANDSCAPE
Part of the picture *The Crucifixion of Christ*, by Antonello da Messina
Antwerp Museum

consistories or received ambassadors under huge old chestnut-trees, or beneath the olives on the green sward by some gurgling spring. A view like that of a narrowing gorge, with a bridge arched boldly over it, awakens at once his artistic sense. Even the smallest details give him delight through something beautiful, or perfect, or characteristic in them—the blue fields of waving flax, the yellow gorse which covers the hills, even tangled thickets, or single trees, or springs, which seem to him like wonders of nature.

The height of his enthusiasm for natural beauty was reached during his stay on Monte Amiata in the summer of 1462, when plague and heat made the lowlands uninhabitable. Half-way up the mountain, in the old Lombard monastery of S. Salvatore, he and his Court took up their quarters. There, between the chestnuts which clothe the steep declivity, the eye may wander over all Southern Tuscany, with the towers of Siena in the distance. The ascent of the highest peak he left to his companions, who were joined by the Venetian envoy; they found at the top two vast blocks of stone one upon the other—perhaps the sacrificial altar of a prehistoric people—and fancied that in the far

FIG. 142. LANDSCAPE IN RAIN
Drawing by Leonardo da Vinci
Windsor

distance they saw Corsica and Sardinia [1] rising above the sea. In the cool air of the hills, among the old oaks and chestnuts, on the green meadows where there were no thorns to wound the feet and no snakes or insects to hurt or to

[1] So we must suppose it to have been written, not Sicily.

annoy, the Pope passed days of unclouded happiness. For the "Segnatura," which took place on certain days of the week, he selected on each occasion some new shady retreat [1] "novas in convallibus fontes et novas inveniens umbras, quæ dubiam facerent electionem." At such times the dogs would perhaps start a great stag from his lair, who, after defending himself awhile with hoofs

FIG. 143. THE FAMILY
By Giorgione
Venice, Palazzo Giovanelli

and antlers, would fly at last up the mountain. In the evening the Pope was accustomed to sit before the monastery on the spot from which the whole valley of the Paglia was visible, holding lively conversations with the cardinals. The courtiers who ventured down from the heights on their hunting expeditions found the heat below intolerable and the scorched plains like a very hell, while the monastery, with its cool, shady woods, seemed like an abode of the blessed.

All this is genuine modern enjoyment, not a reflection of antiquity. As surely as the ancients themselves felt in the same manner, so surely, nevertheless,

[1] He calls himself, with an allusion to his name, " Silvarum amator et varia videndi cupidus."

were the scanty expressions of the writers whom Pius knew insufficient to awaken in him such enthusiasm.[1]

The second great age of Italian poetry, which now followed at the end of the fifteenth and the beginning of the sixteenth century, as well as the Latin poetry of the same period, is rich in proofs of the powerful effect of nature on the human mind. The first glance at the lyric poets of that time will suffice to convince us. Elaborate descriptions of natural scenery, it is true, are very rare, for the reason that in this energetic age the novels and the lyric or epic poetry had something else to deal with. Bojardo and Ariosto paint nature vigorously, but as briefly as possible, and with no effort to appeal by their descriptions to the feelings of the reader,[2] which they endeavour to reach solely by their narrative and characters. Letter-writers and the authors of philosophical dialogues are, in fact, better evidence of the growing love of nature than the poets. The novelist Bandello, for example, observes rigorously the rules of his department of literature; he gives us in his novels themselves not a word more than is necessary on the natural scenery amid which the action of his tales takes place,[3] but in the dedications which always precede them we meet with charming descriptions of nature as the setting for his dialogues and social pictures. Among letter-writers, Aretino[4] unfortunately must be named as the first who has fully painted in words the splendid effect of light and shadow in an Italian sunset.

We sometimes find the feeling of the poets also attaching itself with tenderness to graceful scenes of country life. Tito Strozzi, about 1480, describes in a Latin elegy[5] the dwelling of his mistress. We are shown an old ivy-clad house, half hidden in trees, and adorned with weather-stained frescoes of the saints, and near it a chapel much damaged by the violence of the river Po, which flowed hard by; not far off the priest ploughs his few barren roods with borrowed cattle. This is no reminiscence of the Roman elegists, but true modern sentiment; and the parallel to it—a sincere, unartificial description of country life in general—will be found at the end of this part of our work.

It may be objected that the German painters at the beginning of the sixteenth century succeed in representing with perfect mastery these scenes of country life, as, for instance, Albrecht Dürer, in his engraving of *The Prodigal Son*.[6] But it is one thing if a painter, brought up in a school of realism, introduces such scenes, and quite another thing if a poet, accustomed to an ideal or mythological framework, is driven by inward impulse into realism. Besides which priority in point of time is here, as in the descriptions of country life, on the side of the Italian poets.

[1] On Leon Battista Alberti's feeling for landscapes see above, pp. 149 *sqq.* Alberti, a younger contemporary of Æneas Sylvius (*Trattato del Governo della Famiglia*, p. 90; see above, p. 145, note 2), is delighted when in the country with " the bushy hills," " the fair plains and rushing waters." Mention may here be made of a little work *Ætna*, by P. Bembus, first published at Venice, 1495, and often printed since, in which, among much that is rambling and prolix, there are remarkable geographical descriptions and notices of landscapes.

[2] A most elaborate picture of this kind in Ariosto; his sixth canto is all foreground.

[3] He deals differently with his architectural framework, and in this modern decorative art can learn something from him even now.   [4] *Lettere Pittoriche*, iii, 36, to Titian, May 1544.

[5] *Strozzii Poetæ*, in the *Erotica*, lib. vi, fol. 182 *sqq.*; in the poem " Hortatur se ipse, ut ad amicam properet."

[6] *Cf.* Thausing, *Dürer*, p. 166 (Leipzig, 1876).

CHAPTER IV

The Discovery of Man—Spiritual Description in Poetry

TO the discovery of the outward world the Renaissance added a still greater achievement by first discerning and bringing to light the full, whole nature of man.[1]

This period, as we have seen, first gave the highest development to individuality, and then led the individual to the most zealous and thorough study of himself in all forms and under all conditions. Indeed, the development of personality is essentially involved in the recognition of it in oneself and in others. Between these two great processes our narrative has placed the influence of ancient literature, because the mode of conceiving and representing both the individual and human nature in general was defined and coloured by that influence. But the power of conception and representation lay in the age and in the people.

The facts which we shall quote in evidence of our thesis will be few in number. Here, if anywhere in the course of this discussion, the author is conscious that he is treading on the perilous ground of conjecture, and that what seems to him a clear, if delicate and gradual, transition in the intellectual movement of the fourteenth and fifteenth centuries may not be equally plain to others. The gradual awakening of the soul of a people is a phenomenon which may produce a different impression on each spectator. Time will judge which impression is the most faithful.

Happily the study of the intellectual side of human nature began not with the search after a theoretical psychology—for that Aristotle still sufficed—but with the endeavour to observe and to describe. The indispensable ballast of theory was limited to the popular doctrine of the four temperaments, in its then habitual union with the belief in the influence of the planets. Such conceptions may remain ineradicable in the minds of individuals without hindering the general progress of the age. It certainly makes on us a singular impression when we meet them at a time when human nature in its deepest essence and in all its characteristic expressions was not only known by exact observation, but represented by an immortal poetry and art. It sounds almost ludicrous when an otherwise competent observer considers Clement VII to be of a melancholy temperament, but defers his judgment to that of the physicians, who declare the Pope of a sanguine-choleric nature;[2] or when we read that the same Gaston de Foix, the victor of Ravenna, whom Giorgione painted and Bambaja carved,

[1] These striking expressions are taken from the seventh volume of Michelet's *Histoire de France* (Introduction).
[2] Tomm. Gar, *Relaz. della Corte di Roma*, i, pp. 278 and 279. In the *Rel.* of Soriano, year 1533.

and whom all the historians describe, had the saturnine temperament.[1]   No
doubt those who use these expressions mean something by them; but the terms

FIG. 144. DANTE
Part of Raphael's *Disputa*
Rome, Vatican

in which they tell us their meaning are strangely out of date in the Italy of the
sixteenth century.

As examples of the free delineation of the human spirit we shall first speak
of the great poets of the fourteenth century.

[1] Prato, *Archiv. Stor.*, iii, pp. 295 *sqq.*   The word *saturnico* means " unhappy " as well as " bringing misfortune."   For the influence of the planets on human character in general see Corn. Agrippa, *De Occulta Philosophia*, c. 52.

THE DISCOVERY OF MAN

If we were to collect the pearls from the courtly and knightly poetry of all he countries of the West during the two preceding centuries we should have a mass of wonderful divinations and single pictures of the inward life, which at first sight would seem to rival the poetry of the Italians. Leaving lyrical poetry out of account, Godfrey of Strasburg gives us, in *Tristram and Isolt*, a representation of human passion, some features of which are immortal. But these pearls lie scattered in the ocean of artificial convention, and they are altogether something very different from a complete objective picture of the inward man and his spiritual wealth.

Italy too in the thirteenth century had, through the *trovatori*, its share in the poetry of the Courts and of chivalry. To them is mainly due the *canzone*, whose construction is as difficult and artificial as that of the songs of any Northern minstrel. Their subject and mode of thought represents simply the conventional tone of the Courts, be the poet a burgher or a scholar.

But two new paths at length showed themselves, along which Italian poetry could advance to another and a characteristic future. They are not the less important for being concerned only with the formal and external side of the art.

To the same Brunetto Latini—the teacher of Dante—who in his *canzoni* adopts the customary manner of the *trovatori*, we owe the first-known *versi sciolti*, or blank hendecasyllabic verses,[1] and in his apparent absence of form a true and genuine passion suddenly showed itself. The same voluntary renunciation of outward effect, through confidence in the power of the inward conception, can be observed some years later in fresco-painting, and later still in painting of all kinds, which began to cease to rely on colour for its effect, using simply a lighter or darker shade. For an age which laid so much stress on artificial form in poetry these verses of Brunetto mark the beginning of a new epoch.[2]

About the same time, or even in the first half of the thirteenth century, one of the many strictly balanced forms of metre, in which Europe was then so fruitful, became a normal and recognized form in Italy—the sonnet. The order of rhymes and even the number of the lines varied for a whole century,[3] till Petrarch fixed them permanently. In this form all higher lyrical or meditative subjects, and at a later time subjects of every possible description, were treated, and the madrigals, the sestines, and even the *canzoni* were reduced to a subordinate place. Later Italian writers complain, half jestingly, half resentfully, of this inevitable mould, this Procrustean bed, to which they were compelled to make their thoughts and feelings fit. Others were, and still are, quite satisfied with this particular form of verse, which they use freely to express any personal reminiscence or idle sing-song without necessity or serious purpose. For which reason there are many more bad or insignificant sonnets than good ones.

[1] See Trucchi, *Poesie Ital. Ined.*, i, pp. 165 *sqq.* The entire poem will be found in Grion in the *Propugnatore*, i, pp. 608 *sqq.* (1869).
[2] Blank verse became at a later time the usual form for dramatic compositions. Trissino, in the dedication of his *Sofonisba* to Leo X, expressed the hope that the Pope would recognize this style for what it was—as better, nobler, and *less easy* than it looked. Roscoe, *Leo X*, ed. Bossi, viii, 174.
[3] *Cf.*, for example, the striking forms adopted by Dante, *La Vita Nuova*, ed. Witte, pp. 13 *sqq.*, 16 *sqq.* Each has twenty irregular lines; in the first, one rhyme occurs eight times.

Nevertheless, the sonnet must be held to have been an unspeakable blessing for Italian poetry. The clearness and beauty of its structure, the invitation it gave to elevate the thought in the second and more rapidly moving half, and the ease with which it could be learned by heart made it valued even by the greatest masters. In fact, they would not have kept it in use down to our own

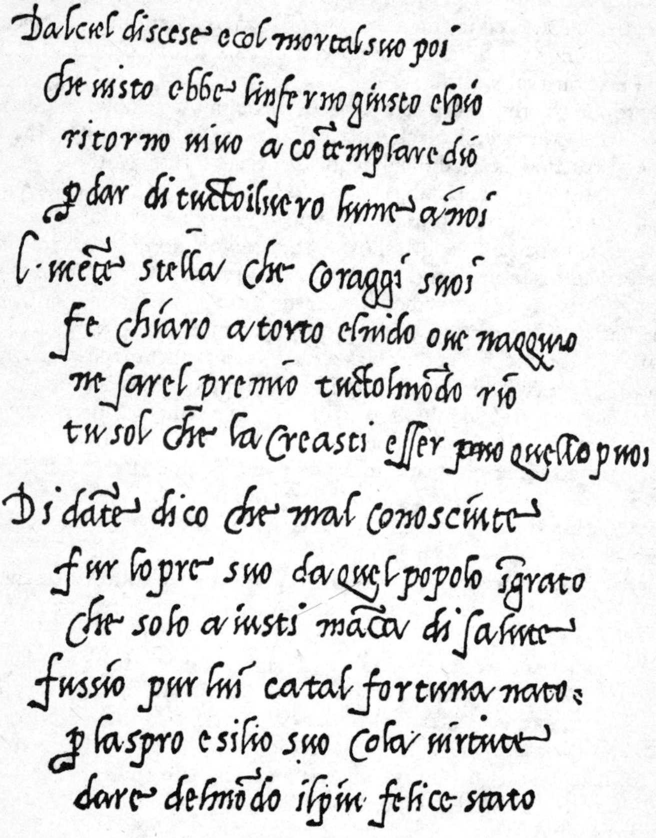

Dal ciel discese e col mortal suo poi
che visto ebbe linferno giusto e pio
ritorno vivo a contemplare dio
p dar di tuttoilvero lume a noi

l mete stella che coraggi suoi
fe chiaro a torto elnido ove nacquo
me sarel premio tuttolmodo rio
tu sol che la creasti esser p questo puoi

Di dante dico che mal conosciute
fur lopre suo da quel popolo igrato
che solo a iusti maca di salute
fussio pur lui catal fortuna nato
p laspro esilio suo cola virtute
dare delmodo ilpiu felice stato

FIG. 145. MICHELANGELO'S SONNET TO DANTE
Photo G. Grote'sche Verlagsbuchhandlung, Berlin

century had they not been impressed with a sense of its singular worth. These masters could have given us the same thoughts in other and wholly different forms. But when once they had made the sonnet the normal type of lyrical poetry many other writers of great, if not the highest, gifts, who otherwise would have lost themselves in a sea of diffusiveness, were forced to concentrate their feelings. The sonnet became for Italian literature a condenser of thoughts and emotions such as was possessed by the poetry of no other modern people.

Thus the world of Italian sentiment comes before us in a series of pictures, clear, concise, and most effective in their brevity. Had other nations possessed a form of expression of the same kind we should perhaps have known more of their inward life; we might have had a number of pictures of inward and outward situations—reflections of the national character and temper—and should not be dependent for such knowledge on the so-called lyrical poets of the fourteenth and fifteenth centuries, who can hardly ever be read with any serious

FIG. 146. DANTE AND HIS WORK
By Domenico di Michelino
Florence, Cathedral

enjoyment. In Italy we can trace an undoubted progress from the time when the sonnet came into existence. In the second half of the thirteenth century the *trovatori della transizione*, as they have been named,[1] mark the passage from the troubadours to the poets—that is, to those who wrote under the influence of antiquity. The simplicity and strength of their feeling, the vigorous delineation of fact, the precise expression and rounding off of their sonnets and other poems, herald the coming of a Dante. Some political sonnets of the Guelphs and Ghibellines (1260–70) have about them the ring of his passion, and others remind us of his sweetest lyrical notes.

Of his own theoretical view of the sonnet we are unfortunately ignorant, since the last books of his work *De Vulgari Eloquentia*, in which he proposed to treat of ballads and sonnets, either remained unwritten or have been lost. But, as a matter of fact, he has left us in his sonnets and *canzoni* a treasure of inward experience. And in what a framework he has set them! The prose of

[1] Trucchi, *op. cit.*, i, 181 *sqq.*

La Vita Nuova, in which he gives an account of the origin of each poem, is as wonderful as the verses themselves, and forms with them a uniform whole, inspired with the deepest glow of passion. With unflinching frankness and sincerity he lays bare every shade of his joy and sorrow, and moulds it resolutely into the strictest forms of art. Reading attentively these sonnets and *canzoni*, and the marvellous fragments of the diary of his youth which lie between them, we fancy that throughout the Middle Ages the poets have been purposely fleeing from themselves, and that he was the first to seek his own soul. Before his time we meet with many an artistic verse; but he is the first artist in the full sense of the word—the first who consciously cast immortal matter into an immortal form. Subjective feeling has here a full objective truth and greatness, and most of it is so set forth that all ages and peoples can make it their own.[1] Where he writes in a thoroughly objective spirit, and lets the force of his sentiment be guessed at only by some outward fact, as in the magnificent sonnets *Tanto gentile*, etc., and *Vedi perfettamente*, etc., he seems to feel the need of excusing himself.[2] The most beautiful of these poems really belongs to this class—the *Deh Peregrini che Pensosi Andate*.

Even apart from the *Divine Comedy* Dante would have marked by these youthful poems the boundary between medievalism and modern times. The human spirit had taken a mighty step toward the consciousness of its own secret life.

The revelations in this matter which are contained in the *Divine Comedy* itself are simply immeasurable; and it would be necessary to go through the whole poem, one canto after another, in order to do justice to its value from this point of view. Happily we have no need to do this, as it has long been a daily food of all the countries of the West. Its plan and the ideas on which it is based belong to the Middle Ages, and appeal to our interest only historically; but it is nevertheless the beginning of all modern poetry, through the power and richness shown in the description of human nature in every shape and attitude.[3]

From this time forward poetry may have experienced unequal fortunes, and may show for half a century together a so-called relapse. But its nobler and more vital principle was saved for ever; and whenever in the fourteenth, fifteenth, and in the beginning of the sixteenth century an original mind devotes himself to it he represents a more advanced stage than any poet out of Italy, given—what is certainly not always easy to settle satisfactorily—an equality of natural gifts to start with.

Here, as in other things in Italy, culture—to which poetry belongs—precedes the plastic arts and, in fact, gives them their chief impulse. More than a century elapsed before the spiritual element in painting and sculpture attained a power of expression in any way analogous to that of the *Divine Comedy*.

[1] These were the *canzoni* and sonnets which every blacksmith and donkey-driver sang and parodied—which made Dante not a little angry (*cf.* Franco Sachetti, *Nov.* 114, 115), so quickly did these poems find their way among the people.

[2] *La Vita Nuova*, ed. Witte, pp. 81, 82 *sqq.*; *Deh Peregrini, ibid.*, 116.

[3] For Dante's psychology the beginning of *Purgatorio*, iv, is one of the most important passages. See also the parts of the *Convivio* bearing on the subject.

FIG. 147. DRAWING BY BOTTICELLI FOR DANTE'S "DIVINA COMMEDIA," "PURGATORIO," XVIII

Berlin, Collection of Copper Engravings

How far the same rule holds good for the artistic development of other nations,[1] and of what importance the whole question may be, does not concern us here. For Italian civilization it is of decisive weight.

FIG. 148. PETRARCH
By Andrea del Castagno
Florence, S. Apollonia

The position to be assigned to Petrarch in this respect must be settled by the many readers of the poet. Those who come to him in the spirit of a cross-examiner, and busy themselves in detecting the contradictions between the poet and the man, his infidelities in love, and the other weak sides of his character, may perhaps, after sufficient effort, end by losing all taste for his poetry. In place, then, of artistic enjoyment we may acquire a knowledge of the man in his ' totality.' What a pity that Petrarch's letters from Avignon contain so little gossip to take hold of, and that the letters of his acquaintances and of the friends of these acquaintances have either been lost or never existed! Instead of heaven being thanked when we are not forced to inquire how and through what struggles a poet has rescued something immortal from his own poor life and lot, a biography which reads like an indictment has been stitched together for Petrarch out of these so-called ' remains.' But the poet may take comfort. If the printing and editing of the correspondence of celebrated people goes on he will have illustrious company enough sitting with him on the stool of repentance.

---

[1] The portraits of the school of Van Eyck would prove the contrary for the North. They remained for a long period far in advance of all descriptions in words.

Without shutting our eyes to much that is forced and artificial in his poetry, where the writer is merely imitating himself and singing on in the old strain, we cannot fail to admire the marvellous abundance of pictures of the inmost soul—descriptions of moments of joy and sorrow which must have been thoroughly his own, since no one before him gives us anything of the kind, and on which rests his significance for his country and for the world. His verse is not in all places equally transparent; by the side of his most beautiful thoughts stand at times some allegorical conceit, or some sophistical trick of logic, altogether foreign to our present taste. But the balance is on the side of excellence.

FIG. 149. BOCCACCIO
By Andrea del Castagno
Florence, S. Apollonia

Boccaccio too, in his imperfectly known sonnets,[1] succeeds sometimes in giving a most powerful and effective picture of his feeling. The return to a spot consecrated by love (Sonnet 22), the melancholy of spring (Sonnet 33), the sadness of the poet who feels himself growing old (Sonnet 65), are admirably treated by him. And in the *Ameto* he has described the ennobling and transfiguring power of love in a manner which would hardly be expected from the author of the *Decamerone*.[2] In the *Fiammetta* we have another great and minutely painted picture of the human soul, full of the keenest observation, though executed

---

[1] Printed in the sixteenth volume of his *Opere Volgari*. See M. Landau, *Giov. Boccaccio*, pp. 36–40 (Stuttgart, 1877); he lays special stress on Boccaccio's dependence on Dante and Petrarch.

[2] In the song of the shepherd Teogape, after the feast of Venus, *Opp.*, ed. Moutier, vol. xv, 2, pp. 67 *sqq.* *Cf.* Landau, pp. 58–64; on the *Fiammetta* see Landau, pp. 96–105.

with anything but uniform power, and in parts marred by the passion for high-sounding language and an unlucky mixture of mythological allusions and learned quotations. The *Fiammetta*, if we are not mistaken, is a sort of feminine counterpart to *La Vita Nuova* of Dante, or, at any rate, owes its origin to it.

That the ancient poets, particularly the elegists, and Virgil in the fourth book of the *Æneid*, were not without influence [1] on the Italians of this and the following generation is beyond a doubt; but the spring of sentiment within the latter was nevertheless powerful and original. If we compare them in this respect with their contemporaries in other countries we shall find in them the earliest complete expression of modern European feeling. The question, be it remembered, is not whether eminent men of other nations did not feel as deeply and as nobly, but who first gave documentary proof of the widest knowledge of the movements of the human heart.

Why did the Italians of the Renaissance do nothing above the second rank in tragedy? That was the field on which to display human character, intellect, and passion in the thousand forms of their growth, their struggles, and their decline. In other words, why did Italy produce no Shakespeare? For with the stage of other Northern countries besides England the Italians of the sixteenth and seventeenth centuries had no reason to fear a comparison; and with the Spaniards they could not enter into competition, since Italy had long lost all traces of religious fanaticism, treated the chivalrous code of honour only as a form, and was both too proud and too intelligent to bow down before its tyrannical and illegitimate masters. [2] We have therefore only to consider the English stage in the period of its brief splendour.

It is an obvious reply that all Europe produced but one Shakespeare, and that such a mind is the rarest of heaven's gifts. It is further possible that the Italian stage was on the way to something great when the Counter-Reformation broke in upon it, and, aided by the Spanish rule over Naples and Milan, and indirectly over the whole peninsula, withered the best flowers of the Italian spirit. It would be hard to conceive of Shakespeare himself under a Spanish viceroy, or in the neighbourhood of the Holy Inquisition at Rome, or even in his own country a few decades later, at the time of the English Civil War. The stage, which in its perfection is a late product of every civilization, must wait for its own time and fortune.

We must not, however, quit this subject without mentioning certain circumstances which were of a character to hinder or retard a high development of the drama in Italy, till the time for it had gone by.

As the most weighty of these causes we must certainly mention that the scenic tastes of the people were occupied elsewhere, and chiefly in the mysteries

---

[1] The famous Leonardo Aretino, the leader of the humanists at the beginning of the fifteenth century, admits: " Che gli antichi Greci d' umanità e di gentilezza di cuore abbino avanzato di gran lungo i nostri Italiani "; but he says it at the beginning of a novel which contains the sentimental story of the invalid Prince Antiochus and his stepmother Stratonice—a document of an ambiguous and half-Asiatic character. (Printed as an appendix to the *Cento Novelle Antiche*.)

[2] No doubt the Court and prince received flattery enough from their occasional poets and dramatists.

and religious processions. Throughout all Europe dramatic representations of sacred history and legend form the origin of the secular drama; but Italy, as it will be shown more fully in the sequel, had spent on the mysteries such a wealth of decorative splendour as could not but be unfavourable to the dramatic element. Out of all the countless and costly representations there sprang not

even a branch of poetry like the *Autos Sagramentales* of Calderon and other Spanish poets, much less any advantage or foundation for the legitimate drama.[1]

And when the latter did at length appear it at once gave itself up to magnificence of scenic effects, to which the mysteries had already accustomed the public taste to far too great an extent. We learn with astonishment how rich and splendid the scenes in Italy were at a time when in the North the simplest indication of the place was thought sufficient. This alone might have had no such unfavourable effect on the drama if the attention of the audience had not been drawn away from the poetical conception of the play partly by the splendour of the costumes, partly and chiefly by fantastic interludes (*intermezzi*).

That in many places, particularly in Rome and Ferrara, Plautus and Terence, as well as pieces by the old tragedians, were given in Latin or in Italian (pp. 246, 257),

FIG. 150. THEATRICAL PERFORMANCE
From the Venice edition of Terence, 1497
Photo Kurt Schroeder, Bonn

that the academies (p. 277), of which we have already spoken, made this one of their chief objects, and that the poets of the Renaissance followed these models too servilely were all untoward conditions for the Italian stage at the period in question. Yet I hold them to be of secondary importance. Had not the Counter-Reformation and the rule of foreigners intervened these very disadvantages might have been turned into useful means of transition. At all events, by the year 1520 the victory of the mother-tongue in tragedy and comedy was, to the great disgust of the humanists, as good as won.[2] On this

[1] *Cf.* the contrary view taken by Gregorovius, *Gesch. Roms*, vii, 619.
[2] Paul. Jovius, *Dialog. de Viris Lit. Illustr.*, in Tiraboschi, tom. vii, iv; Lil. Greg. Gyraldus, *De Poetis nostri Temp.*, ed. K. Wotke, p. 40.

side, then, no obstacle stood in the way of the most developed people in Europe, to hinder them from raising the drama, in its noblest forms, to be a true reflection of human life and destiny. It was the Inquisitors and Spaniards who cowed the Italian spirit, and rendered impossible the representation of the greatest and most sublime themes, most of all when they were associated with patriotic memories. At the same time, there is no doubt that the distracting *intermezzi* did serious harm to the drama. We must now consider them a little more closely.

FIG. 151. SETTING FOR TRAGEDY
From Serlio's *Architettura*, 1545
Photo Kurt Schroeder, Bonn

When the marriage of Alfonso of Ferrara with Lucrezia Borgia was celebrated Duke Hercules in person showed his illustrious guests the hundred and ten costumes which were to serve at the representation of five comedies of Plautus, in order that all might see that not one of them was used twice.[1] But all this display of silk and camlet was nothing to the ballets and pantomimes which served as interludes between the acts of the Plautine dramas. That in comparison Plautus himself seemed mortally dull to a lively young lady like Isabella Gonzaga, and that while the play was going on everybody was longing for the interludes, is quite intelligible when we think of the picturesque brilliancy with which they were put on the stage. There were to be seen combats of Roman warriors, who brandished their weapons to the sound of music, torch-dances executed by Moors, a dance of savages with horns of plenty, out of

[1] Isabella Gonzaga to her husband, February 3, 1502, *Archiv. Stor.*, App. II, pp. 306 *sqq. Cf.* Gregorovius, *Lucrezia Borgia*, i, 255–266, 3rd ed. In the French *mystères* the actors themselves first marched before the audience in procession, which was called the *montre*.

which streamed waves of fire—all as the ballet of a pantomime in which a maiden was delivered from a dragon. Then came a dance of fools, got up as Punches, beating one another with pigs' bladders, with more of the same kind. At the Court of Ferrara they never gave a comedy without its ballet (*moresca*).[1] In what style the *Amphitruo* of Plautus was there represented (1491, at the first marriage of Alfonso, with Anna Sforza) is doubtful. Possibly it was given rather as a pantomime with music than as a drama.[2] In any case, the accessories were more considerable than the play itself. There was a choral dance of ivy-clad youths moving in intricate figures, done to the music of a ringing orchestra; then came Apollo, striking the lyre with the plectrum, and singing an ode to the praise of the house of Este; then followed, as an interlude within an interlude, a kind of rustic farce, after which the stage was again occupied by classical mythology—Venus, Bacchus, and their followers—and by a pantomime representing the judgment of Paris. Not till then was the second half of the fable of Amphitruo performed, with unmistakable references to the future birth of a Hercules of the house of Este. At a former representation of the same piece in the courtyard of the palace (1487) " a paradise with stars and other wheels " was constantly burning, by which is probably meant an illumination with fireworks that, no doubt, absorbed most of the attention of the spectators. It was certainly better when such performances were given separately, as was the case at other Courts. We shall have to speak of the entertainments given by Cardinal Pietro Riario, by the Bentivogli at Bologna, and by others when we come to treat of the festivals in general.

This scenic magnificence, now become universal, had a disastrous effect on Italian tragedy. Francesco Sansovino [3] writes:

> In Venice formerly, besides comedies, tragedies by ancient and modern writers were put on the stage with great pomp. The fame of the scenic arrangements [*apparati*] brought spectators from far and near. Nowadays performances are given by private individuals in their own houses, and the custom of passing the carnival in comedies and other cheerful entertainments has long been fixed.

In other words, scenic display had helped to kill tragedy.

---

[1] *Diario Ferrarese*, in Murat., xxiv, col. 404. Other passages referring to the stage in that city, cols. 278, 279, 282–285, 361, 380, 381, 393, 397, from which it appears that Plautus was the dramatist most popular on these occasions, that the performances sometimes lasted till three o'clock in the morning, and were even given in the open air. The ballets were without any meaning or reference to the persons present and the occasion solemnized. Isabella Gonzaga, who was certainly at the time longing for her husband and child, and was dissatisfied with the union of her brother with Lucrezia, spoke of the "coldness and frostiness" of the marriage and the festivities which attended it.

[2] *Strozzii Poetæ*, fol. 232, in the fourth book of the *Æolosticha* of Tito Strozzi. The lines run:

> " Ecce superveniens rerum argumenta retexit
> Mimus, et ad populum verba diserta refert.
> Tum similes habitu formaque et voce Menæchmi
> Dulcibus oblectant lumina nostra modis."

The *Menæchmi* was also given at Ferrara in 1486, at the cost of more than a thousand ducats (Murat., xxiv, 278).

[3] Franc. Sansovino, *Venezia*, fol. 169. The passage in the original is as follows : " Si sono anco spesso recitate delle tragedie con grandi apparecchi, comporte da poeti antichi o da moderni. Alle quali per la fama degli apparati concorrevano le genti estere a circonvicine per vederle e udirle. Ma hoggi le feste da particolari si fanno fra i parenti et essendosi la città regolata per se medesima da certi anni in quà, si passano i tempi del Carnevale in comedie e in altri più lieti e honorati diletti." The passage is not altogether clear. Perhaps for *parenti* we should read *pareti*.

The various starts or attempts of these modern tragedians, among which the *Sofonisba* of Trissino was the most celebrated, belong to the history of literature. The same may be said of genteel comedy, modelled on Plautus and Terence. Even Ariosto could do nothing of the first order in this style. On the other hand, popular prose-comedy, as treated by Machiavelli, Bibbiena, and Aretino, might have had a future if its matter had not condemned it to destruction. This was, on the one hand, licentious to the last degree, and, on the other, aimed at certain classes in society, which after the middle of the sixteenth century ceased to afford a ground for public attacks. If in the *Sofonisba* the portrayal of character gave place to brilliant declamation, the latter, with its half-sister caricature, was used far too freely in comedy also. Nevertheless, these Italian comedies, if we are not mistaken, were the first written in prose and copied from real life, and for this reason deserve mention in the history of European literature.

The writing of tragedies and comedies, and the practice of putting both ancient and modern plays on the stage, continued without intermission; but they served only as occasions for display. The national genius turned elsewhere for living interest. When the opera and the pastoral fable came up these attempts were at length wholly abandoned.

One form of comedy only was and remained national—the unwritten, improvised *commedia dell' arte*. It was of no great service in the delineation of character, since the masks used were few in number and familiar to everybody. But the talent of the nation had such an affinity for this style that often in the middle of written comedies the actors would throw themselves on their own inspiration,[1] so that a new mixed form of comedy came into existence in some places. The plays given in Venice by Burchiello, and afterward by the company of Armonio, Val. Zuccato, Lod. Dolce, and others, were perhaps of this character.[2] Of Burchiello we know expressly that he used to heighten the comic effect by mixing Greek and Slavonic words with the Venetian dialect. A complete *commedia dell' arte*, or very nearly so, was represented by Angelo Beolco, known as Il Ruzzante (1502–42), who enjoyed the highest reputation as poet and actor, was compared as poet to Plautus, and as actor to Roscius, and who formed a company with several of his friends, who appeared in his pieces as Paduan peasants, with the names Menato, Vezzo, Billora, etc. He studied their dialect when spending the summer at the villa of his patron Luigi Cornaro (Aloysius Cornelius) at Codevico.[3] Gradually all the famous local masks made their appearance, whose remains still delight the Italian populace of our day: Pantalone, the Doctor, Brighella, Pulcinella, Arlecchino, and the rest. Most

---

[1] This must be the meaning of Sansovino, *Venezia*, fol. 168, when he complains that the " recitanti " ruined the comedies " con invenzioni o personaggi troppo ridicoli."

[2] Sansovino, *loc. cit.* [who, however, as Geiger has established, does not speak of companies under the leadership of a definite person.—W. G.].

[3] Scardeonius, *De Urb. Patav. Antiq.*, in Græv., *Thesaur.*, vi, iii, col. 288 *sqq.* An important passage for the literature of the dialects generally. One of the passages is as follows: " Hinc ad recitandas comœdias socii scenici et gregales et æmuli fuere nobiles juvenes Patavini, Marcus Aurelius Alvarotus quem in comœdiis suis Menatum appellitabat, et Hieronymus Zanetus quem Vezzam, et Castegnola quem Billoram vocitabat, et alii quidam qui sermonem agrestium imitando præ ceteris callebant."

of them are of great antiquity, and possibly are historically connected with the masks in the old Roman farces; but it was not till the sixteenth century that several of them were combined in one piece. At the present time this is less often the case; but every great city still keeps to its local mask—Naples to the Pulcinella, Florence to the Stentorello, Milan to its often so admirable Meneghino.[1]

This is, indeed, scanty compensation for a people which possessed the

FIG. 152. SETTING FOR COMEDY
From Serlio's *Architettura*, 1545
Photo Kurt Schroeder, Bonn

power, perhaps to a greater degree than any other, to reflect and contemplate its own highest qualities in the mirror of the drama. But this power was destined to be marred for centuries by hostile forces, for whose predominance the Italians were only in part responsible. The universal talent for dramatic representation could not, indeed, be uprooted, and in music Italy long made good her claim to supremacy in Europe. Those who can find in this world of sound a compensation for the drama, to which all future was denied, have, at all events, no meagre source of consolation.

But perhaps we can find in epic poetry what the stage fails to offer us. Yet

[1] That the latter existed as early as the fifteenth century may be inferred from the *Diario Ferrarese*, February 2, 1501: "Il duca Hercole fece una festa di Menechino secondo il suo uso." Murat., xxiv, col. 393. There cannot be a confusion with the *Menæchmi* of Plautus, which is correctly written, *loc. cit.*, col. 278. See above, p. 315, note 2.

the chief reproach made against the heroic poetry of Italy is precisely on the score of the insignificance and imperfect representation of its characters.

Other merits are allowed to belong to it, among the rest that for three centuries it has been actually read and constantly reprinted, while nearly the whole of the epic poetry of other nations has become a mere matter of literary or historical curiosity. Does this perhaps lie in the taste of the readers, who demand something different from what would satisfy a Northern public?

FIG. 153. SETTING FOR THE SATYRIC DRAMA
From Serlio's *Architettura*, 1545
Photo Kurt Schroeder, Bonn

Certainly, without the power of entering to some degree into Italian sentiment, it is impossible to appreciate the characteristic excellence of these poems, and many distinguished men declare that they can make nothing of them. And in truth, if we criticize Pulci, Bojardo, Ariosto, and Berni solely with an eye to their thought and matter we shall fail to do them justice. They are artists of a peculiar kind, who write for a people which is distinctly and eminently artistic.

The medieval legends had lived on after the gradual extinction of the poetry of chivalry, partly in the form of rhyming adaptations and collections, and partly of novels in prose. The latter was the case in Italy during the fourteenth century; but the newly awakened memories of antiquity were rapidly growing up to a gigantic size, and soon cast into the shade all the fantastic creations of the Middle Ages. Boccaccio, for example, in his *Amorosa Visione* names among the heroes in his enchanted palace Tristram, Arthur, Galeotto, and others, but briefly, as if he were ashamed to speak of them (p. 214); and following writers either do not name them at all, or name them only for purposes of ridicule. But the people kept them in its memory, and from the people they passed into the hands of the poets of the fifteenth century. These were now able to conceive and represent their subject in a wholly new manner. But they did more. They introduced into it a multitude of fresh elements, and, in fact, recast it from beginning to end. It must not be expected of them that they should treat such subjects with the respect once felt for them. All other countries must envy them the advantage of having a popular interest of this kind to appeal to; but they could not without hypocrisy treat these myths with any respect.[1]

Instead of this they moved with victorious freedom in the new field which poetry had won. What they chiefly aimed at seems to have been that their poems, when recited, should produce the most harmonious and exhilarating effect. These works, indeed, gain immensely when they are repeated not as a whole, but piecemeal, and with a slight touch of comedy in voice and gesture. A deeper and more detailed portrayal of character would do little to enhance this effect; though the reader may desire it, the hearer, who sees the rhapsodist standing before him, and who hears only one piece at a time, does not think about it at all. With respect to the figures which the poet found ready made for him, his feeling was of a double kind; his humanistic culture protested against their medieval character, and their combats as counterparts of the battles and tournaments of the poet's own age exercised all his knowledge and artistic power, while at the same time they called forth all the highest qualities in the reciter. Even in Pulci,[2] accordingly, we find no parody, strictly speaking, of chivalry, nearly as the rough humour of his paladins at times approaches it. By their side stands the ideal of pugnacity—the droll and jovial Morgante—who masters whole armies with his bell-clapper, and who is himself thrown into relief by contrast with the grotesque and most interesting monster Margutte. Yet Pulci lays no special stress on these two rough and vigorous characters, and his story, long after they had disappeared from it, maintains its singular course. Bojardo[3] treats his characters with the same mastery, using them for serious or comic purposes as he pleases; he has his fun even out of supernatural beings, whom he sometimes intentionally depicts as louts. But there is one artistic aim which he pursues as earnestly as Pulci—namely, the lively and exact description of all that goes forward. Pulci recited his poem, as one book after another was finished, before the society of Lorenzo the Magnificent, and in the same way Bojardo recited his at the Court of Hercules of Ferrara. It may

[1] Pulci mischievously invents a solemn old-world legend for his story of the giant Margutte (*Morgante*, canto xix, str. 153 *sqq.*). The critical introduction of Limerno Pitocco is still droller (*Orlandino*, cap. i, str. 12–22).

[2] The *Morgante* was written in 1460 and the following years, and first printed at Venice in 1481. For the tournaments see Part V, Chapter I. See for what follows Ranke, *Zur Geschichte der italienischen Poesie* (Berlin, 1837).

[3] The *Orlando Inamorato* was first fully published in 1494; the first two-thirds as early as 1487.

be easily imagined what sort of excellence such an audience demanded, and how little thanks a profound exposition of character would have earned for the poet. Under these circumstances the poems naturally formed no complete whole, and might just as well be half or twice as long as they now are. Their composition is not that of a great historical picture, but rather that of a frieze, or of some rich festoon entwined among groups of picturesque figures. And precisely as in the figures or tendrils of a frieze we do not look for minuteness of execution in the individual forms, or for distant perspectives and different planes, so we must as little expect anything of the kind from these poems.

The varied richness of invention which continually astonishes us, most of all in the case of Bojardo, turns to ridicule all our school definitions as to the essence of epic poetry. For that age, this form of literature was the most agreeable diversion from archæological studies, and, indeed, the only possible means of re-establishing an independent class of narrative poetry. For the versification of ancient history could only lead to the false tracks which were trodden by Petrarch in his *Africa*, written in Latin hexameters, and a hundred and fifty years later by Trissino in his *Italy Delivered from the Goths*, composed in *versi sciolti*—a never-ending poem of faultless language and versification, which only makes us doubt whether an unlucky alliance has been most disastrous to history or to poetry.[1]

FIG. 154. LUIGI PULCI
Part of the fresco *The Resurrection of the King's Son*,
by Filippino Lippi
Florence, S. Maria del Carmine
Photo Alinari

And whither did the example of Dante beguile those who imitated him? The visionary *Trionfi* of Petrarch were the last of the works written under this influence which satisfy our taste. The *Amorosa Visione* of Boccaccio is at bottom no more than an enumeration of historical or fabulous characters, arranged under allegorical categories.[2] Others preface what they have to tell

---

[1] *L'Italia Liberata da Goti* (Rome, 1547).
[2] See above, p. 319, and Landau's *Boccaccio*, 64–69. It must, nevertheless, be observed that the work of Boccaccio here mentioned was written before 1344, while that of Petrarch was written after Laura's death—that is, after 1348.

with a baroque imitation of Dante's first canto, and provide themselves with some allegorical comparison, to take the place of Virgil. Uberti, for example, chose Solinus for his geographical poem—*Il Dittamondo*—and Giovanni Santi

FIG. 155. ARIOSTO
By Titian
London, National Gallery

Plutarch for his encomium on Federigo of Urbino.[1] The only salvation of the time from these false tendencies lay in the new epic poetry which was represented by Pulci and Bojardo. The admiration and curiosity with which it was received, and the like of which will perhaps never again fall to the lot of epic

[1] Vasari, viii, 71, in the Commentary to the *Vita di Rafaelle*.

poetry to the end of time, is a brilliant proof how great was the need of it. It is idle to ask whether that epic ideal which our own day has formed from Homer and the *Nibelungenlied* is or is not realized in these works; an ideal of their own age certainly was. By their endless descriptions of combats, which to us are the most fatiguing part of these poems, they satisfied, as we have already said, a practical interest of which it is hard for us to form a just conception [1]—as hard, indeed, as of the esteem in which a lively and faithful reflection of the passing moment was then held.

Nor can a more inappropriate test be applied to Ariosto than the degree in which his *Orlando Furioso* [2] serves for the representation of character. Characters, indeed, there are, and drawn with an affectionate care; but the poem does not depend on these for its effect, and would lose rather than gain if more stress were laid upon them. But the demand for them is part of a wider and more general desire which Ariosto fails to satisfy as our day would wish it satisfied. From a poet of such fame and such mighty gifts we would gladly receive something better than the adventures of Orlando. From him we might have hoped for a work expressing the deepest conflicts of the human soul, the highest thoughts of his time on human and divine things—in a word, one of those supreme syntheses like the *Divine Comedy* or *Faust*. Instead of which he goes to work like the plastic artists of his own day, not caring for originality in our sense of the word, simply reproducing a familiar circle of figures, and even, when it suits his purpose, making use of the details left him by his predecessors. The excellence which, in spite of all this, can nevertheless be attained will be the more incomprehensible to people born without the artistic sense, the more learned and intelligent in other respects they are. The artistic aim of Ariosto is brilliant, living action, which he distributes equally through the whole of his great poem. For this end he needs to be excused not only from all deeper expression of character, but also from maintaining any strict connexion in his narrative. He must be allowed to take up lost and forgotten threads when and where he pleases; his heroes must come and go not because their character, but because the story, requires it. Yet in this apparently irrational and arbitrary style of composition he displays a harmonious beauty, never losing himself in description, but giving only such a sketch of scenes and persons as does not hinder the flowing movement of the narrative. Still less does he lose himself in conversation and monologue,[3] but maintains the lofty privilege of the true epos, by transforming all into living narrative. His pathos does not lie in the words,[4] not even in the famous twenty-third and following cantos, where Roland's madness is described. That the love-stories in the heroic poem are without all lyrical tenderness must be reckoned a merit, though from a moral point of view they cannot always be approved. Yet at times they are of such truth and reality, notwithstanding all the magic and romance which surrounds

---

[1] Much of this kind in the *Iliad* our present taste could dispense with.
[2] First edition 1516.
[3] The speeches inserted are themselves narratives.
[4] As was the case with Pulci, *Morgante*, canto xix, str. 20 *sqq*.

them, that we might think them personal affairs of the poet himself. In the full consciousness of his own genius he does not scruple to interweave the events of his own day into the poem, and to celebrate the fame of the house of Este in visions and prophecies. The wonderful stream of his octaves bears it all forward in even and dignified movement.

With Teofilo Folengo, or, as he here calls himself, Limerno Pitocco, the parody of the whole system of chivalry attained the end it has so long desired.[1] But here comedy, with its realism, demanded of necessity a stricter delineation of character. Exposed to all the rough usage of the half-savage street-lads in a Roman country town, Sutri, the little Orlando grows up before our eyes into the hero, the priest-hater, and the disputant. The conventional world which had been recognized since the time of Pulci, and had served as framework for the epos, falls here to pieces. The origin and position of the paladins are openly ridiculed, as in the tournament of donkeys in the second book, where the knights appear with the most ludicrous armament. The poet utters his ironical regrets over the inexplicable faithlessness which seems implanted in the house of Gano of Mainz, over the toilsome acquisition of the sword Durindana, and so forth. Tradition, in fact, serves him only as a substratum for episodes, ludicrous fancies, allusions to events of the time (among which some, like the close of cap. vi, are exceedingly fine), and indecent jokes. Mixed with all this, a certain derision of Ariosto is unmistakable, and it was fortunate for the Orlando Furioso that the Orlandino, with its Lutheran heresies, was soon put out of the way by the Inquisition. The parody is evident when (cap. v, str. 28) the house of Gonzaga is deduced from the paladin Guidone, since the Colonna claimed Orlando, the Orsini Rinaldo, and the house of Este—according to Ariosto—Ruggiero as their ancestors. Perhaps Ferrante Gonzaga, the patron of the poet, was a party to this sarcasm on the house of Este.

That in the *Jerusalem Delivered* of Torquato Tasso the delineation of character is one of the chief tasks of the poet proves only how far his mode of thought differed from that prevalent half a century before. His admirable work is a true monument of the Counter-Reformation, which had been accomplished meanwhile, and of the spirit and tendency of that movement.

[1] The *Orlandino*, first edition 1526.

CHAPTER V

BIOGRAPHY

UTSIDE the sphere of poetry also the Italians were the first of all European nations who displayed any remarkable power and inclination accurately to describe man as shown in history, according to his inward and outward characteristics.

It is true that in the Middle Ages considerable attempts were made in the same direction; and the legends of the Church, as a kind of standing biographical task, must, to some extent, have kept alive the interest and the gift for such descriptions. In the annals of the monasteries and cathedrals many of the Churchmen, such as Meinwerk of Paderborn, Godehard of Kildesheim, and others, are brought vividly before our eyes; and descriptions exist of several of the German Emperors, modelled after old authors—particularly Suetonius—which contain admirable features. Indeed, these and other profane *vitæ* came in time to form a continuous counterpart to the sacred legends. Yet neither Eginhard nor Radevicus [1] can be named by the side of Joinville's picture of St Louis, which certainly stands almost alone as the first complete spiritual portrait of a modern European nature. Characters like St Louis are rare at all times, and his was favoured by the rare good fortune that a sincere and naïve observer caught the spirit of all the events and actions of his life and represented it admirably. From what scanty sources are we left to guess at the inward nature of Frederick II or Philip the Fair! Much of what, till the close of the Middle Ages, passed for biography is, properly speaking, nothing but contemporary narrative, written without any sense of what is individual in the subject of the memoir.

Among the Italians, on the contrary, the search for the characteristic features of remarkable men was a prevailing tendency; and this it is which separates them from the other Western peoples, among whom the same thing happens but seldom, and in exceptional cases. This keen eye for individuality belongs only to those who have emerged from the half-conscious life of the race and become themselves individuals.

Under the influence of the prevailing conception of fame (pp. 151 *sqq.*), an art of comparative biography arose which no longer found it necessary, like Anastasius,[2]

---

[1] Radevicus, *De Gestis Frederici Imp.*, especially ii, 76. The admirable *Vita Henrici IV* contains very little personal description, as is also the case with the *Vita Chuonradi Imp.* by Wipo.

[2] The librarian Anastasius (middle of ninth century) is here meant. The whole collection of the lives of the Popes (*Liber Pontificalis*) was formerly ascribed to him, but erroneously. *Cf.* Wattenbach, *Deutschlands Geschichtsquellen*, i, 223 *sqq.*, 3rd ed.

Agnellus,[1] and their successors, or like the biographers of the Venetian Doges, to adhere to a dynastic or ecclesiastical succession. It felt itself free to describe a man if and because he was remarkable. It took as models Suetonius, Nepos (the *Viri Illustres*), and Plutarch, so far as he was known and translated; for sketches of literary history, the lives of the grammarians, rhetoricians, and poets, known to us as the " Appendices " to Suetonius,[2] seem to have served as patterns, as well as the widely read life of Virgil by Donatus.

FIG. 156. FRESCO CYCLE OF THE LIFE OF ÆNEAS SYLVIUS (PIUS II)
By Pinturicchio
Siena, Cathedral Library
Photo Alinari

It has been already mentioned that biographical collections—lives of famous men and famous women—began to appear in the fourteenth century (p. 158). Where they do not describe contemporaries they are naturally dependent on earlier narratives. The first great original effort is the life of Dante by Boccaccio. Lightly and rhetorically written, and full, as it is, of arbitrary fancies, this work nevertheless gives us a lively sense of the extraordinary

---

[1] Lived about the same time as Anastasius; author of a history of the bishopric of Ravenna. Wattenbach, *loc. cit.*, p. 227.

[2] How early Philostratus was used in the same way I am unable to say. Suetonius was no doubt taken as a model in times still earlier. Besides the life of Charles the Great written by Eginhard, examples from the twelfth century are offered by William of Malmesbury in his descriptions of William the Conqueror (pp. 452 *sqq.*, 466 *sqq.*), of William II (pp. 494, 504), and of Henry I (p. 640).

features in Dante's nature.[1]   Then follow, at the end of the fourteenth century, the *vite* of illustrious Florentines by Filippo Villani.   They are men of every calling: poets, jurists, physicians, scholars, artists, statesmen, and soldiers, some of them then still living.   Florence is here treated like a gifted family, in which all the members are noticed in whom the spirit of the house expresses itself vigorously.   The descriptions are brief, but show a remarkable eye for what is characteristic, and are noteworthy for including the inward and outward physiognomy in the same sketch.[2]   From that time forward[3] the Tuscans never ceased to consider the description of man as lying within their special competence, and to them we owe the most valuable portraits of the Italians of the fifteenth and sixteenth centuries.   Giovanni Cavalcanti, in the appendices to his Florentine history, written before 1450,[4] collects instances of civil virtue and abnegation, of political discernment and of military valour, all shown by Florentines.   Pius II gives us in his *Commentaries* valuable portraits of famous contemporaries; and a separate work of his earlier years,[5] which seems preparatory to these portraits, but which has colours and features that are very singular, has been reprinted.   To Jacob of Volterra we owe piquant sketches of members of the Curia[6] in the time of Sixtus IV.   Vespasiano Fiorentino has been often referred to already, and as a historical authority a high place must be assigned to him; but his gift as a painter of character is not to be compared with that of Machiavelli, Niccolò Valori, Guicciardini, Varchi, Francesco Vettori, and others, by whom European history has been probably as much influenced as by the ancients.   It must not be forgotten that some of these authors soon found their way into Northern countries by means of Latin translations.   And without Giorgio Vasari of Arezzo and his all-important work we should perhaps to this day have no history of Northern art, or of the art of modern Europe, at all.[7]

Among the biographers of North Italy in the fifteenth century Bartolommeo Facio of Spezzia holds a high rank (p. 159).   Platina, born in the territory of Cremona, gives us in his *Life of Paul II* (p. 236) examples of biographical caricatures.   The description of the last Visconti,[8] written by Piercandido Decembrio—an enlarged imitation of Suetonius—is of special importance.

[1] See the admirable criticism in Landau, *Boccaccio*, pp. 180-182.

[2] See above, p. 145.   The original (Latin) was first published in 1847 at Florence, by Galletti, with the title *Philippi Villani Liber de Civitatis Florentiæ Famosis Civibus*; an old Italian translation has been often printed since 1747.   The first book, which treats of the earliest history of Florence and Rome, has never been printed.   The chapter in Villani, *De Semipoetis*—that is, those who wrote in prose as well as in verse, or those who wrote poems besides following some other profession—is specially interesting.

[3] Here we refer the reader to the biography of L. B. Alberti, from which extracts are given above, and to the numerous Florentine biographies in Muratori, in the *Archivio Storico*, and elsewhere.   The life of Alberti is probably an autobiography: p. 149, note 2.

[4] *Storia Fiorentina*, ed. F. L. Polidori (Florence, 1838).

[5] *De Viris Illustribus*, in the publications of the *Stuttgarter Liter. Vereins*, No. I (Stuttgart, 1839).   *Cf.* G. Voigt, ii, 324.   Of the sixty-five biographies twenty-one are lost.

[6] His *Diarium Romanum* from 1472 to 1484, in Murat., xiii, 81-202.

[7] *Ugolini Verini Poetæ Florentini* (a contemporary of Lorenzo, a pupil of Landinus, fol. 13, and teacher of Petrus Crinitus, fol. 14).   *De Illustratione Urbis Florentinæ Libri Tres* (Paris, 1583), deserves mention, especially lib. 2.   Dante, Petrarch, Boccaccio, are spoken of and characterized without a word of blame.   For several women see fol. 11.

[8] *Petri Candidi Decembrii Vita Philippi Mariæ Vicecomitis*, in Murat., xx.   *Cf.* above, p. 53.

Sismondi regrets that so much trouble has been spent on so unworthy an object, but the author would hardly have been equal to deal with a greater man, while he was thoroughly competent to describe the mixed nature of Filippo Maria, and in and through it to represent with accuracy the conditions, the

FIG. 157. SELF-PORTRAIT BY LUCA SIGNORELLI
Part of the fresco *The Antichrist*
Orvieto, Cathedral
Photo Anderson, Rome

forms, and the consequences of this particular kind of despotism. The picture of the fifteenth century would be incomplete without this unique biography, which is characteristic down to its minutest details. Milan afterward possessed, in the historian Corio, an excellent portrait-painter; and after him came Paolo Giovio of Como, whose larger biographies and shorter *Elogia* have achieved a world-wide reputation, and have become models for future writers in all countries. It is easy to prove by a hundred passages how superficial and even dishonest he was; nor from a man like him can any high and serious purpose

327

be expected. But the breath of the age moves in his pages, and his Leo, his Alfonso, his Pompeo Colonna, live and act before us with such perfect truth and reality that we seem admitted to the deepest recesses of their nature.

Among Neapolitan writers, Tristano Caracciolo (p. 51), so far as we are able to judge, holds indisputably the first place in this respect, although his purpose was not strictly biographical. In the figures which he brings before us guilt and destiny are wondrously mingled. He is a kind of unconscious tragedian. That genuine tragedy which then found no place on the stage swept by in the palace, the street, and the public square. The *Words and Deeds of Alfonso the Great*, written by Antonio Panormita [1] during the lifetime of the king, and consequently showing more of the spirit of flattery than is consistent with historical truth, is remarkable as one of the first of such collections of anecdotes and of wise and witty sayings.

The rest of Europe followed the example of Italy in this respect but slowly, although great political and religious movements had broken so many bonds and had awakened so many thousands to new spiritual life. Italians, whether scholars or diplomatists, still remained, on the whole, the best source of information for the characters of the leading men all over Europe. It is well known how speedily and unanimously in recent times the reports of the Venetian embassies in the sixteenth and seventeenth centuries have been recognized as authorities of the first order for personal description. [3] Even autobiography takes here and there in Italy a bold and vigorous flight, and puts before us, together with the most varied incidents of external life, striking revelations of the inner man. Among other nations, even in Germany at the time of the Reformation, it deals only with outward experiences, and leaves us to guess at the spirit within from the style of the narrative. [4] It seems as though Dante's *La Vita Nuova*, with the inexorable truthfulness which runs through it, had shown his people the way.

The beginnings of autobiography are to be traced in the family histories of the fourteenth and fifteenth centuries, which are said to be not uncommon as manuscripts in the Florentine libraries—unaffected narratives written for the sake of the individual or of his family, like that of Buonaccorso Pitti.

A profound self-analysis is not to be looked for in the *Commentaries* of Pius II. What we here learn of him as a man seems at first sight to be chiefly confined to the account which he gives of the different steps in his career. But further reflection will lead us to a different conclusion with regard to this remarkable book. There are men who are by nature mirrors of what surrounds

---

[1] See above, p. 231.

[2] On Comines see above, p. 114, note 3. While Comines, as is there indicated, owes his power of objective criticism partly to intercourse with Italians, the German humanists and statesmen, notwithstanding the prolonged residence of some of them in Italy, and their diligent and often most successful study of the classical world, acquired little or nothing of the gift of biographical representation or of the analysis of character. The travels, biographies, and historical sketches of the German humanists in the fifteenth and often in the early part of the sixteenth century are mostly either dry catalogues or empty, rhetorical declamations.

[3] See above, p. 114.

[4] Here and there we find exceptions. Letters of Hutten, containing autobiographical notices, bits of the chronicle of Barth. Sastrow, and the *Sabbata* of Joh. Kessler introduce us to the inward conflicts of the writers, mostly, however, bearing the specifically religious character of the Reformation.

FIG. 158. SELF-PORTRAIT BY RAPHAEL
Florence, Uffizi
Photo Deutsche Verlagsanstalt, Stuttgart

them. It would be irrelevant to ask incessantly after their convictions, their spiritual struggles, their inmost victories and achievements. Æneas Sylvius lived wholly in the interest which lay near, without troubling himself about the problems and contradictions of life. His Catholic orthodoxy gave him all the help of this kind that he needed. And at all events, after taking part in every intellectual movement which interested his age, and notably furthering some of them, he still, at the close of his earthly course, retained character enough to preach a crusade against the Turks, and to die of grief when it came to nothing.

Nor is the autobiography of Benvenuto Cellini, any more than that of Pius II, founded on introspection. And yet it describes the whole man—not always willingly—with marvellous truth and completeness. It is no small matter that Benvenuto, whose most important works have perished half finished, and who, as an artist, is perfect only in his little decorative speciality, but in other respects, if judged by the works of him which remain, is surpassed by so many of his greater contemporaries—that Benvenuto as a man will interest mankind to the end of time. It does not spoil the impression when the reader often detects him bragging or lying; the stamp of a mighty, energetic, and thoroughly developed nature remains. By his side Northern autobiographers, though their tendency and moral character may stand much higher, appear incomplete beings. He is a man who can do all and dares do all, and who carries his measure in himself.[1] Whether we like him or not, he lives, such as he was, as a significant type of the modern spirit.

Another man deserves a brief mention in connexion with this subject, a man who, like Benvenuto, was not a model of veracity—Girolamo Cardano of Milan (b. 1500). His little book *De Propria Vita*[2] will outlive and eclipse his fame in philosophy and natural science, just as Benvenuto's life, though its value is of another kind, has thrown his works into the shade. Cardano is a physician who feels his own pulse and describes his own physical, moral, and intellectual nature, together with all the conditions under which it had developed, and this, to the best of his ability, honestly and sincerely. The work which he avowedly took as his model—the *Meditations* of Marcus Aurelius—he was able, hampered as he was by no stoical maxims, to surpass in this particular. He desires to spare neither himself nor others, and begins the narrative of his career with the statement that his mother tried, and failed, to procure abortion. It is worth remark that he attributes to the stars which presided over his birth only the events of his life and his intellectual gifts, but not his moral qualities; he confesses (cap. 10) that the astrological prediction that he would not live to the age of forty or fifty years did him much harm in his youth. But there is no need to quote from so well-known and accessible a book; whoever opens it will not lay it down till the last page. Cardano admits that he cheated at play, that he was vindictive, incapable of all compunction, purposely cruel in his speech. He confesses it without impudence and without

[1] Among Northern autobiographies we might, perhaps, select for comparison that of Agrippa d'Aubigné (though belonging to a later period) as a living and speaking picture of human individuality.

[2] Written in his old age, about 1576. On Cardano as an investigator and discoverer see Libri, *Histoire des Sciences Mathématiques*, iii, pp. 167 *sqq.*

feigned contrition, without even wishing to make himself an object of interest, but with the same simple and sincere love of fact which guided him in his scientific researches. And, what is to us the most repulsive of all, the old man, after the most shocking experiences [1] and with his confidence in his fellow-men

FIG. 159. LUIGI CORNARO
By Tintoretto
Florence, Palazzo Pitti

gone, finds himself after all tolerably happy and comfortable. He has still left him a grandson, immense learning, the fame of his works, money, rank and credit, powerful friends, the knowledge of many secrets, and, best of all, belief in God. After this he counts the teeth in his head, and finds that he has fifteen.

Yet when Cardano wrote Inquisitors and Spaniards were already busy in Italy, either hindering the production of such natures, or, where they existed,

---

[1] For example, the execution of his eldest son, who had taken vengeance for his wife's infidelity by poisoning her (cap. 27, 50).

by some means or other putting them out of the way. There lies a gulf between this book and the memoirs of Alfieri.

Yet it would be unjust to close this list of autobiographers without listening to a word from one man who was both worthy and happy. This is the well-known philosopher of practical life, Luigi Cornaro, whose dwelling at Padua, classical as an architectural work, was at the same time the home of all the Muses. In his famous treatise *On the Sober Life* [1] he describes the strict regimen by which he succeeded, after a sickly youth, in reaching an advanced and healthy age, then of eighty-three years. He goes on to answer those who despise life after the age of sixty-five as a living death, showing them that his own life had nothing deadly about it.

Let them come and see, and wonder at my good health, how I mount on horseback without help, how I run upstairs and up hills, how cheerful, amusing, and contented I am, how free from care and disagreeable thoughts. Peace and joy never quit me. . . . My friends are wise, learned, and distinguished people of good position, and when they are not with me I read and write, and try thereby, as by all other means, to be useful to others. Each of these things I do at the proper time, and at my ease, in my dwelling, which is beautiful and lies in the best part of Padua, and is arranged both for summer and winter with all the resources of architecture, and provided with a garden by the running water. In the spring and autumn I go for a while to my hill in the most beautiful part of the Euganean mountains, where I have fountains and gardens, and a comfortable dwelling; and there I amuse myself with some easy and pleasant chase, which is suitable to my years. At other times I go to my villa on the plain; [2] there all the paths lead to an open space, in the middle of which stands a pretty church; an arm of the Brenta flows through the plantations—fruitful, well-cultivated fields, now fully peopled, which the marshes and the foul air once made fitter for snakes than for men. It was I who drained the country; then the air became good, and people settled there and multiplied, and the land became cultivated as it now is, so that I can truly say: " On this spot I gave to God an altar and a temple and souls to worship Him." This is my consolation and my happiness whenever I come here. In the spring and autumn I also visit the neighbouring towns, to see and converse with my friends, through whom I make the acquaintance of other distinguished men, architects, painters, sculptors, musicians, and cultivators of the soil. I see what new things they have done, I look again at what I know already, and learn much that is of use to me. I see palaces, gardens, antiquities, public grounds, churches, and fortifications. But what most of all delights me when I travel is the beauty of the country and the cities, lying now on the plain, now on the slopes of the hills, or on the banks of rivers and streams, surrounded by gardens and villas. And these enjoyments are not diminished through weakness of the eyes or the ears; all my senses (thank God!) are in the best condition, including the sense of taste; for I enjoy more the simple food which I now take in moderation than all the delicacies which I ate in my years of disorder.

After mentioning the works he had undertaken on behalf of the republic for draining the marshes, and the projects which he had constantly advocated for preserving the lagoons, he thus concludes:

[1] *Discorsi della Vita Sobria*, consisting of the *trattato*, of a *compendio*, of an *esortazione*, and of a *lettera* to Daniel Barbaro. The book has been often reprinted.

[2] Was this the villa of Codevico mentioned above, p. 316? *Cf.* Lovarini, *Le Ville edificate da Al. Cornaro*, *L'Arte*, ii, pp. 189 *sqq.* (1898).

These are the true recreations of an old age which God has permitted to be healthy, and which is free from those mental and bodily sufferings to which so many young people and so many sickly older people succumb. And if it be allowable to add the little to the great, to add jest to earnest, it may be mentioned as a result of my moderate life that in my eighty-third year I have written a most amusing comedy, full of blameless wit. Such works are generally the business of youth, as tragedy is the business of old age. If it is reckoned to the credit of the famous Greek that he wrote a tragedy in his seventy-third year, must I not, with my ten years more, be more cheerful and healthy than he ever was? And that no consolation may be wanting in the overflowing cup of my old age, I see before my eyes a sort of bodily immortality in the persons of my descendants. When I come home I see before me not one or two, but eleven grandchildren, between the ages of two and eighteen, all from the same father and mother, all healthy, and, so far as can already be judged, all gifted with the talent and disposition for learning and a good life. One of the younger I have as my playmate [*buffoncello*], since children from the third to the fifth year are born to tricks; the elder ones I treat as my companions, and, as they have admirable voices, I take delight in hearing them sing and play on different instruments. And I sing myself, and find my voice better, clearer, and louder than ever. These are the pleasures of my last years. My life, therefore, is alive, and not dead; nor would I exchange my age for the youth of such as live in the service of their passions.

In the *Exhortation* which Cornaro added at a much later time, in his ninety-fifth year, he reckons it among the elements of his happiness that his treatise had made many converts. He died at Padua in 1565, at the age of over a hundred years.

CHAPTER VI

The Description of Nations and Cities

THIS national gift did not, however, confine itself to the criticism and description of individuals, but felt itself competent to deal with the qualities and characteristics of whole peoples. Throughout the Middle Ages the cities, families, and nations of all Europe were in the habit of making insulting and derisive attacks on one another, which, with much caricature, contained commonly a kernel of truth. But from the first the Italians surpassed all others in their quick apprehension of the mental differences among cities and populations. Their local patriotism, stronger probably than in any other medieval people, soon found expression in literature, and allied itself with the current conception of 'fame.' Topography became the counterpart of biography (p. 157); while all the more important cities began to celebrate their own praises in prose and verse,[1] writers appeared who made the chief towns and districts the subject partly of a serious comparative description, partly of satire, and sometimes of notices in which jest and earnest are not easily to be distinguished. Brunetto Latini must first be mentioned. Besides his own country, he knew France, from a residence of seven years, and gives a long list of the characteristic differences in costume and modes of life between Frenchmen and Italians, noticing the distinction between the monarchical Government of France and the republican constitution of the Italian cities.[2] After this, next to some famous passages in the *Divine Comedy*, comes the *Dittamondo* of Uberti (about 1360). As a rule only single remarkable facts and characteristics are here mentioned: the Feast of the Crows at S. Apollinare in Ravenna, the springs at Treviso, the great cellar near Vicenza, the high duties at Mantua, the forest of towers at Lucca. Yet mixed up with all this we find laudatory and satirical criticisms of every kind. Arezzo figures with the crafty disposition of its citizens, Genoa with the artificially blackened eyes and teeth (?) of its women, Bologna with its prodigality, Bergamo with its coarse dialect and hard-headed people.[3] In the fifteenth century the fashion was to

---

[1] In some cases very early; in the Lombard cities as early as the twelfth century. *Cf.* Landulfus Senior, Ricobaldus, and (in Murat., xi) the remarkable anonymous work, probably by Giovanni Inagnono, *De Laudibus Papiæ*, of the fourteenth century. Also (in Murat., i) *Liber de Situ Urbis Mediol.* Some notices on Italian local history in O. Lorenzo, *Deutschlands Geschichtsquellen im Mittelalter seit dem 13ten Jahr* (Berlin, 1877); but the author expressly refrains from an original treatment of the subject.

[2] *Il Tesoro*, ed. Chabaille, pp. 179–180 (Paris, 1863). *Cf. ibid.*, p. 577 (lib. iii, p. ii, c. 1).

[3] On Paris, which was a much more important place to the medieval Italian than to his successor a hundred years later, see *Dittamondo*, iv, cap. 18. The contrast between France and Italy is accentuated by Petrarch in his *Invectivæ contra Gallum*.

FIG. 160. THE APOTHEOSIS OF VENICE
Ceiling-piece in the Palace of the Doges by Paolo Veronese
Venice

belaud one's own city even at the expense of others. Michele Savonarola allows that, in comparison with his native Padua, only Rome and Venice are more splendid, and Florence perhaps more joyous [1]—by which our knowledge

[1] Savonarola, in Murat., xxiv, col. 1186 (above, p. 157). On Venice see above, pp. 82 *sqq.* The oldest description of Rome, by Signorili (manuscript), was written in the pontificate of Martin V (1417); see

is naturally not much extended. At the end of the century Jovianus Pontanus in his *Antonius*, writes an imaginary journey through Italy, simply as a vehicle for malicious observations. But in the sixteenth century we meet with a series of exact and profound studies of national characteristics such as no other people of that time could rival.[1] Machiavelli sets forth in some of his valuable essays the character and the political condition of the Germans and French in such a way that the born Northerner, familiar with the history of his own country, is grateful to the Florentine thinker for his flashes of insight. The Florentines (pp. 95 *sqq.*) begin to take pleasure in describing themselves;[2] and, basking in the well-earned sunshine of their intellectual glory, their pride seems to attain its height when they derive the artistic pre-eminence of Tuscany among Italians not from any special gifts of nature, but from hard, patient work.[3] The homage of famous men from other parts of Italy, of which the sixteenth *capitolo* of Ariosto is a splendid example, they accepted as a merited tribute to their excellence.

An admirable description of the Italians, with their various pursuits and characteristics, though in few words and with special stress laid on the Lucchese, to whom the work was dedicated, was given by Ortensio Landi, who, however, is so fond of playing hide-and-seek with his own name, and fast-and-loose with historical facts, that even when he seems to be most in earnest he must be accepted with caution and only after close examination.[4] The same Landi

Gregorovius, vii, 569; the oldest by a German is that of H. Muffel (middle of fifteenth century), ed. by Voigt (Tübingen, 1876).

[1] The character of the restless and energetic Bergamasque, full of curiosity and suspicion, is charmingly described in Bandello, i, *Nov.* 34.

[2] For example, Varchi, in the ninth book of the *Storie Fiorentine* (vol. iii, pp. 56 *sqq.*).

[3] Vasari, xii, p. 158. *V. di Michelangelo,* at the beginning. At other times Mother Nature is praised loudly enough, as in the sonnet of Alfonso de' Pazzi to the non-Tuscan Annibale Caro (in Trucchi, *loc. cit.,* iii, p. 187):

> " Misero il Varchi! e più infelici noi,
> Se a vostri virtudi accidentali
> Aggiunto fosse 'l natural, ch' è in noi! "

[4] *Forcianæ Quæstiones, in quibus varia Italorum ingenia explicantur multaque alia scitu non indigna. Autore Philalette Polytopiensi cive.* Among them, *Mauritii Scævæ Carmen.*

> " Quos hominum mores varios quas denique mentes
> Diverso profert Itala terra solo,
> Quisve vinis animus, mulierum et strenua virtus
> Pulchre hoc exili codice lector habes."

Neapoli excudebat Martinus de Ragusia, anno MDXXXVI. This little work, made use of by Ranke, *Päpste,* i, 385, passes as being from the hand of Ortensio Landi (*cf.* Tiraboschi, vii, 800–812), although in the work itself no hint is given of the author. The title is explained by the circumstance that conversations are reported which were held at Forcium, a bath near Lucca, by a large company of men and women, on the question whence it comes that there are such great differences among mankind. The question receives no answer, but many of the differences among the Italians of that day are noticed—in studies, trade, warlike skill (the point quoted by Ranke), the manufacture of warlike implements, modes of life, distinctions in costume, in language, in intellect, in loving and hating, in the way of winning affection, in the manner of receiving guests, and in eating. At the close come some reflections on the differences among philosophical systems. A large part of the work is devoted to women—their differences in general, the power of their beauty, and especially the question whether women are equal or inferior to men. The work has been made use of in various passages below. The following extract may serve as an example (fol. 7*b sqq.*): " Aperiam nunc quæ sint in consilio aut dando aut accipiendo dissimilitudo. Præstant consilio Mediolanenses, sed aliorum gratia potius quam sua. Sunt nullo consilio Genuenses. Rumor est Venetos abundare. Sunt perutili consilio Lucenses, idque aperte indicarunt, cum in tanto totius Italiæ ardore, tot hostibus circumsepti suam libertatem, ad quam nati videntur semper tutati sint, nulla, quidem, aut capitis aut fortunarum ratione habita. Quis porro non vehementer admiretur? Quis callida consilia non stupeat? Equidem quotiescunque cogito, quanta prudentia ingruentes procellas evitarint,

ublished an anonymous *Commentario* some ten years later,[1] which contains
mong many follies not a few valuable hints on the unhappy ruined condition
f Italy in the middle of the century.[2] Leandro Alberti[3] is not so fruitful as
ight be expected in his description of the character of the different cities.

To what extent this comparative study of national and local characteristics
nay, by means of Italian humanism, have influenced the rest of Europe we
annot say with precision. To Italy, at all events, belongs the priority in this
espect, as in the description of the world in general.

---

uanta solertia impendentia pericula effugerint, adducor in stuporem. Lucanis vero summum est studium, eos
eludere qui consilii captandi gratia adeunt, ipsi vero omnia inconsulte ac temere faciunt. Brutii optimo sunt
onsilio, sed ut incommodent, aut perniciem afferant, in rebus quæ magnæ deliberationis dictu mirum quam stupidi
nt, eisdem plane dotibus instructi sunt Volsci quod ad cædes et furta paulo propensiores sint. Pisani bono
uidem sunt consilio, sed parum constanti, si quis diversum ab eis senserit, mox acquiescunt, rursus si aliter
uadeas, mutabunt consilium, illud in caussa fuit quod tam duram ac diutinam obsidionem ad extremum usque
on pertulerint. Placentini utrisque abundant consiliis, scilicet salutaribus ac pernitiosis, non facile tamen
b iis impetres pestilens consilium, apud Regienses neque consilii copiam invenies. Si sequare Mutinensium
onsilia, raro cedet infeliciter, sunt enim peracutissimo consilio, et voluntate plane bona. Providi sunt
lorentini (si unumquemque seorsum accipias) si vero simul conjuncti sint, non admodum mihi consilia eorum
robabuntur; feliciter cedunt Senensium consilia, subita sunt Perusinorum; salutaria Ferrariensium, fideli sunt
onsilio Veronenses, semper ambigui sunt in consiliis aut dandis aut accipiendis Patavini. Sunt pertinaces in
o quod cœperint consilio Bergomates, respuunt omnium consilia Neapolitani, sunt consultissimi Bononienses."

[1] *Commentario delle Più Notabili, e Mostruose Cose d' Italia e Altri Luoghi, di Lingua Aramæa in Italiana tradotta.*
Con *un Breve Catalogo degli Inventori delle Cose che si Mangiano et Beveno, novamente ritrovato* (Venice, 1553; first
rinted 1548; based on a journey taken by Ortensio Landi through Italy in 1543 and 1544). That Landi was
eally the author of this *Commentario* is clear from the concluding remarks of Niccolò Morra (fol. 46a): "Il
resente commentario nato del constantissimo cervello di M.O.L.," and from the signature of the whole (fol.
oa): SVISNETROH SVDNAL, ROTUA TSE, "Hortensius Landus autor est." After a declaration as to
taly from the mouth of a mysterious grey-haired sage a journey is described from Sicily through Italy to the
East. All the cities of Italy are more or less fully discussed: that Lucca should receive special praise is intelli-
ible from the writer's way of thinking. Venice, where he claims to have been much with Pietro Aretino
p. 170), and Milan are described in detail, and in connexion with the latter the maddest stories are told (fol. 25
qq.). There is no want of such elsewhere—of roses which flower all the year round, stars which shine at mid-
lay, birds which are changed into men, and men with bulls' heads on their shoulders, mermen, and men who
pit fire from their mouths. Among all these there are often authentic bits of information, some of which will
e used in the proper place; short mention is made of the Lutherans (fol. 32a, 38a), and frequent complaints
re heard of the wretched times and unhappy state of Italy. We there read (fol. 22a): "Son questi quelli
taliani li quali in un fatto d' armi uccisero ducento mila Francesi? sono finalmente quelli che di tutto il mondo
' impadronirono? Hai quanto (per quel che io vego) degenerati sono. Hai quanto dissimili mi paiono dalli
ntichi padri loro, li quali e singolar virtù di cuore e disciplina militare ugualmente monstrarno havere." On
he catalogue of eatables which is added see below.

[2] *Descrizione di Tutta l' Italia* (1562).

[3] Satirical lists of cities are frequently met with later—for example, *Macaroneide*, *Phantas*. ii. For France
Rabelais, who knew the *Macaroneide*, is the chief source of all the jests and malicious allusions of this local sort.

CHAPTER VII

DESCRIPTION OF THE OUTWARD MAN

BUT the discoveries made with regard to man were no confined to the spiritual characteristics of individuals an nations; his outward appearance was in Italy the subject of an entirely different interest from that shown in it b Northern peoples.[1]

Of the position held by the great Italian physicians wit respect to the progress of physiology we cannot venture to speak; and th artistic study of the human figure belongs not to a work like the present, bu to the history of art. But something must here be said of that universa education of the eye which rendered the judgment of the Italians as to bodil beauty or ugliness perfect and final.

On reading the Italian authors of that period attentively we are astounded at the keenness and accuracy with which outward features are seized, and at th completeness with which personal appearance in general is described.[2] Eve to-day the Italians, and especially the Romans, have the art of sketching a man' picture in a couple of words. This rapid apprehension of what is charac teristic is an essential condition for detecting and representing the beautiful In poetry, it is true, circumstantial description may be a fault, not a merit since a single feature, suggested by deep passion or insight, will often awaken in the reader a far more powerful impression of the figure described. Dante gives us nowhere a more splendid idea of his Beatrice than where he describes only the influence which goes forth from her upon all around. But here we have not to treat particularly of poetry, which follows its own laws and pursues its own ends, but rather of the general capacity to paint in words real or imaginary forms.

In this Boccaccio is a master—not in the *Decamerone*, where the character of the tales forbids lengthy description, but in the romances, where he is free to take his time. In his *Ameto*[3] he describes a blonde and a brunette much as an artist a hundred years later would have painted them—for here too culture long precedes art. In the account of the brunette—or, strictly speaking, of the less blonde of the two—there are touches which deserve to be called classical. In the words " la spaziosa testa e distesa " lies the feeling for grander forms, which go beyond a graceful prettiness; the eyebrows with him no longer

[1] It is true that many decaying literatures are full of painfully minute descriptions. See, for example, in Sidonius Apollinaris the descriptions of a Visigoth king (*Epist.*, i, 2), of a personal enemy (*Epist.*, iii, 13), and in his poems the types of the different German tribes.

[2] On Filippo Villani see above, p. 326.　　　　　　　[3] *Parnasso Teatrale*, Introd., p. vii (Lipsia, 1829).

338

esemble two bows, as in the Byzantine ideal, but a single wavy line; the nose eems to have been meant to be aquiline;[1] the broad, full breast, the arms of

FIG. 161. VENUS
Part of Botticelli's picture *Mars and Venus*
London, National Gallery

moderate length, the effect of the beautiful hand as it lies on the purple mantle —all both foretell the sense of beauty of a coming time and unconsciously approach to that of classical antiquity. In other descriptions Boccaccio mentions a flat (not medievally rounded) brow, a long, earnest, brown eye, and

[1] The reading is here evidently corrupt. The passage is as follows (*Ameto*, p. 54, Venezia, 1856): " Del mezo de' quali non camuso naso in linea diretta discende, quanto ad aquilineo non essere dimanda il dovere."

round, not hollowed neck, as well as—in a very modern tone—the " little feet " and the " two roguish eyes " of a black-haired nymph.[1]

Whether the fifteenth century has left any written account of its ideal of beauty I am not able to say. The works of the painters and sculptors do not render such an account as unnecessary as might appear at first sight, since possibly, as opposed to their realism, a more ideal type might have been favoured and preserved by the writers.[2] In the sixteenth century Firenzuola came forward with his remarkable work on female beauty.[3] We must clearly distinguish in it what he had learned from old authors or from artists, such as the fixing of proportions according to the length of the head, and certain abstract conceptions. What remains is his own genuine observation, illustrated with examples of women and girls from Prato. As his little work is a kind of lecture, delivered before the women of this city—that is to say, before very severe critics—he must have kept pretty closely to the truth. His principle is avowedly that of Zeuxis and of Lucian—to piece together an ideal beauty out of a number of beautiful parts. He defines the shades of colour which occur in the hair and skin, and gives to the *biondo* the preference, as the most beautiful colour for the hair,[4] understanding by it a soft yellow inclining to brown. He requires that the hair should be thick, long, and locky; the forehead serene, and twice as broad as high; the skin bright and clear (*candida*), but not of a dead white (*bianchezza*); the eyebrows dark, silky, most strongly marked in the middle, and shading off toward the ears and the nose; the white of the eye faintly touched with blue, the iris not actually black, though all the poets praise *occhi neri* as a gift of Venus, despite that even goddesses were known for their eyes of heavenly blue, and that soft, joyous, brown eyes were admired by everybody. The eye itself should be large and full, and brought well forward; the lids white, and marked with almost invisible tiny red veins; the lashes neither too long, nor too thick, nor too dark. The hollow round the eye should have the same colour as the cheek.[5] The ear, neither too large nor

---

[1] " Due occhi ladri nel loro movimento." The whole work is rich in such descriptions.

[2] The charming book of songs by Giusto de' Conti, *La Bella Mano* (best ed. Florence, 1715), does not tell us as many details of this famous hand of his beloved as Boccaccio in a dozen passages of the *Ameto* of the hands of his nymphs.

[3] *Della Bellezza delle Donne*, in the first vol. of the *Opere di Firenzuola* (Milan, 1802). For his view of bodily beauty as a sign of beauty of soul *cf.* vol. ii, pp. 48-52, in the *ragionamenti* prefixed to his novels. Among the many who maintain this doctrine, partly in the style of the ancients, we may quote one, Castiglione, *Il Cortigiano*, lib. iv, fol. 176. [4] This was a universal opinion, not only the professional opinion of painters. See below.

[5] This may be an opportunity for a word on the eyes of Lucrezia Borgia, taken from the distichs of a Ferrarese Court poet, Ercole Strozzi (*Strozzii Poeta*, fol. 85-88). The power of her glance is described in a manner only explicable in an artistic age, and which would not now be permitted. Sometimes it turns the beholder to fire, sometimes to stone. He who looks long at the sun becomes blind; he who beheld Medusa became a stone; but he who looks at the countenance of Lucrezia

" Fit primo intuitu cæcus et inde lapis."

Even the marble Cupid sleeping in her halls is said to have been petrified by her gaze:

" Lumine Borgiado saxificatur Amor."

Critics may dispute, if they please, whether the so-called Eros of Praxiteles or that of Michelangelo is meant, since she was the possessor of both.

And the same glance appeared to another poet, Marcello Filosseno, only mild and lofty, " mansueto e altero " (Roscoe, *Leo X*, ed. Bossi, vii, p. 306).

Comparisons with ideal figures of antiquity occur (p. 30). Of a boy ten years old we read in the *Orlandino* (ii, str. 47), " ed ha capo romano."

FIG. 162. LODOVICA TORNABUONI

Part of the fresco *The Birth of Mary*, by Ghirlandaio

Florence, S. Maria Novella

Photo Anderson, Rome

too small, firmly and neatly joined, should show a stronger colour in the winding than in the even parts, with an edge of the transparent ruddiness of the pomegranate. The temples must be white and even, and for the most perfect beauty ought not to be too narrow.[1] The red should grow deeper as the cheek gets rounder. The nose, which chiefly determines the value of the profile, must recede gently and uniformly in the direction of the eyes; where the cartilage ceases there may be a slight elevation, but not so marked as to make the nose aquiline, which is not pleasing in women; the lower part must be less strongly coloured than the ears, but not of a chilly whiteness, and the middle partition above the lips lightly tinted with red. The mouth our author would have rather small, and neither projecting to a point nor quite flat, with the lips not too thin, and fitting neatly together; an accidental opening—that is, when the woman is neither speaking nor laughing—should not display more than six upper teeth. As delicacies of detail, he mentions a dimple in the upper lip, a certain fullness of the under lip, and a tempting smile in the left corner of the mouth—and so on. The teeth should not be too small, regular, well marked off from one another, and of the colour of ivory; and the gums must not be too dark or even like red velvet. The chin is to be round, neither pointed nor curved outward, and growing slightly red as it rises; its glory is the dimple. The neck should be white and round and rather long than short, with the hollow and the Adam's apple but faintly marked; and the skin at every movement must show pleasing lines. The shoulders he desires broad, and in the breadth of the bosom sees the first condition of its beauty. No bone may be visible upon it, its fall and swell must be gentle and gradual, its colour *candidissimo*. The leg should be long and not too hard in the lower parts, but not without flesh on the shin, which must be provided with white, full calves. He likes the foot small, but not bony, the instep (it seems) high, and the colour white as alabaster. The arms are to be white, and in the upper parts tinted with red; in their consistence fleshy and muscular, but soft as those of Pallas when she stood before the shepherd on Mount Ida—in a word, ripe, fresh, and firm. The hand should be white, especially toward the wrist, but large and plump, feeling soft as silk, the rosy palm marked with a few but distinct and not intricate lines; the elevations in it should not be too great, the space between thumb and forefinger brightly coloured and without wrinkles, the fingers long, delicate, and scarcely at all thinner toward the tips, with nails clear, even, not too long or too square, and cut so as to show a white margin about the breadth of a knife's back.

Æsthetic principles of a general character occupy a very subordinate place to these particulars. The ultimate principles of beauty, according to which the eye judges *senza appello*, are for Firenzuola a secret, as he frankly confesses; and his definitions of *leggiadria*, *grazia*, *vaghezza*, *venustà*, *aria*, and *maestà* are partly, as has been remarked, philological, and partly vain attempts to utter the

[1] Referring to the fact that the appearance of the temples can be altogether changed by the arrangement of the hair, Firenzuola makes a comical attack on the overcrowding of the hair with flowers, which causes the head to " look like a pot of pinks or a quarter of goat on the spit." He is, as a rule, thoroughly at home in caricature.

VENUS
By Giorgione
Picture Gallery, Dresden

DIVES AND LAZARUS
By Bonifacio Veronese
The Academy, Venice

unutterable.   Laughter he prettily defines, probably following some old author, as a radiance of the soul.

The literature of all countries can, at the close of the Middle Ages, show single attempts to lay down theoretic principles of beauty; [1] but no other work can be compared to that of Firenzuola.   Brantôme, who came a good half-century later, is a bungling critic by his side, because governed by lasciviousness and not by a sense of beauty.

[1] For the ideal of the *Minnesänger* see Falke, *Die deutsche Trachtenund Modenwelt*, i, pp. 85 *sqq.*

CHAPTER VIII

Descriptions of Life in Movement

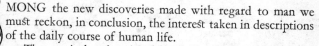MONG the new discoveries made with regard to man we must reckon, in conclusion, the interest taken in descriptions of the daily course of human life.

The comical and satirical literature of the Middle Ages could not dispense with pictures of everyday events. But it is another thing when the Italians of the Renaissance dwelt on this picture for its own sake—for its inherent interest—and because it forms part of that great universal life of the world whose magic breath they felt everywhere around them. Instead of and together with the satirical comedy, which wanders through houses, villages, and streets, seeking food for its derision in parson, peasant, and burgher, we now see in literature the beginnings of a true *genre* long before it found any expression in painting. That *genre* and satire are often met with in union does not prevent them from being wholly different things.

How much of earthly business must Dante have watched with attentive interest before he was able to make us see with our own eyes all that happened in his spiritual world![1] The famous pictures of the busy movement in the arsenal at Venice, of the blind men laid side by side before the church door,[2] and the like, are by no means the only instances of this kind; for the art, in which he is a master, of expressing the inmost soul by the outward gesture cannot exist without a close and incessant study of human life.

The poets who followed rarely came near him in this respect, and the novelists were forbidden by the first laws of their literary style to linger over details. Their prefaces and narratives might be as long as they pleased, but what we understand by *genre* was outside their province. The taste for this class of description was not fully awakened till the time of the revival of antiquity.

And here again we are met by the man who had a heart for everything—Æneas Sylvius. Not only natural beauty, not only that which has an antiquarian or a geographical interest, finds a place in his descriptions (p. 248; ii, p. 28), but any living scene of daily life.[3] Among the numerous passages in his memoirs in which scenes are described which hardly one of his contemporaries

---

[1] On the accuracy of his sense of form, p. 283.

[2] *Inferno*, xxi, 7; *Purgatorio*, xiii, 61.

[3] We must not take it too seriously if we read (in Platina, *Vitæ Pontiff.*, p. 310) that he kept at his Court a sort of buffoon, the Florentine Greco, " hominem certe cuiusvis mores, naturam, linguam cum maximo omnium qui audiebant risu facile exprimentem."

FIG. 163. THE JOURNEY OF THE MAGI
By Benozzo Gozzoli
Florence Palazzo Medici-Riccardi

would have thought worth a line of notice, we will here mention only the boat-race on the Lake of Bolsena.[1] We are not able to detect from what old letter-writer or story-teller the impulse was derived to which we owe such lifelike pictures. Indeed, the whole spiritual communion between antiquity and the Renaissance is full of delicacy and of mystery.

To this class belong those descriptive Latin poems of which we have already spoken (p. 264)—hunting-scenes, journeys, ceremonies, and so forth. In Italian we also find something of the same kind, as, for example, the descriptions of the famous Medicean tournament by Politian and Luca Pulci.[2] The true epic poets, Luigi Pulci, Bojardo, and Ariosto are carried on more rapidly by the stream of their narrative; yet in all of them we must recognize the lightness and precision of their descriptive touch as one of the chief elements of their greatness. Franco Sacchetti amuses himself with repeating the short speeches of a troop of pretty women caught in the woods by a shower of rain.[3]

Other scenes of moving life are to be looked for in the military historians (p. 118). In a lengthy poem [4] dating from an earlier period we find a faithful picture of a combat of mercenary soldiers in the fourteenth century, chiefly in the shape of the orders, cries of battle, and dialogue with which it is accompanied.

But the most remarkable productions of this kind are the realistic descriptions of country life, which are found most abundantly in Lorenzo the Magnificent and the poets of his circle.

Since the time of Petrarch [5] an unreal and conventional style of bucolic poetry had been in vogue, which, whether written in Latin or Italian, was essentially a copy of Virgil. Parallel to this we find the pastoral novel of Boccaccio (p. 261) and other works of the same kind down to the *Arcadia* of Sannazaro, and later still the pastoral comedy of Tasso and Guarino. They are works whose style, whether poetry or prose, is admirably finished and

---

[1] *Pii II Comment.*, viii, p. 391.

[2] Two tournaments must be distinguished, Lorenzo's in 1468 and Giuliano's in 1475 (a third in 1481?). See Reumont, *Lorenzo dei Medici*, i, 264 *sqq.*, 267, note 1, 361; ii, 55, 67, and the works there quoted, which settle the old dispute on these points. The first tournament is treated in the poem of Luca Pulci, ed. *Ciriffo Calvaneo di Luca Pulci Gentilhuomo Fiorentino, con la Giostra del Magnifico Lorenzo de' Medici*, pp. 75, 91 (Florence, 1572); the second is an unfinished poem of Angelo Poliziano, best ed. Carducci, *Le Stanze, l' Orfeo e le Rime di M. A. P.* (Florence, 1863). The description of Politian breaks off at the setting out of Giuliano for the tournament. Pulci gives a detailed account of the combatants and the manner of fighting. The description of Lorenzo is particularly good (p. 82).

[3] This so-called *Caccia* is printed in the Commentary to Castiglione's *Eclogue* from a Roman manuscript. *Lettere del Conte B. Castiglione*, ed. Pierantonio Serassi, ii, p. 269 (Padua, 1771); printed by Carducci, *Cacce in Rime dei Secoli XIV e XV* (Bologna, 1896).

[4] See the *Serventese* of Giannozzo of Florence (probably Sacchetti, a brother of the famous Florentine novelist), in Trucchi, *Poesie Ital. Ined.*, ii, p. 99, or better in Carducci (see previous note), pp. 59 *sqq.* The words are many of them quite unintelligible, borrowed really or apparently from the languages of the foreign mercenaries. Machiavelli's description of Florence during the plague of 1527 belongs, to a certain extent, to this class of works. It is a series of living, speaking pictures of a frightful calamity.

[5] According to Boccaccio (*Vita di Dante*, p. 77) Dante was the author of two eclogues, probably written in Latin. [The authenticity of these poems is, however, very strongly questioned.—W. G.] They are addressed to Joh. de Virgiliis. *Cf.* Fraticelli, *Opp. Min. di Dante*, i, 417. Petrarch's bucolic poem in P. *Carmina Minora*, ed. Rossetti, i. *Cf.* L. Geiger, *Petrarca*, pp. 120–122 and 270, note 6, especially A. Hortis, *Scritti Inediti di F. P.* (Triest, 1874).

FIG. 164. ÆNEAS SYLVIUS'S DEPARTURE FOR THE COUNCIL OF BASEL
By Pinturicchio
Siena, Cathedral Library

perfect, but in which pastoral life is only an ideal dress for sentiments which belong to a wholly different sphere of culture.[1]

But by the side of all this there appeared in Italian poetry, toward the close of the fifteenth century, signs of a more realistic treatment of rustic life. This was not possible out of Italy; for here only did the peasant, whether labourer or proprietor, possess human dignity, personal freedom, and the right of settlement, hard as his lot might sometimes be in other respects.[2] The difference between town and country is far from being so marked here as in Northern countries. Many of the smaller towns are peopled almost exclusively by peasants who, on coming home at nightfall from their work, are transformed into townsfolk. The masons of Como wandered over nearly all Italy; the child Giotto was free to leave his sheep and join a guild at Florence; everywhere there was a human stream flowing from the country into the cities, and some mountain populations seemed born to supply this current.[3] It is true that the pride and local conceit supplied poets and novelists with abundant motives for making game of the *villano*,[4] and what they left undone was taken charge of by the comic improvisers (pp. 316 *sqq*.). But nowhere do we find a trace of that brutal and contemptuous class-hatred against the *vilains* which inspired the aristocratic poets of Provence, and often, too, the French chroniclers. On the contrary,[5] Italian authors of every sort gladly recognize and accentuate what is great or remarkable in the life of the peasant. Gioviano Pontano mentions with admiration instances of the fortitude of the savage inhabitants of the Abruzzi;[6] in the biographical collections and in the novelists we meet with the figure of the heroic peasant-maiden[7] who hazards her life to defend her family and her honour.[8]

---

[1] Boccaccio gives in his *Ameto* (above, p. 338) a kind of mythical *Decamerone*, and sometimes fails ludicrously to keep up the character. One of his nymphs is a good Catholic, and prelates shoot glances of unholy love at her in Rome. Another marries. In the *Ninfale Fiesolano* the nymph Mensola, who finds herself pregnant, takes counsel of an "old and wise nymph."

[2] In general the prosperity of the Italian peasants was greater then than that of the peasantry anywhere else in Europe. *Cf.* Sacchetti, *Nov.* 88 and 222; L. Pulci in the *Beca da Dicamano* (Villari, *Machiavelli*, i, 198, note 2).

[3] "Nullum est hominum genus aptius urbi," says Battista Mantovano (*Ecl.*, viii) of the inhabitants of the Monte Baldo and the Val Cassina, who could turn their hands to anything. Some country populations, as is well known, have even now privileges with regard to certain occupations in the great cities.

[4] Perhaps one of the strongest passages, *Orlandino*, cap. v, str. 54–58. The tranquil and unlearned Vesp. Bisticci says (*Comm. sulla Vita di Giov. Manetti*, p. 96): " Sono due ispezie di uomini difficili a supportare per la loro ignoranza; l' una sono i servi, la seconda i contadini."

[5] In Lombardy, at the beginning of the sixteenth century, the nobles did not shrink from dancing, wrestling, leaping, and racing with the peasants. *Il Cortigiano*, lib. ii, fol. 54. A. Pandolfini (L. B. Alberti) in the *Trattato del Governo della Famiglia*, p. 86, is an instance of a landowner who consoles himself for the greed and fraud of his peasant tenantry with the reflection that he is thereby taught to bear and deal with his fellow-creatures.

[6] Jov. Pontan., *De Fortitudine*, lib. ii.

[7] The famous peasant-woman of the Valtellina—Bona Lombarda, wife of the *condottiere* Pietro Brunoro—is known to us from Jacobus Bergomensis and from Porcellius, in Murat., xxv, col. 43.

[8] On the condition of the Italian peasantry in general, and especially on the details of that condition in several provinces, we are unable to particularize more fully. The proportions between freehold and leasehold property, and the burdens laid on each in comparison with those borne at the present time, must be gathered from special works—for example, Rob. Pöhlmann, *Die Wirtschaftspolitik der Florentiner Renaissance und das Prinzip der Verkehrsfreiheit* (Leipzig, 1878); also Sorbello, *Il Commune Rurale* (Bologna, 1910). In stormy times the country people were apt to have appalling relapses into savagery (*Archiv. Stor.*, xvi, i, pp. 451 *sqq.*, *ad a.* 1440; Corio, fol. 259; *Annales Foroliv.*, in Murat., xxii, col. 227), though nothing in the shape of a general peasants' war occurred. The rising near Piacenza in 1462 was of some importance and interest. *Cf.* Corio, *Storia di Milano*, fol. 409; *Annales Placent.*, in Murat., xx, col. 907; Sismondi, x, p. 138. See below, Part VI, Chapter I.

Such conditions made the poetical treatment of country life possible. The first instance we shall mention is that of Battista Mantovano, whose eclogues, once much read and still worth reading, appeared among his earliest works about 1480. They are a mixture of real and conventional rusticity, but the former tends to prevail. They represent the mode of thought of a well-meaning village clergyman, not without a certain leaning to liberal ideas. As a Carmelite monk, the writer may have had occasion to mix freely with the peasantry.[1]

But it is with a power of a wholly different kind that Lorenzo the Magnificent transports himself into the peasant's world. His *Nencia da Barberino* [2] reads like a crowd of genuine extracts from the popular songs of the Florentine country fused into a great stream of octaves. The objectivity of the writer is such that we are in doubt whether the speaker—the young peasant Vallera, who declares his love to Nencia — awakens his sympathy or ridicule. The deliberate contrast to the

FIG. 165. PASTORAL SCENE, WITH VIRGIL WRITING A POEM
Miniature from a Virgil manuscript
Milan, Ambrosiana

---

[1] *F. Bapt. Mantuani Bucolica seu Adolescentia in Decem Eclogas divisa*; often printed—for example, Strasburg, 1504. The date of composition is indicated by the preface, written in 1498, from which it also appears that the ninth and tenth eclogues were added later. In the heading to the tenth are the words " post religionis ingressum"; in that of the seventh " cum jam autor ad religionem aspiraret." The eclogues by no means deal exclusively with peasant life; in fact, only two of them do so—the sixth, " disceptatione rusticorum et civium," in which the writer sides with the rustics, and the eighth, " de rusticorum religione." The others speak of love, of the relations between poets and wealthy men, of conversion to religion, and of the manners of the Roman Court.

[2] *Poesie di Lorenzo Magnifico*, i, pp. 37 *sqq.* [More recent Italian investigators, in contrast with Burckhardt's opinion, have brought out the satirical tendency of the work.—L. G.] The remarkable poems belonging to the period of the German *Minnesänger*, which bear the name of Neithard von Reuenthal, depict peasant life only in so far as the knight chooses to mix with it for his amusement. The peasants reply to the ridicule of Reuenthal in songs of their own. *Cf.* Karl Schroder, *Die bösisch Dorfpoesie des deutschen Mittelalters*, in Rich. Gosche, *Jahrb. für Literaturgesch.*, pp. 45–98, especially 75 *sqq.* (1 vol., Berlin, 1875).

conventional eclogue is unmistakable. Lorenzo surrenders himself purposely to the realism of simple, rough country life, and yet his work makes upon us the impression of true poetry.

FIG. 166. ANGELO POLIZIANO
Part of the fresco *The Sacrifice of Zacharias*, by Ghirlandaio
Florence, S. Maria Novella
Photo Anderson, Rome

The *Beca da Dicomano* of Luigi Pulci[1] is an admitted counterpart to the *Nencia* of Lorenzo. But the deeper purpose is wanting. The *Beca* is written not so much from the inward need to give a picture of popular life as

[1] *Poesie di Lorenzo Magnifico*, ii, 149.

rom the desire to win the approbation of the educated Florentine world by successful poem. Hence the greater and more deliberate coarseness of the cenes and the indecent jokes. Nevertheless, the point of view of the rustic over is admirably maintained.

Third in this company of poets comes Angelo Poliziano, with his *Rusticus* [1] n Latin hexameters. Keeping clear of all imitation of Virgil's *Georgics*, he describes the year of the Tuscan peasant, beginning with the late autumn, vhen the countryman gets ready his new plough and prepares the seed for he winter. The picture of the meadows in spring is full and beautiful, and he " Summer " has fine passages ; but the vintage feast in autumn is one of he gems of modern Latin poetry. Politian wrote poems in Italian as well as Latin, from which we may infer that in Lorenzo's circle it was possible to give a realistic picture of the passionate life of the lower classes. His gipsy's love-song [2] is one of the earliest products of that wholly modern tendency to put oneself with poetic consciousness into the position of another class. This had probably been attempted for ages with a view to satire,[3] and the opportunity for it was offered in Florence at every carnival by the songs of the maskers. But the sympathetic understanding of the feelings of another class was new; and with it the *Nencia* and this *canzone zingaresca* mark a new starting-point in the history of poetry.

Here, too, we must briefly indicate how culture prepared the way for artistic development. From the time of the *Nencia* a period of eighty years elapses to the rustic *genre*-painting of Jacopo Bassano and his school.

In the next part of this work we shall show how differences of birth had lost their significance in Italy. Much of this was doubtless owing to the fact that men and man were here first thoroughly and profoundly understood. This one single result of the Renaissance is enough to fill us with everlasting thankfulness. The logical notion of humanity was old enough—but here the notion became a fact.

The loftiest conceptions on this subject were uttered by Pico della Mirandola in his speech on the dignity of man,[4] which may justly be called one of the

---

[1] In the *Deliciæ Poetar. Ital.*, and in the works of Politian. First separate ed. Florence, 1493. The didactic poem of Rucellai, *Le Api*, first printed 1519, and of Alamanni, *La Coltivazione* (Paris, 1546), contain something of the same kind.

[2] *Poesie di Lorenzo Magnifico*, ii, 75. [In other editions the poem bears the title of *La Brunetta*, and, according to Carducci, it is not by Politian.—L. G.]

[3] The imitation of different dialects and of the manners of different districts spring from the same tendency. *Cf.* p. 164.

[4] *Jo. Pici Oratio de Hominis Dignitate.* The passage is as follows: " Statuit tandem optimus opifex ut cui dari nihil proprium poterat commune esset quidquid privatum singulis fuerat. Igitur hominem accepit indiscretæ opus imaginis atque in mundi posito meditullio sic est allocutus : Nec certam sedem, nec propriam faciem, nec munus ullum peculiare tibi dedimus, O Adam, ut quam sedem, quam faciem, quæ munera tute optaveris, ea pro voto pro tua sententia habeas et possideas. Definita cæteris natura inter præscriptas a nobis leges coercetur, tu nullis augustiis coercitus pro tuo arbitrio, in cujus manus te posui, tibi illam præfinies. Medium te mundi posui ut circumspiceres inde commodius quidquid est in mundo. Nec te cælestem neque terrenum, neque mortalem neque immortalem fecimus, ut tui ipsius quasi arbitrarius honorariusque plastes et fictor in quam malueris tute formam effingas. Poteris in inferiora quæ sunt bruta degenerare, poteris in superiora quæ sunt divina ex tui animi sententia regenerari. O summam dei patris liberalitatem, summam et admirandam hominis felicitatem. Cui datum id habere quod optat, id esse quod velit. Bruta simulatque nascuntur id secum afferunt, ut ait Lucilius, e bulga matris quod possessura sunt; supremi spiritus aut ab initio aut paulo mox id fuerunt quod sunt futuri in perpetuas æternitates. Nascenti homini omnifaria semina et omnigenæ

noblest bequests of that great age.   God, he tells us, made man at the close
of the Creation, to know the laws of the universe, to love its beauty, to admire
its greatness.   He bound him to no fixed place, to no prescribed form of work
and by no iron necessity, but gave him freedom to will and to move.   " I have
set thee," says the Creator to Adam, " in the midst of the world, that thou
mayst the more easily behold and see all that is therein.   I created thee a being
neither heavenly nor earthly, neither mortal nor immortal only, that thou
mightest be free to shape and to overcome thyself.   Thou mayst sink into
beast, and be born anew to the divine likeness.   The brutes bring from their
mother's body what they will carry with them as long as they live; the higher
spirits are from the beginning, or soon after,[1] what they will be for ever
To thee alone is given a growth and a development depending on thine own
free will.   Thou bearest in thee the germs of a universal life."

vitæ germina indidit pater; quæ quisque excoluerit illa adolescent et fructus suos ferent in illo.   Si vegetal
planta fiet, si sensualia, obbrutescet, si rationalia, cœleste evadet animal, si intellectualia, angelus erit et dei filiu
et si nulla creaturarum sorte contentus in unitatis centrum suæ se receperit, unus cum deo spiritus factus i
solitaria patris caligine qui est super omnia constitutus omnibus antestabit."

The speech first appears in the *Commentationes* of Jo. Picus without any special title; the heading " De Homin
Dignitate " was added later.   It is not altogether suitable, since a great part of the discourse is devoted to th
defence of the peculiar philosophy of Pico, and the praise of the Jewish Kabbalah.   On Pico see above, pp. 21
sqq., and below, Part VI, Chapter IV.   More than two hundred years before Brunetto Latini (*Il Tesoro*, lib. i, cap
13, ed. Chabaille, p. 20) had said: " Toutes choses dou ciel en aval sont faites pour l'ome; mais li hom at fai
pour lui meisme."   The words seemed to a contemporary to have too much human pride in them, and he added
" e por Dieu amer et servir et por avoir la joie pardurable."

[1] An allusion to the fall of Lucifer and his followers.

PART V

SOCIETY AND FESTIVALS

CHAPTER I

The Equalization of Classes

EVERY period of civilization which forms a complete and consistent whole manifests itself not only in political life, in religion, art, and science, but also sets its characteristic stamp on social life. Thus the Middle Ages had their courtly and aristocratic manners and etiquette, differing but little in the various countries of Europe, as well as their peculiar forms of middle-class life.

Italian customs at the time of the Renaissance offer in these respects the sharpest contrast to medievalism. The foundation on which they rest is wholly different. Social intercourse in its highest and most perfect form now ignored all distinctions of caste, and was based simply on the existence of an educated class as we now understand the word. Birth and origin were without influence, unless combined with leisure and inherited wealth. Yet this assertion must not be taken in an absolute and unqualified sense, since medieval distinctions still sometimes made themselves felt to a greater or less degree, if only as a means of maintaining equality with the aristocratic pretensions of the less advanced countries of Europe. But the main current of the time went steadily toward the fusion of classes in the modern sense of the phrase.

The fact was of vital importance that, from certainly the twelfth century onward, the nobles and the burghers dwelt together within the walls of the cities.[1] The interests and pleasures of both classes were thus identified, and the feudal lord learned to look at society from another point of view than that of his mountain-castle. The Church too in Italy never suffered itself, as in Northern countries, to be used as a means of providing for the younger sons of noble families. Bishoprics, abbacies, and canonries were often given from the most unworthy motives, but still not according to the pedigrees of the applicants; and if the bishops in Italy were more numerous, poorer, and, as a rule, destitute of all sovereign rights, they still lived in the cities where their cathedrals stood, and formed, together with their chapters, an important element in the cultivated society of the place. In the age of despots and absolute princes which followed the nobility in most of the cities had the motives and the leisure to give themselves up to a private life (p. 144) free from political

[1] The habit among the Piedmontese nobility of living in their castles in the country struck the other Italians as exceptional. Bandello, ii, *Nov.* 12.

danger and adorned with all that was elegant and enjoyable, but at the same time hardly distinguishable from that of the wealthy burgher. And after the time of Dante, when the new poetry and literature were in the hands of all Italy,[1] when to this was added the revival of ancient culture and the new interest in man as such, when the successful *condottiere* became a prince, and not only good birth, but legitimate birth, ceased to be indispensable for a throne (p. 40), it might well seem that the age of equality had dawned, and the belief in nobility vanished for ever.

FIG. 167. NOTABLES
Part of a picture of the Bernardine Series, by Bartolommeo Caporali (?)
Perugia, Pinacotheca

From a theoretical point of view, when the appeal was made to antiquity the conception of nobility could be both justified and condemned from Aristotle alone. Dante, for example,[2] adapts from the Aristotelian definition, "Nobility rests on excellence and inherited wealth," his own saying, "Nobility rests on personal excellence or on that of predecessors." But elsewhere he is not satisfied with this conclusion. He blames himself,[3] because even in Paradise, while talking with his ancestor Cacciaguida, he made mention of his noble origin, which is but as a mantle from which time is ever cutting something away, unless we ourselves add daily fresh worth to it. And in the *Convivio*[4] he disconnects *nobile* and *nobiltà* from every condition of birth, and identifies the idea with the capacity for moral and intellectual eminence, laying a special stress on high culture by calling *nobiltà* the sister of *filosofia*.

And as time went on the greater the influence of humanism on the Italian mind, the firmer and more widespread became the conviction that birth decides nothing as to the goodness or badness of a man. In the fifteenth century this was the prevailing opinion. Poggio, in his dialogue

---

[1] This was the case long before the invention of printing. A large number of manuscripts, and among them the best, belonged to Florentine artisans. If it had not been for Savonarola's great bonfire many more of them would be left.

[2] Dante, *De Monarchia*, lib. ii, cap. 3.   [3] *Paradiso*, xvi, at the beginning.

[4] Dante, *Convivio*, nearly the whole *Trattato*, iv, and elsewhere. Brunetto Latini says (*Il Tesoro*, lib. i, p. ii, cap. 50, ed. Chabaille, p. 343): "De ce [la vertu] nasqui premierement la nobleté de gentil gent, non pas de ses ancêtres"; and he warns men (lib. ii, p. ii, cap. 196, p. 440) that they may lose true nobility by bad actions. Gaspary, *Geschichte der Ital. Literatur*, p. 518, has pointed out that the sentence " Nobility does not depend on birth, but only upon virtue," was then a commonplace for poets and for the disputes of schools of rhetoric. Similarly Petrarch, *De Rem. utr. Fort.*, lib. i, dial. xvii: " Verus nobilis non nascitur, sed fit."

On Nobility,[1] agrees with his interlocutors—Niccolò Niccoli and Lorenzo de' Medici, brother of the great Cosimo—that there is no other nobility than that of personal merit. The keenest shafts of his ridicule are directed against much of what vulgar prejudice thinks indispensable to an aristocratic life.

A man is all the farther removed from true nobility the longer his forefathers have plied the trade of brigands. The taste for hawking and hunting savours no more of nobility than the nests and lairs of the hunted creatures of spikenard. The cultivation of the soil, as practised by the ancients, would be much nobler than this senseless wandering through the hills and woods, by which men make themselves liker to the brutes than to the reasonable creatures. It may serve well enough as a recreation, but not as the business of a lifetime.

The life of the English and French chivalry in the country or in the woody fastnesses seems to him thoroughly ignoble, and worst of all the doings of the robber-knights of Germany. Lorenzo here begins to take the part of the nobility, not—which is characteristic—appealing to any natural sentiment in its favour, but because Aristotle in the fifth book of the *Politics* recognizes the nobility as existent, and defines it as resting on excellence and inherited wealth. To this Niccoli retorts that Aristotle gives this not as his own conviction, but as the popular impression; in his *Ethics*, where he speaks as he

FIG. 168. YOUTHS OF THE VENETIAN NOBILITY
Part of a painting in the St Ursula Series, by Carpaccio
Venice, Accademia
Photo Anderson, Rome

thinks, he calls him noble who strives after that which is truly good. Lorenzo urges upon him vainly that the Greek word for nobility means good birth; Niccoli thinks the Roman word *nobilis—i.e.*, remarkable—a better one, since it makes nobility depend on a man's deeds.[2] Together with these discussions we find a sketch of the condition of the nobles in various parts of Italy. In

[1] *Poggi Opera, Dial. de Nobilitate.* Aristotle's view is expressly combated by B. Platina, *De Vera Nobilitate* (*Opp.*, ed. Colon., 1573).

[2] This contempt of noble birth is common among the humanists. See the severe passages in Æneas Sylvius, *Opera*, pp. 84 (*Hist. Bohem.*, cap. 2) and 640 (story of Lucretia and Euryalus).

355

Naples they will not work, and busy themselves neither with their own estates nor with trade and commerce, which they hold to be discreditable; they either loiter at home or ride about on horseback.[1] The Roman nobility also despise trade, but farm their own property; the cultivation of the land even opens the way to a title;[2] " it is a respectable but boorish nobility." In Lombardy the nobles live upon the rent of their inherited estates; descent and the abstinence from any regular calling constitute nobility.[3] In Venice the *nobili*, the ruling caste, were all merchants. Similarly in Genoa the nobles and non-nobles were alike merchants and sailors, and separated only by their birth; some few of the former, it is true, still lurked as brigands in their mountain-castles. In Florence a part of the old nobility had devoted themselves to trade; another and certainly by far the smaller part enjoyed the satisfaction of their titles and spent their time either in doing nothing at all or else in hunting and hawking.[4]

The decisive fact was that nearly everywhere in Italy even those who might be disposed to pride themselves on their birth could not make good the claims against the power of culture and of wealth, and that their privileges in politics and at Court were not sufficient to encourage any strong feeling of caste. Venice offers only an apparent exception to this rule, for there the *nobili* led the same life as their fellow-citizens, and were distinguished by few honorary privileges. The case was certainly different at Naples, which the strict isolation and the ostentatious vanity of its nobility excluded, above all other causes, from the spiritual movement of the Renaissance. The traditions of medieval Lombardy and Normandy, and the French aristocratic influences which followed, all tended in this direction; and the Aragonese Government, which was established by the middle of the fifteenth century, completed the work, and accomplished in Naples what followed a hundred years later in the rest of Italy—a social transformation in obedience to Spanish ideas, of which the chief features were the contempt for work and the passion for titles. The effect of this new influence was evident, even in the smaller towns, before the year 1500. We hear complaints from La Cava that the place had been proverbially rich as long as it was filled with masons and weavers; while now, since instead of looms and trowels nothing but spurs, stirrups, and gilded belts was to be seen, since everybody was trying to become Doctor of Laws or of Medicine, notary, officer, or knight, the most intolerable poverty prevailed.[5]

[1] This is the case in the capital itself. See Bandello, ii, *Nov.* 7; Jov. Pontan., *Antonius,* where the decline of energy in the nobility is dated from the coming of the Aragonese dynasty.

[2] Throughout Italy it was universal that the owner of large landed property stood on an equality with the nobles. It is only flattery when J. A. Campanus adds to the statement of Pius II (*Commentarii,* p. 1) that as a boy he had helped his poor parents in their rustic labours the further assertion that he only did so for his amusement, and that this was the custom of the young nobles (Voigt, ii, 339).

[3] For an estimate of the nobility in North Italy Bandello, with his repeated rebukes of *mésalliances,* is of importance (i, *Nov.* 4, 26; iii, *Nov.* 60; also iv, *Nov.* 8). The Milanese noble who is also a merchant is exceptional (iii, *Nov.* 37). For the participation of the nobles in the games of the peasants see above.

[4] The severe judgment of Machiavelli, *Discorsi,* i, 55, refers only to those of the nobility who still retained feudal rights, and who were thoroughly idle and politically mischievous. Agrippa of Nettesheim, who owes his most remarkable ideas chiefly to his life in Italy, has a chapter on the nobility and princes (*De Incert. et Vanit. Scient.,* cap. 80, *Opp.,* ed. Lugd., ii, 212–230), the bitterness of which exceeds anything to be met with elsewhere, and is due to the social ferment then prevailing in the North.

[5] Massuccio, *Nov.* 19 (ed. Settembrini, p. 220, Naples, 1874). The first edition of the novels appeared in 1476.

In Florence an analogous change appears to have taken place by the time of Cosimo, the first Grand Duke; he is thanked for adopting the young people, who now despise trade and commerce, as knights of his Order of St Stephen.[1] This goes straight in the teeth of the good old Florentine custom,[2] by which fathers left property to their children on the condition that they should have some occupation (p. 100). But a mania for title of a curious and ludicrous sort sometimes crossed and thwarted, especially among the Florentines, the levelling influence of art and culture. This was the passion for knighthood, which became one of the most striking follies of the day, at a time when the dignity itself had lost every shadow of significance.

Toward the end of the fourteenth century Franco Sacchetti[3] writes:

> A few years ago everybody saw how all the workpeople down to the bakers, how all the wool-carders, usurers, money-changers, and blackguards of all descriptions became knights. Why should an official need knighthood when he goes to preside over some little provincial town? What has this title to do with any ordinary bread-winning pursuit? How art thou sunken, unhappy dignity! Of all the long list of knightly duties what single one do these knights of ours discharge? I wished to speak of these things that the reader might see that knighthood is dead.[4] And as we have gone so far as to confer the honour upon dead men, why not upon figures of wood and stone, and why not upon an ox?

The stories which Sacchetti tells by way of illustration speak plainly enough. There we read how Bernabò Visconti knighted the victor in a drunken brawl, and then did the same derisively to the vanquished; how German knights with their decorated helmets and devices were ridiculed—and more of the same kind. At a later period Poggio[5] makes merry over the many knights of his day without a horse and without military training. Those who wished to assert the privilege of the order and ride out with lance and colours found in Florence that they might have to face the Government as well as the jokers.[6]

On considering the matter more closely we shall find that this belated chivalry, independent of all nobility of birth, though partly the fruit of an insane passion for title, had nevertheless another and a better side. Tournaments had not yet ceased to be practised, and no one could take part in them who was not a knight. But the combat in the lists, and especially the difficult and perilous tilting with the lance, offered a favourable opportunity for the display of strength, skill, and courage, which no one, whatever might be his origin, would willingly neglect in an age which laid such stress on personal merit.[7]

---

[1] Jacopo Pitti to Cosimo I, *Archiv. Stor.*, iv, ii, p. 99. In North Italy the Spanish rule brought about the same results. Bandello, ii, *Nov.* 40, dates from this period.

[2] When, in the fifteenth century, Vespasiano Fiorentino (pp. 518, 632) implies that the rich should not try to increase their inherited fortune, but should spend their whole annual income, this can only, in the mouth of a Florentine, refer to the great landowners.

[3] Franco Sacchetti, *Nov.* 153. *Cf. Nov.* 82 and 150.   [4] " Che la cavalleria è morta."

[5] Poggius, *De Nobilitate*, fol. 27. See above, p. 38. Æneas Sylvius (*Hist. Fried. III*, ed. Kollar, p. 294) finds fault with the readiness with which Frederick conferred knighthood in Italy.

[6] Vasari, iii, 49, and note, *Vita di Dello*. The city of Florence claimed the right of conferring knighthood. On the ceremonies of this kind in 1378 and 1389 see Reumont, *Lorenzo dei Medici*, ii, 444 *sqq.* There is in existence a *Ceremoniale della Repubblica Fiorentina nel far Cavalieri e Ricever Oratori compilato da Francisco Filarete Araldo* (*Nozze*) (Pisa, 1884).

[7] Senarega, *De Reb. Gen.*, in Murat., xxiv, col. 525. At a wedding of Joh. Adurnus with Leonora di

It was in vain that from the time of Petrarch downward the tournament was denounced as a dangerous folly. No one was converted by the pathetic appeal of the poet: " In what book do we read that Scipio and Cæsar were skilled at the joust? " [1] The practice became more and more popular in Florence. Every honest citizen came to consider his tournament—now, no doubt, less dangerous than formerly—as a fashionable sport. Franco

FIG. 169. A VENETIAN NOBLEMAN
Part of a painting of the St Ursula Series, by Carpaccio
Venice, Accademia. Photo Anderson, Rome

Sacchetti [2] has left us a ludicrous picture of one of these holiday cavaliers— a notary seventy years old. He rides out on horseback to Peretola, where the tournament was cheap, on a jade hired from a dyer. A thistle is stuck by some wag under the tail of the steed, which takes fright, runs away, and carries the helmeted rider, bruised and shaken, back into the city. The inevitable conclusion of the story is a severe curtain-lecture from the wife, who is not a little enraged at these breakneck follies of her husband. [3]

It may be mentioned in conclusion that a passionate interest in this sport was displayed by the Medici, as if they wished to show—private citizens as

Sanseverino, " certamina equestria in Sarzano edita sunt . . . proposita et data victoribus præmia. Ludi multiformes in palatio celebrati a quibus tanquam a re nova pendebat plebs et integros dies illis spectantibus impendebat."

[1] Petrarch, *Epist. Senil.*, xi, 13, to Ugo d'Este. Another passage in the *Epist. Fam.*, lib. v, Ep. 6, December 1, 1343, describes the disgust he felt at seeing a knight fall at a tournament in Naples. For legal prescriptions as to the tournament at Naples see Fracassetti's Italian translation of Petrarch's letters, ii, p. 34 (Florence, 1864). L. B. Alberti also points out the danger, uselessness, and expense of tournaments. *Della Famiglia, Opp. Volg.*, ii, 229.

[2] *Nov.* 64. With reference to this practice it is said expressly in the *Orlandino* (ii, str. 7) of a tournament under Charlemagne: " Here they were no cooks and scullions, but kings, dukes, and marquises, who fought."

[3] This is one of the oldest parodies of the tournament. Sixty years passed before Jacques Cœur, the burgher-minister of finance under Charles VII, gave a tournament of donkeys in the courtyard of his palace at Bourges (about 1450). The most brilliant of all these parodies—the second canto of the *Orlandino*, just quoted —was not published till 1526.

FIG. 170. TOURNAMENT ON THE PIAZZA S. CROCE, FLORENCE (1439)

Jarves Collection, Newhaven

they were without noble blood in their veins—that the society which surrounded them was in no respects inferior to a Court.[1] Even under Cosimo (1459), and afterward under the elder Pietro, brilliant tournaments were held at Florence. The younger Pietro neglected the duties of government for these amusements, and would never suffer himself to be painted except clad in armour. The same practice prevailed at the Court of Alexander VI, and when the Cardinal Ascanio Sforza asked the Turkish Prince Djem (pp. 126, 132) how he liked the spectacle the barbarian replied with much discretion that such combats in his country only took place among slaves, since then, in the case of accident, nobody was the worse for it. The Oriental was unconsciously in accord with the old Romans in condemning the manners of the Middle Ages.

Apart, however, from this particular prop of knighthood, we find here and there in Italy—for example, at Ferrara (pp. 66 *sqq.*)—orders of Court service whose members had a right to the title.

But great as were individual ambitions and the vanities of nobles and knights, it remains a fact that the Italian nobility took its place in the centre of social life, and not at the extremity. We find it habitually mixing with other classes on a footing of perfect equality, and seeking its natural allies in culture and intelligence. It is true that for the courtier a certain rank of nobility was required,[2] but this exigence is expressly declared to be caused by a prejudice rooted in the public mind—" per l'oppenion universale "—and never was held to imply the belief that the personal worth of one who was not of noble blood was in any degree lessened thereby, nor did it follow from this rule that the prince was limited to the nobility for his society. It was meant simply that the perfect man—the true courtier—should not be wanting in any conceivable advantage, and therefore not in this. If in all the relations of life he was specially bound to maintain a dignified and reserved demeanour the reason was not found in the blood which flowed in his veins, but in the perfection of manner which was demanded from him. We are here in the presence of a modern distinction, based on culture and on wealth, but on the latter solely because it enables men to devote their lives to the former, and effectually to promote its interests and advancement.

---

[1] *Cf.* the poetry, already quoted, of Politian and Luca Pulci (p. 346, note 1). Further, Paul. Jovius, *Vita Leonis X*, lib. i ; Machiavelli, *Storie Fiorent.*, lib. vii ; Paul Jovius, *Elogia*, pp. 187 *sqq.*, and 332 *sqq.*, speaking of Pietro de' Medici, who neglected his public duties for these amusements, and of Franc. Borbonius, who lost his life in them ; Vasari, ix, 219, *Vita di Granacci*. In the *Morgante* of Pulci, written under the eyes of Lorenzo, the knights are comical in their language and actions, but their blows are sturdy and scientific. Bojardo too writes for those who understand the tournament and the art of war. *Cf.* p. 319. In earlier Florentine history we read of a tournament in honour of the King of France, about 1380, in Leonardo Aretino, *Hist. Flor.*, lib. xi, p. 222 (ed. Argent.). The tournaments at Ferrara in 1464 are mentioned in the *Diario Ferrarese*, in Murat., xxiv, col. 208 ; at Venice, see Sansovino, *Venezia*, fol. 153 *sqq.*; at Bologna in 1470 and after, see Bursellis, *Annal. Bonon.*, in Murat., xxiii, col. 898, 903, 906, 908, 911, where it is curious to note the odd mixture of sentimentalism attaching to the celebration of Roman triumphs ; " ut antiquitas Romana renovata videretur," we read in one place. Federigo of Urbino (pp. 63 *sqq.*) lost his right eye at a tournament " ab ictu lanceæ." On the tournament as held at that time in Northern countries see Olivier de la Marche, *Mémoires, passim*, and especially cap. 8, 9, 14, 16, 18, 19, 21, etc. For the first public caricature of the tournament in a Florentine pen-and-ink drawing of the fourteenth century see *Rep. f. Kunstwiss* (1899).

[2] Bald. Castiglione, *Il Cortigiano*, lib. i, fol. 18.

CHAPTER II

THE OUTWARD REFINEMENT OF LIFE

BUT in proportion as distinctions of birth ceased to confer any special privilege was the individual himself compelled to make the most of his personal qualities, and society to find its worth and charm in itself. The demeanour of individuals and all the higher forms of social intercourse became ends pursued with a deliberate and artistic purpose.

Even the outward appearance of men and women and the habits of daily life were more perfect, more beautiful, and more polished than among the other nations of Europe. The dwellings of the upper classes fall rather within the province of the history of art; but we may note how far the castle and the city mansion in Italy surpassed in comfort, order, and harmony the dwellings of the Northern noble. The style of dress varied so continually that it is impossible to make any complete comparison with the fashions of other countries, all the more because since the close of the fifteenth century imitations of the latter were frequent. The costumes of the time, as given us by the Italian painters, are the most convenient and the most pleasing to the eye which were then to be found in Europe; but we cannot be sure if they represent the prevalent fashion, or if they are faithfully reproduced by the artist. It is nevertheless beyond a doubt that nowhere was so much importance attached to dress as in Italy. The people was, and is, vain; and even serious men among it looked on a handsome and becoming costume as an element in the perfection of the individual. At Florence, indeed, there was a brief period when dress was a purely personal matter, and every man set the fashion for himself (p. 144, note 1), and till far into the sixteenth century there were exceptional people who still had the courage to do so;[1] and the majority at all events showed themselves capable of varying the fashion according to their individual tastes. It is a symptom of decline when Giovanni della Casa warns his readers not to be singular or to depart from existing fashions.[2] Our own age, which, in men's dress at any rate, treats uniformity as the supreme law, gives up by so doing far more than it is itself aware of. But it saves itself much time, and this, according to our notions of business, outweighs all other disadvantages.

In Venice[3] and Florence at the time of the Renaissance there were rules

---

[1] Paul. Jovius, *Elogia*, under " Petrus Gravina," " Alex. Achillinus," " Balth. Castellio," etc., pp. 138 *sqq.*, 112 *sqq.*, 143 *sqq.* L. Bruni made famous the red gown reaching to the ankle.

[2] Casa, *Il Galateo*, p. 78.

[3] See on this point the Venetian books of fashions, and Sansovino, *Venezia*, fol. 150 *sqq.* The bridal dress at the betrothal—white, with the hair falling freely on the shoulders—is that of Titian's Flora. The

and regulations prescribing the dress of the men and restraining the luxury of the women. Where the fashions were less free, as in Naples, the moralists confess with regret that no difference can be observed between noble and

FIG. 171. THE PALAZZO MEDICI-RICCARDI, FLORENCE
By Michelozzi

"Proveditori alle pompe" at Venice established 1514. Extracts from their decisions in Armand Baschet, *Souvenirs d'une Mission* (Paris, 1857). Prohibition of gold-embroidered garments in Venice, 1481, which had formerly been worn even by the bakers' wives; they were now to be decorated "gemmis unionibus," so that "frugalissimus ornatus" cost four thousand gold florins. M. Ant. Sabellici, *Epist.*, lib. iii (to M. Anto. Barbavarus).

ourgher.[1] They further deplore the rapid changes of fashion, and—if we rightly understand their words—the senseless idolatry of whatever comes from France, though in many cases the fashions which were received back from the French were originally Italian. It does not further concern us how far these frequent changes and the adoption of French and Spanish ways [2] contributed to the national passion for external display; but we find in them additional evidence of the rapid movement of life in Italy in the decades before and after the year 1500. The occupation of different parts of Italy by foreigners caused the inhabitants not only to adopt foreign fashions, but sometimes to abandon all luxury in matters of dress. Such a change in public feeling at Milan is recorded by Landi. But the differences in costume, he tells us, continued to exist, Naples distinguishing itself by splendour, and Florence, to the eye of the writer, by absurdity.[3]

We may note in particular the efforts of the women to alter their appearance by all the means which the toilette could afford. In no country of Europe since the fall of the Roman Empire was so much trouble taken to modify the face, the colour of skin, and the growth of the hair as in Italy at this time.[4] All tended to the formation of a conventional type, at the cost of the most striking and transparent deceptions. Leaving out of account costume in general, which in the fourteenth century [5] was in the highest degree varied in

[1] Jov. Pontan., *De Principe*: " Utinam autem non eo impudentiæ perventum esset, ut inter mercatorem et patricium nullum sit in vestitu ceteroque ornatu discrimen. Sed hæc tanta licentia reprehendi potest, coerceri non potest, quanquam mutari vestes sic quotidie videamus, ut quas quarto ante mense in deliciis habebamus, nunc repudiemus et tanquam veteramenta abjiciamus. Quodque tolerari vix potest, nullum fere vestimenti genus probatur, quod e Galliis non fuerit adductum, in quibus levia pleraque in pretio sunt, tametsi nostri persæpe homines modum illis et quasi formulam quandam præscribant."

[2] See, for example, the *Diario Ferrarese*, in Murat., xxiv, col. 297, 320, 376 *sqq.*, in which the last German fashions are spoken of; the chronicler says: " Che pareno buffoni tali portatori."

[3] This interesting passage from a very rare work may be here quoted. See above, p. 336, note 4. The historical event referred to is the conquest of Milan by Antonio Leiva, the general of Charles V, in 1522. " Olim splendidissime vestiebant Mediolanenses. Sed postquam Carolus Cæsar in eam urbem tetram et monstruosam bestiam immisit, ita consumpti et exhausti sunt, ut vestimentorum splendorem omnium maxime oderint et quemadmodum ante illa durissima Antoniana tempora nihil aliud fere cogitabant quam de mutandis vestibus, nunc alia cogitant ac in mente versant. Non potuit tamen illa Leviana rabies tantum perdere, neque illa in exhausta deprædandi libidine tantum expilare, quin a re familiari adhuc belle parati fiant atque ita vestiant quemadmodum decere existimant. Et certe nisi illa Antonii Levæ studia egregios quosdam imitatores invenisset, meo quidem judicio, nulli cederent. Neapolitani nimium exercent in vestitu sumptus. Genuensium vestitum perelegantem judico neque sagati sunt neque togati. Ferme oblitus eram Venetorum. Ii togati omnes. Decet quidem ille habitus adulta ætate homines, juvenes vero (si quid ego judico) minime utuntur panno quem ipsi vulgo Venetum appellant, ita probe confecto ut perpetuo durare existimes, sæpissime vero eas vestes gestant nepotes, quas olim tritavi gestarunt. Noctu autem dum scortantur ac potant, Hispanicis palliolis utuntur. Ferrarienses ac Mantuani nihil tam diligenter curant, quam ut pileos habeant aureis quibusdam frustillis adornatos, atque nutanti capite incedunt seque quovis honore dignos existimant, Lucenses neque superbo, neque abjecto vestitu. Florentinorum habitus mihi quidem ridiculus videtur. Reliquos omitto, ne nimius sim." Ugolinus Verinus, *De Illustratione Urbis Florentiæ*, says of the simplicity of the good old time:

" non externis advecta Britannis
Lana erat in pretio, non concha aut coccus in usu."

[4] *Cf.* the passages on the same subject in Falke, *Die deutsche Trachten- und Modenwelt* (Leipzig, 1858).

[5] On the Florentine women see the chief references in Giov. Villani, x, 10 and 150 (regulations as to dress and their repeal); Matteo Villani, i, 4 (extravagant living in consequence of the plague). In the celebrated edict on fashions of the year 1330 embroidered figures only were allowed on the dresses of women, to the exclusion of those which were painted (*dipinto*). What was the nature of these decorations appears doubtful. There is a list of the arts of the toilette practised by women in Boccaccio, *De Cas. Vir.*, lib. i, cap. 18, *in mulieres.*

colour and loaded with ornament, and at a later period assumed a character of more harmonious richness, we here limit ourselves more particularly to the toilette in the narrower sense.

No sort of ornament was more in use than false hair, often made of white or yellow silk.[1] The law denounced and forbade it in vain, till some preacher

of repentance touched the worldly minds of the wearers. Then was seen, in the middle of the public square, a lofty pyre (*talamo*), on which, beside lutes, dice-boxes, masks, magical charms, song-books, and other vanities, lay masses of false hair,[2] which the purging fire soon turned into a heap of ashes. The ideal colour sought for both in natural and artificial hair was blond. And as the sun was supposed to have the power of making the hair of this colour[3] many ladies would pass their whole time in the open air on sunshiny days.[4] Dyes and other mixtures were also used freely for the same purpose. Besides all these we meet with an endless list of beautifying waters, plasters, and paints for every single part of the face—even for the teeth and eyelids—of which in our day we can form no conception. The ridicule of the poets,[5] the invectives of the preachers, and the experience of the baneful effects of these cosmetics on the skin were powerless to hinder women from giving their faces an unnatural form and colour. It is possible that the frequent and splendid representations of mysteries,[6] at which hundreds

[1] Those of real hair were called *capelli morti*. Wigs were also worn by men, as by Giannozzo Manetti, Vesp. Bist., *Commentario*, p. 103; so at least we explain this somewhat obscure passage. For an instance of false teeth made of ivory, and worn though only for the sake of clear articulation, by an Italian prelate, see Anshelm, *Berner Chronik*, iv, p. 30 (1508). Ivory teeth in Boccaccio, *loc. cit.*: "Dentes casu sublatos reformare ebore fuscatos pigmentis gemmisque in albedinem revocare pristinam."

[2] Infessura, in Eccard, *Scriptores*, ii, col. 1874; Allegretto, in Murat., xxiii, col. 823. For the writers on Savonarola see below.

[3] Sansovino, *Venezia*, fol. 152: "Capelli biondissimi per forza di sole." *Cf.* p. 89, and the rare works quoted by Yriarte, *Vie d'un Patricien de Venise*, p. 56 (1874).

[4] As was the case in Germany too. *Poesie Satiriche*, p. 119 (Milan, 1808). From the satire of Bern Giambullari, *Per prendere Moglie* (pp. 107-126), we can form a conception of the chemistry of the toilette, which was founded largely on superstition and magic.

[5] The poets spared no pains to show the ugliness, danger, and absurdity of these practices. *Cf.* Ariosto *Sat.*, iii, 202 *sqq.*; Aretino, *Il Marescalco*, atto ii, scena 5; and several passages in the *Ragionamenti*, *loc. cit.*; Phil. Beroald. Sen., *Carmina*; also Filelfo in his *Satires*, iv, 2-5 *sqq.* (Venice, 1502).

[6] Cennino Cennini, *Trattato della Pittura*, gives in cap. 161 a recipe for painting the face, evidently for the purpose of mysteries or masquerades, since in cap. 162 he solemnly warns his readers against the general use of cosmetics and the like, which was peculiarly common, as he tells us, in Tuscany.

f people appeared painted and masked, helped to further this practice in
daily life. It is certain that it was widely spread, and that the countrywomen
vied in this respect with their sisters in the towns.[1] It was vain to preach
that such decorations were the mark of the courtesan; the most honourable

FIG. 173. PILLARED COURT IN THE PALAZZO GONDI
By Giuliano da Sangallo
Florence

matrons, who all the year round never touched paint, used it nevertheless on
holidays when they showed themselves in public.[2] But whether we look on
this bad habit as a remnant of barbarism, to which the painting of savages
is a parallel, or as a consequence of the desire for perfect youthful beauty in

[1] Cf. *La Nencia da Barberino*, str. 20 and 40. The lover promises to bring his beloved cosmetics from the
town (see on this poem of Lorenzo de' Medici, above, p. 349).

[2] Agnolo Pandolfini (L. B. Alberti), *Trattato della Governo della Famiglia*, p. 118. He condemns this practice
most energetically.

features and in colour, as the art and complexity of the toilette would lead us to think—in either case there was no lack of good advice on the part of the men.

The use of perfumes too went beyond all reasonable limits. They were applied to everything with which human beings came into contact. At festivals

FIG. 174. INNER APARTMENTS (THE BIRTH OF MARY)
By Carpaccio
Bergamo, Accademia Carrara
Photo Anderson, Rome

even the mules were treated with scents and ointments.[1] Pietro Aretino thanks Cosimo I for a perfumed roll of money.[2]

The Italians of that day lived in the belief that they were more cleanly than other nations. There are, in fact, general reasons which speak rather for than against this claim. Cleanliness is indispensable to our modern notion of social perfection, which was developed in Italy earlier than elsewhere. That the Italians were one of the richest of existing peoples is another presumption in their favour. Proof either for or against these pretensions can, of course,

[1] Tristan. Caracciolo, in Murat., xxii, col. 87. Bandello, ii, *Nov.* 47.
[2] Cap. i, to Cosimo: " Quei cento scudi nuovi e profumati che l' altro di mi mandaste a donare." Some objects which date from that period have not yet lost their odour. Can *profumati* have been used figuratively to mean ' handsome '?

ever be forthcoming, and if the question were one of priority in establishing
rules of cleanliness the chivalrous poetry of the Middle Ages is perhaps in
advance of anything that Italy can produce. It is nevertheless certain that the
singular neatness and cleanliness of some distinguished representatives of the

FIG. 175. BEDROOM (URSULA'S DREAM)
By Carpaccio
Venice, Accademia

Renaissance, especially in their behaviour at meals, was noticed expressly,[1]
and that 'German' was the synonym in Italy for all that was filthy.[2] The dirty

---

[1] Vespas. Fiorent., p. 453, in the life of Donato Acciajuoli, and p. 625, in the life of Niccoli.

[2] Giraldi, *Hecatommithi*, Introduz., *Nov.* 6. A few notices on the Germans in Italy may not here be out of
place. On the German invasion, see p. 138, note 5; on Germans as copyists and printers, pp. 201 *sqq.*
and the notes; on the ridicule of Adrian VI as a German, p. 169 and notes. The Italians were in general ill-
disposed to the Germans, and showed their ill-will by ridicule. Boccaccio (*Decamerone*, viii, 1) says: "Un

367

habits which Massimiliano Sforza picked up in the course of his German education, and the notice they attracted on his return to Italy, are recorded by Giovio.[1] It is at the same time very curious that, at least in the fifteenth century, the inns and hotels were left chiefly in the hands of Germans,[2] who probably, however, made their profit mostly out of the pilgrims journeying to Rome. Yet the statements on this point may refer rather to the country districts, since it is notorious that in the great cities Italian hotels held the first

FIG. 176. WORKROOM OF A SCHOLAR (ST JEROME)
By Carpaccio
Venice, S. Giorgio degli Schiavoni

Tedesco in soldo . . . pro della persona e assai leale a coloro ne' cui servigi si mettea; il che rade volte suol de' Tedeschi avvenire." The tale is given as an instance of German cunning. The Italian humanists are full of attacks on the German barbarians, and especially those who, like Poggio, had seen Germany. *Cf.* Voigt, *Wiederbelebung*, pp. 374 *sqq.*; Geiger, *Beziehungen zwischen Deutschland und Italien Zeit des Humanismus*, in *Zeitschrift für deutsche Kulturgeschichte*, pp. 104–124 (1875); see also Janssen, *Gesch. der deutschen Volkes*, i, 262. One of the chief opponents of the Germans was Joh. Ant. Campanus. See his works, ed. Mencken, who delivered a discourse *De Campani Odio in Germanos*. The hatred of the Germans was strengthened by the conduct of Adrian VI, and still more by the conduct of the troops at the sack of Rome (Gregorovius, viii, 548, note). Bandello, iii, *Nov.* 30, chooses the German as the type of the dirty and foolish man (see iii, 51, for another German). When an Italian wishes to praise a German he says, as Petrus Alcyonius in the dedication to his dialogue *De Exilio*, to Nicolaus Schomberg, p. 9: "Itaque etsi in Misnensi clarissima Germaniæ provinciæ illustribus natalibus ortus es, tamen in Italiæ luce cognosceris." Unqualified praise is rare—for example, of German women at the time of Marius, *Cortigiano*, iii, cap. 33.

It must be added that the Italians of the Renaissance, like the Greeks of antiquity, were filled with aversion for all barbarians. Boccaccio, *De Claris Mulieribus*, in the article *Carmenta*, speaks of "German barbarism, French savagery, English craft, and Spanish coarseness."

[1] Paul. Jovius, *Elogia*, p. 289, who, however, makes no mention of the German education. Maximilian could not be induced, even by celebrated women, to change his underclothing,

[2] Æneas Sylvius (*Vitæ Paparum*, in Murat., iii, i, col. 880) says, in speaking of Baccano: "Pauca sunt mapalia eaque hospitia faciunt Theutonici; hoc hominum genus totam fere Italiam hospitalem facit; ubi non repereris hos, neque diversorium quæras."

place.[1] The want of decent inns in the country may also be explained by the general insecurity of life and property.

To the first half of the sixteenth century belongs the manual of politeness which Giovanni della Casa, a Florentine by birth, published under the title *Il Galateo*. Not only cleanliness in the strict sense of the word, but the dropping of all the tricks and habits which we consider unbecoming, is here prescribed with the same unfailing tact with which the moralist discerns the highest ethical truths. In the literature of other countries the same lessons are taught, though less systematically, by the indirect influence of repulsive descriptions.[2]

In other respects also the *Galateo* is a graceful and intelligent guide to good manners —a school of tact and delicacy. Even now it may be read with no small profit by people of all classes, and the politeness of European nations is not likely to outgrow its precepts. So far as tact is an

FIG. 177. VENETIAN COSTUMES
Part of a painting in the St Ursula Series, by Carpaccio
Venice, Accademia

affair of the heart, it has been inborn in some men from the dawn of civilization, and acquired through force of will by others; but the Italian first recognized it as a universal social duty and a mark of culture and education. And Italy itself had altered much in the course of two centuries. We feel at their close that the time for practical jokes between friends and acquaintances—for *burle* and *beffe* (pp. 163 *sqq.*)—was over in good

[1] Franco Sacchetti, *Nov.* 21. Padua, about 1450, boasted of a great inn—the Ox—like a palace, containing stabling for two hundred horses. Michele Savonarola, in Murat., xxiv, col. 1175. At Florence, outside the Porta S. Gallo, there was one of the largest and most splendid inns then known, but which served, it seems, only as a place of amusement for the people of the city. Varchi, *Stor. Fiorent.*, iii, p. 86. At the time of Alexander VI the best inn at Rome was kept by a German. See the remarkable notices taken from the manuscript of Burcardus, in Gregorovius, vii, 361, note 2. *Cf. ibid.*, p. 93, notes 2 and 3.

[2] *Cf.*, for example, the passages in Sebastian Brant's *Narrenschiff*, in the *Colloquies* of Erasmus, in the Latin poem of Grobianus, in Wimpfeling's pedagogical writings and poems on behaviour at table, where, besides descriptions of bad habits, rules are given for good behaviour. *Cf.* Bömer, *Anstand und Etikette nach den Theorien der Humanisten*, in *N. Jahrb. f. d. klass Altert.*, xiv (1904). See C. Weller, *Deutsche Gedichte des Jahrhunderts* (Tübingen, 1875).

THE RENAISSANCE IN ITALY

society,[1] that the people had emerged from the walls of the cities and had learned a cosmopolitan politeness and consideration. We shall speak later on of the intercourse of society in the narrower sense.

Outward life, indeed, in the fifteenth and the early part of the sixteenth century was polished and ennobled as among no other people in the world. A countless number of those small things and great things which combine to make up what we mean by comfort we know to have first appeared in Italy. In the well-paved streets of the Italian cities [2] driving was universal, while elsewhere in Europe walking or riding was the custom, and at all events no one drove for amusement. We read in the novelists of soft, elastic beds, of costly carpets and bedroom furniture, of which we hear nothing in other countries. We often hear especially of the abundance and beauty of the linen. Much of all this is drawn within the sphere of art. We note with admiration the thousand ways in which art ennobles luxury, not only adorning the massive sideboard or the light brackets with noble vases and clothing the walls with the moving splendour of tapestry, and covering the toilet-table with numberless graceful trifles, but absorbing whole branches of mechanical work—especially carpentry—into its province. All Western Europe, as soon as its wealth enabled it to do so, set to work in the same way at the close of the Middle Ages. But its efforts produced either childish and fantastic toy-work, or were bound by the chains of a narrow and purely Gothic art, while the Renaissance moved freely, entering into the spirit of every task it undertook and working for a far larger circle of patrons and admirers than the Northern artist. The rapid victory of Italian decorative art over Northern in the course of the sixteenth century is due partly to this fact, though partly the result of wider and more general causes.

[1] The diminution of the *burla* is evident from the instances in the *Cortigiano*, lib. ii, fol. 96. The Florentine practical jokes kept their ground tenaciously. See, for evidence, the tales of Lasca (Ant. Franc. Grazini, b. 1503, d. 1582), which appeared at Florence in 1550.

[2] For Milan see Bandelloi, *Nov.* 9. There were more than sixty carriages with four, and numberless others with two, horses; many of the carriages were carved and richly gilt and had silken tops. *Cf. ibid., Nov.* 4; Ariosto, *Sat.*, iii, 127.

[3] Bandello, i, *Nov.* 3; iii, 42; iv, 25.

CHAPTER III

LANGUAGE AS THE BASIS OF SOCIAL INTERCOURSE

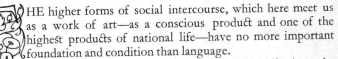THE higher forms of social intercourse, which here meet us as a work of art—as a conscious product and one of the highest products of national life—have no more important foundation and condition than language.

In the most flourishing period of the Middle Ages the nobility of Western Europe had sought to establish a 'courtly' speech for social intercourse as well as for poetry. In Italy too, where the dialects differed so greatly from one another, we find in the thirteenth century a so-called *curiale* which was common to the Courts and to the poets. It is of decisive importance for Italy that the attempt was there seriously and deliberately made to turn this into the language of literature and society. The introduction to the *Cento Novelle Antiche*, which were put into their present shape before 1300, avow this object openly. Language is here considered apart from its uses in poetry; its highest function is clear, simple, intelligent utterance in short speeches, epigrams, and answers. This faculty was admired in Italy as nowhere else but among the Greeks and Arabians: "How many in the course of a long life have scarcely produced a single *bel parlare*!"

But the matter was rendered more difficult by the diversity of the aspects under which it was considered. The writings of Dante transport us into the midst of the struggle. His work on "the Italian language" [1] is not only of the utmost importance for the subject itself, but is also the first complete treatise on any modern language. His method and results belong to the history of linguistic science, in which they will always hold a high place. We must here content ourselves with the remark that long before the appearance of this book the subject must have been one of daily and pressing importance, that the various dialects of Italy had long been the objects of eager study and dispute, and that the birth of the one classical language was not accomplished without many throes. [2]

Nothing certainly contributed so much to this end as the great poem of

[1] *De Vulgari Eloquentia*, ed. Corbinelli (Paris, 1577), best ed. L. Bertalot (Friedrichsdorf, 1917). According to Boccaccio, *Vita di Dante*, p. 77, it was written shortly before his death, but now it is more probably dated 1303–9. He mentions in the *Convivio* the rapid and striking changes which took place in the Italian language during his lifetime.

[2] See on this subject the investigations of Leonardo Aretino (*Epist.*, ed. Mehus., ii, 62 *sqq.*; vi, 10) and Poggio (*Historia Disceptativæ Convivales Tres*, in the *Opp.*, fol. 14 *sqq.*), whether in earlier times the language of the people and of scholars was the same. Leonardo maintains the negative; Poggio expressly maintains the affirmative against his predecessor. See also the detailed argument of L. B. Alberti in the introduction to *Della Famiglia*, iii, on the necessity of Italian for social intercourse.

Dante. The Tuscan dialect became the basis of the new national speech. If this assertion may seem to some to go too far, as foreigners we may be excused, in a matter on which much difference of opinion prevails, for following the general belief.

Literature and poetry probably lost more than they gained by the contentious

FIG. 178. FIGURE OF A BOY FROM A PAINTING IN THE BERNARDINE SERIES
By Perugino (?)
Perugia, Pinacotheca

purism which was long prevalent in Italy, and which marred the freshness and vigour of many an able writer. Others, again, who felt themselves masters of this magnificent language, were tempted to rely upon its harmony and flow, apart from the thought which it expressed. A very insignificant melody, played upon such an instrument, can produce a very great effect. But however this may be, it is certain that socially the language had great value. It was, as it were, the crown of a noble and dignified behaviour, and compelled the gentleman, both in his ordinary bearing and in exceptional moments, to observe external propriety. No doubt this classical garment, like the language of Attic society, served to drape much that was foul and malicious; but it was also the adequate expression of all that is noblest and most refined. But politically and nationally it was of supreme importance, serving as an ideal home for the educated classes in all the states of the divided peninsula.[2] Nor was it the special property of the nobles or of any one class, but the poorest and humblest might learn it if they would. Even now—and perhaps more than ever—in those parts of Italy where, as a rule, the most unintelligible dialect prevails, the stranger is often astonished at hearing pure and well-spoken Italian from the mouths of peasants or artisans, and looks in vain for anything analogous in France or in Germany, where even the educated classes retain traces of a provincial speech. There are certainly a larger number of people able to read in Italy than we should be

[1] The gradual progress which this dialect made in literature and social intercourse could be tabulated without difficulty by a native scholar. It could be shown to what extent in the fourteenth and fifteenth centuries the various dialects kept their places, wholly or partly, in correspondence, in official documents, in historical works, and in literature generally. The relations between the dialects and a more or less impure Latin, which served as the official language, would also be discussed. The modes of speech and pronunciation in the different cities of Italy are noticed in Landi, *Forcianæ Quæstiones*, fol. 7a. Of the former he says: " Hetrusci vero quanquam cæteris excellant, effugere tamen non possunt, quin et ipsi ridiculi sint, aut saltem quin se mutuo lacerent"; as regards pronunciation, the Sienese, Lucchese, and Florentines are specially praised; but of the Florentines it is said: " Plus [jucunditatis] haberet si voces non ingurgitaret aut non ita palato lingua jungeretur."

[2] It is so felt to be by Dante, *De Vulgari Eloquentia*, i, c. 17 and 18.

led to expect from the condition of many parts of the country—as, for instance, the States of the Church—in other respects; but what is of more importance is the general and undisputed respect for pure language and pronunciation as something precious and sacred. One part of the country after another came to adopt the classical dialect officially. Venice, Milan,

and Naples did so at the noontime of Italian literature, and partly through its influences. It was not till the nineteenth century that Piedmont became of its own free will a genuine Italian province by sharing in this chief treasure of the people—pure speech.[1] The dialects were from the beginning of the sixteenth century purposely left to deal with a certain class of subjects, serious as well as comic,[2] and the style which was thus developed proved equal to all its tasks. Among other nations a conscious separation of this kind did not occur till a much later period.

The opinion of educated people as to the social value of language is fully set forth in the *Cortigiano*.[3] There were then persons, at the beginning of the sixteenth century, who purposely kept to the antiquated expressions of Dante and the other Tuscan writers of his time, simply because they were old. Our author forbids the use of them altogether in speech, and is un-

FIG. 179. FLORENTINE COSTUMES
Part of the painting *The Birth of Mary*, by Ghirlandaio
Florence, S. Maria Novella

willing to permit them even in writing, which he considers a form of speech. Upon this follows the admission that the best style of speech is that which most resembles good writing. We can clearly recognize the author's feeling that people who have anything of importance to say must shape their own speech,

---

[1] Tuscan, it is true, was read and written long before this in Piedmont—but very little reading and writing was done at all.

[2] The place, too, of the dialect in the usage of daily life was clearly understood. Gioviano Pontano ventured especially to warn the prince of Naples against the use of it (Jov. Pontan., *De Principe*). The last Bourbons were notoriously less scrupulous in this respect. For the way in which a Milanese cardinal who wished to retain his native dialect in Rome was ridiculed see Bandello, ii, *Nov.* 31.

[3] Bald. Castiglione, *Il Cortigiano*, lib. i, fol. 27 *sqq.* Throughout the dialogue we are able to gather the personal opinion of the writer. The opposition to Petrarch and Boccaccio is very curious (Dante is not once mentioned). We read that Politian, Lorenzo de' Medici, and others were also Tuscans, and as worthy of imitation as they, " e forse di non minor dottrina e guidizio."

373

and that language is something flexible and changing because it is something living. It is allowable to make use of any expression, however ornate, as long as it is used by the people; nor are non-Tuscan words, or even French and Spanish words, forbidden, if custom has once applied them to definite purposes.[1] Thus care and intelligence will produce a language which, if not the pure old Tuscan, is still Italian, rich in flowers and fruit like a well-kept garden.

FIG. 180. PORTRAIT OF A LADY
By Bernardino de' Conti
London, Alfred Morrison

It belongs to the completeness of the Cortigiano that his wit, his polished manners, and his poetry must be clothed in this perfect dress.

When style and language had once become the property of a living society all the efforts of purists and archaists failed to secure their end. Tuscany itself was rich in writers and talkers of the first order, who ignored and ridiculed these endeavours. Ridicule in abundance awaited the foreign scholar who explained to the Tuscans how little they understood their own language.[2] The life and influence of a writer like Machiavelli was enough to sweep away all these cobwebs. His vigorous thoughts, his clear and simple mode of expression, wore a form which had any merit but that of the *trecentisti*. And on the other hand there were too many North Italians, Romans, and Neapolitans who were thankful if the demand for purity of style in literature and conversation was not pressed too far. They repudiated, indeed, the forms and idioms of their dialect; and Bandello, with what a foreigner might suspect to be false modesty, is never tired of declaring: " I have no style; I do not write like a Florentine, but like a barbarian; I am not ambitious of giving new graces to my language; I am a Lombard, and from the Ligurian border into the bargain." [3]   But the

---

[1] There was a limit, however, to this. The satirists introduce bits of Spanish, and Folengo (under the pseudonym Limerno Pitocco, in his *Orlandino*) of French, but only by way of ridicule. It is an exceptional fact that a street in Milan, which at the time of the French (1500-12, 1515-22) was called Rue Belle, now bears the name Rugabella. The long Spanish rule has left almost no traces on the language, and but rarely the name of some governor in streets and public buildings. It was not till the eighteenth century that, together with French modes of thought, many French words and phrases found their way into Italian. The purism of our time is still busy in removing them.

[2] Firenzuola, *Opera*, i, in the preface to the discourse on female beauty, and ii, in the *Ragionamenti*, which precede the novels.

[3] Bandello, i, *Proemio*, and *Nov.* 1 and 2. Another Lombard, the above-mentioned Teofilo Folengo, in his *Orlandino*, treats the whole matter with ridicule.

claims of the purists were most successfully met by the express renunciation of the higher qualities of style, and the adoption of a vigorous, popular language in their stead. Few could hope to rival Pietro Bembo, who, though born in Venice, nevertheless wrote the purest Tuscan, which to him was a foreign

FIG. 181. PORTRAIT OF A YOUNG WOMAN
By Bastiano Mainardi
Berlin, Kaiser Friedrich Museum

language, or the Neapolitan Sannazaro, who did the same. But the essential point was that language, whether spoken or written, was held to be an object of respect. As long as this feeling was prevalent the fanaticism of the purists—their linguistic congresses and the rest of it [1]—did little harm. Their bad influence was not felt till much later, when the original power of Italian literature

[1] Such a congress appears to have been held at Bologna at the end of 1531, under the presidency of Bembo. See the letter of Claud. Tolomei, in Firenzuola, *Opere*, vol. ii, App., pp. 231 *sqq.* This was not so much a matter of purism, but rather the old quarrel between Lombards and Tuscans.

relaxed, and yielded to other and far worse influences. At last it became possible for the Accademia della Crusca to treat Italian like a dead language. But this association proved so helpless that it could not even hinder the invasion of Gallicism in the eighteenth century.

This language—loved, tended, and trained to every use—now served as the basis of social intercourse. In Northern countries the nobles and the princes passed their leisure either in solitude, or in hunting, fighting, drinking, and the

FIG. 182. CHEST BELONGING TO THE STROZZI FAMILY
Berlin, Schlossmuseum

like; the burghers in games and bodily exercises, with a mixture of literary or festive amusement. In Italy there existed a neutral ground, where people of every origin, if they had the needful talent and culture, spent their time in conversation and the polished interchange of jest and earnest. As eating and drinking formed a small part of such entertainments [1] it was not difficult to keep at a distance those who sought society for these objects. If we are to take the writers of dialogues literally, the loftiest problems of human existence were not excluded from the conversation of thinking men, and the production of noble thoughts was not, as was commonly the case in the North, the work of solitude, but of society. But we must here limit ourselves to the less serious side of social intercourse—to the side which existed only for the sake of amusement.

[1] Luigi Cornaro complains about 1550 (at the beginning of his *Trattato della Vita Sobria*) that latterly Spanish ceremonies and compliments, Lutheranism, and gluttony had been gaining ground in Italy. With immoderation in respect to the entertainment offered to guests, the freedom and ease of social intercourse disappeared.

CHAPTER IV

THE HIGHER FORMS OF SOCIETY

THIS society, at all events at the beginning of the sixteenth century, was a matter of art, and had and rested on tacit or avowed rules of good sense and propriety, which are the exact reverse of all mere etiquette. In less polished circles, where society took the form of a permanent corporation, we meet with a system of formal rules and a prescribed mode of entrance, as was the case with those wild sets of Florentine artists of whom

FIG. 183. DISTINGUISHÉD COMPANY IN THE OPEN (MIDDLE OF THE FOURTEENTH CENTURY)
Part of the fresco *The Triumph of Death*
Pisa, Camposanto

Vasari tells us that they were capable of giving representations of the best comedies of the day.[1] In the easier intercourse of society it was not unusual

---

[1] Vasari, xii, pp. 9 and 11, *Vita di Rustici*. For the School for Scandal of needy artists see xi, 216 *sqq.*, *Vita d' Aristotele*. Machiavelli's *capitoli* for a circle of pleasure-seekers (*Opere Minori*, p. 407) are a ludicrous caricature of these social statutes. The well-known description of the evening meeting of artists in Rome in Benvenuto Cellini, i, cap. 30, is incomparable.

to select some distinguished lady as president, whose word was law for the evening. Everybody knows the introduction to Boccaccio's *Decamerone*, and looks on the presidency of Pampinea as a graceful fiction. That it was so in this particular case is a matter of course; but the fiction was nevertheless based on a practice which often occurred in reality. Firenzuola, who nearly two

FIG. 184. THE WEDDING OF ADIMARI—I (FIRST HALF OF THE FIFTEENTH CENTURY)
Florence, Accademia
Photo Anderson, Rome

centuries later (1523) prefaces his collection of tales in a similar manner, with express reference to Boccaccio, comes assuredly nearer to the truth when he puts into the mouth of the queen of the society a formal speech on the mode of spending the hours during the stay which the company proposed to make in the country. The day was to begin with a stroll among the hills passed in philosophical talk; then followed breakfast,[1] with music and singing, after which came the recitation, in some cool, shady spot, of a new poem, the subject of which had been given the night before; in the evening the whole party walked to a spring of water where they all sat down and each one told a tale; last of all came supper and lively conversation " of such a kind that the women

---

[1] Which must have been taken about ten or eleven o'clock. See Bandello, ii, *Nov.* 10.

might listen to it without shame and the men might not seem to be speaking under the influence of wine." Bandello, in the introductions and dedications to single novels, does not give us, it is true, such inaugural discourses as this, since the circles before which the stories are told are represented as already formed; but he gives us to understand in other ways how rich, how manifold,

FIG. 185. THE WEDDING OF ADIMARI—II
Florence, Accademia
Photo Anderson, Rome

and how charming the conditions of society must have been. Some readers may be of opinion that no good was to be got from a world which was willing to be amused by such immoral literature. It would be juster to wonder at the secure foundations of a society which, notwithstanding these tales, still observed the rules of order and decency, and which knew how to vary such pastimes with serious and solid discussion. The need of noble forms of social intercourse was felt to be stronger than all others. To convince ourselves of it we are not obliged to take as our standard the idealized society which Castiglione depicts as discussing the loftiest sentiments and aims of human life at the Court of Guidobaldo of Urbino and Pietro Bembo at the castle of Asolo. The society described by Bandello, with all the frivolities which may be laid to its

379

charge, enables us to form the best notion of the easy and polished dignity, of the urbane kindliness, of the intellectual freedom, and of the wit and the graceful dilettantism which distinguished these circles. A significant proof of the value of such circles lies in the fact that the women who were the centres of them could become famous and illustrious without in any way compromising their reputation. Among the patronesses of Bandello, for example, Isabella Gonzaga (born an Este, p. 61) was talked of unfavourably not through any fault of her own, but on account of the too free-lived young ladies who filled

FIG. 186. VILLA MEDICI AT CAREGGI, NEAR FLORENCE
The Platonic Academy often met here

her Court.[1] Giulia Gonzaga Colonna, Ippolita Sforza married to a Bentivoglio, Bianca Rangoni, Cecilia Gallerina, Camilla Scarampi, and others were either altogether irreproachable, or their social fame threw into the shade whatever they may have done amiss. The most famous woman of Italy, Vittoria Colonna[2] (b. 1490, d. 1547), the friend of Castiglione and Michelangelo, enjoyed the reputation of a saint. It is hard to give such a picture of the unconstrained intercourse of these circles in the city, at the baths, or in the country, as will furnish literal proof of the superiority of Italy in this respect over the rest of Europe. But let us read Bandello,[3] and then ask ourselves if anything of the same kind would have been then possible, say, in France,

[1] Prato, *Archiv. Stor.*, iii, p. 309, calls the ladies " alquante ministre di Venere." *Cf.* Luzio Renier, pp. 100–101, *passim*.

[2] Biographical information and some of her letters in A. von Reumont's *Briefe heiliger und gottesfürchtiger Italiener*, pp. 22 *sqq.* (Freiburg, 1877).

[3] Important passages: Parte i, *Nov.* 1, 3, 21, 30, 44; ii, 10, 34, 55; iii, 17, etc.

before this kind of society was there introduced by people like himself. No doubt the supreme achievements of the human mind were then produced independently of the helps of the drawing-room. Yet it would be unjust to rate the influence of the latter on art and poetry too low, if only for the reason that society helped to shape that which existed in no other country—a widespread interest in artistic production and an intelligent and critical public opinion. And apart from this, society of the kind we have described was in itself a natural flower of that life and culture which then was purely Italian, and which since then has extended to the rest of Europe.

In Florence society was powerfully affected by literature and politics. Lorenzo the Magnificent was supreme over his circle, not, as we might be led to believe, through the princely position which he occupied, but rather through the wonderful tact he displayed in giving perfect freedom of action to the many and varied natures which surrounded him.[1] We see how gently he dealt with his great tutor, Politian, and how the sovereignty of the poet and scholar was reconciled, though not without difficulty, with the inevitable reserve prescribed by the approaching change in the position of the house of Medici and by consideration for the sensitiveness of the wife. In return for the treatment he received Politian became the herald and the living symbol of Medicean glory. Lorenzo, after the fashion of a true Medici, delighted in giving an outward and artistic expression to his social amusements. In his brilliant improvisation —*The Hawking-party*—he gives us a humorous description of his comrades, and in the *Symposium* a burlesque of them, but in both cases in such a manner that we clearly feel his capacity for more serious companionship.[2] Of this intercourse his correspondence and the records of his literary and philosophical conversation give ample proof. Some of the social unions which were afterward formed in Florence were in part political clubs, though not without a certain poetical and philosophical character also. Of this kind was the so-called Platonic Academy which met after Lorenzo's death in the gardens of the Ruccellai.[3]

At the Courts of the princes society naturally depended on the character of the ruler. After the beginning of the sixteenth century they became few in number, and these few soon lost their importance. Rome, however, possessed in the unique Court of Leo X a society to which the history of the world offers no parallel.

---

[1] Cf. *Lorenzo Magn. dei Med., Poesie*, i, 204 (the *Symposium*), 291 (*The Hawking-party*). Roscoe, *Lorenzo de' Medici*, iii, p. 140, and App. 17-19.

[2] The title *Simposio* is inaccurate; it should be called *The Return from the Vintage*. Lorenzo, in a parody of Dante's hell, gives an amusing account of his meeting in the Via Faenza all his good friends coming back from the country more or less tipsy. There is a most comical picture in the eighth chapter of Piovanno Arlotto, who sets out in search of his lost thirst, armed with dry meat, a herring, a piece of cheese, a sausage, and four sardines, " e tutte si cocevan nel sudore."

[3] On Cosimo Ruccellai as centre of this circle at the beginning of the sixteenth century see Machiavelli, *Arte della Guerra*, lib. i.

CHAPTER V

THE PERFECT MAN OF SOCIETY

T was for this society—or rather for his own sake—that the Cortigiano, as described to us by Castiglione, educated himself. He was the ideal man of society, and was regarded by the civilization of that age as its choicest flower; and the Court existed for him far rather than he for the Court. Indeed, such a man would have been out of place at any Court, since he himself possessed all the gifts and the bearing of an accomplished ruler, and because his calm supremacy in all things, both outward and spiritual, implied a too independent nature. The inner impulse which inspired him was directed, though our author does not acknowledge the fact, not to the service of the prince, but to his own perfection. One instance will make this clear.[1] In time of war the courtier refuses even useful and perilous tasks, if they are not beautiful and dignified in themselves, such as, for instance, the capture of a herd of cattle; what urges him to take part in war is not duty, but *l'onore*. The moral relation to the prince, as prescribed in the fourth book, is singularly free and independent. The theory of well-bred love-making set forth in the third book is full of delicate psychological observation, which perhaps would be more in place in a treatise on human nature generally; and the magnificent praise of ideal love, which occurs at the end of the fourth book, and which rises to a lyrical elevation of feeling, has no connexion whatever with the special object of the work. Yet here, as in the *Asolani* of Bembo, the culture of the time shows itself in the delicacy with which this sentiment is represented and analysed. It is true that the writers are not in all cases to be taken literally; but that the discourses they give us were actually frequent in good society cannot be doubted, and that it was no affectation, but genuine passion, which appeared in this dress, we shall see farther on.

Among outward accomplishments, the so-called knightly exercises were expected in thorough perfection from the courtier, and besides these much that could only exist at Courts highly organized and based on personal emulation, such as were not to be found out of Italy. Other points obviously rest on an abstract notion of individual perfection. The courtier must be at home in all noble sports, among them running, leaping, swimming, and wrestling; he must, above all things, be a good dancer, and, as a matter of course, an accomplished rider. He must be master of several languages; at all events, of Latin

[1] *Il Cortigiano*, lib. ii, fol. 53.

amiliar with literature and have some knowledge of
a certain practical skill was expected of him, which he
s, to keep as secret as possible. All this is not to be
cept what relates to the use of arms. The mutual inter-

FIG. 187. CASTIGLIONE
By Raphael
Paris, Louvre

action of these gifts and accomplishments results in the perfect man, in whom
no one quality usurps the place of the rest.

So much is certain, that in the sixteenth century the Italians had all Europe
for their pupils, both theoretically and practically, in every noble bodily exercise
and in the habits and manners of good society. Their instructions and their
illustrated books on riding, fencing, and dancing served as the model to other
countries. Gymnastics as an art, apart from military training and from mere
amusement, was probably first taught by Vittorino da Feltre (p. 220), and after

his time became essential to a complete education.[1] The important fact
that they were taught systematically, though what exercises were most in favou
and whether they resembled those now in use, we are unable to say.   But w
may infer not only from the general character of the people, but from positiv
evidence which has been left for us, that not only strength and skill but gra
of movement was one of the main objects of physical training.   It is enoug

FIG. 188. ANGELS MAKING MUSIC
By Luca della Robbia
Florence, Cathedral Museum

to remind the reader of the great Federigo of Urbino (p. 63) directing the
evening games of the young people committed to his care.

The games and contests of the popular classes did not differ essentially from
those which prevailed elsewhere in Europe.   In the maritime cities boat-racing
was among the number, and the Venetian regattas were famous at an early

[1] Cælius Calcagninus (*Opere*, p. 514) describes the education of a young Italian of position about the year
1506 in the funeral speech on Antonio Costabili: first, " artes liberales et ingenuæ disciplinæ; tum adolescentia
in iis exercitationibus acta, quæ ad rem militarem corpus et animum præmuniunt.   Nunc gymnastæ [that is,
the teachers of gymnastics] operam dare, luctari, excurrere, natare, equitare, venari, aucupari, ad palum et apud
lanistam ictus inferre aut declinare, cæsim punctimve hostem ferire, hastam vibrare, sub armis hyemem juxta et
æstatem traducere, lanceis occursare, veri ac communis Martis simulacra imitari." Cardanus (*De Prop. Vita*,
c. 7) names among his gymnastic exercises the springing on to a wooden horse. *Cf.* Rabelais, *Gargantua*, i,
23, 24, for education in general, and 35 for gymnastic art.   Even for the philologists Marsilius Ficinus (*Epist.*,
iv, 171, Galeotto) requires gymnastics, and Maffeo Vegio (*De Puerorum Educatione*, lib. iii, c. 5) for boys.

period.[1]   The classical game of Italy was and is the ball; and this was probably played at the time of the Renaissance with more zeal and brilliancy than elsewhere.   But on this point no distinct evidence is forthcoming.

A few words on music will not be out of place in this part of our work.[2] Musical composition down to the year 1500 was chiefly in the hands of the Flemish school, whose originality and artistic dexterity were greatly admired. Side by side with this there nevertheless existed an Italian school, which probably stood nearer to our present taste.   Half a century later came Palestrina, whose genius still works powerfully among us.   We learn among other facts that he was a great innovator; but whether he or others took the decisive part in shaping the musical language of the modern world lies beyond the judgment of the unprofessional critic.   Leaving on one side the history of musical composition, we shall confine ourselves to the position which music held in the social life of the day.

A fact most characteristic of the Renaissance and of Italy is the specialization of the orchestra, the search for new instruments and modes of sound, and, in close connexion with this tendency, the formation of a class of *virtuosi* who devoted their whole attention to particular instruments or particular branches of music.

Of the more complex instruments, which were perfected and widely diffused

[1] Sansovino, *Venezia*, fol. 172 *sqq.*   They are said to have arisen through the rowing out to the Lido, where the practice with the crossbow took place.   The great regatta on the feast of St Paul was prescribed by law from 1315 onward.   In early times there was much riding in Venice, before the streets were paved and the level wooden bridges turned into arched stone ones.   Petrarch (*Epist. Seniles*, ii, 2, p. 783) describes a brilliant tournament held in 1364 on the Square of St Mark, and the Doge Steno, about the year 1400, had as fine a stable as any prince in Italy.   But riding in the neighbourhood of the square was prohibited as a rule after the year 1291.   At a later time the Venetians naturally had the name of bad riders.   See Ariosto, *Sat.*, v, 208.

[2] See on this subject *Ueber den Einfluss der Renaissance auf die Entwickelung der Musik*, by Bernhard Loos (Basel, 1875), which, however, hardly offers for this period more than is given here.   On Dante's position with regard to music, and on the music to Petrarch's and Boccaccio's poems, see Trucchi, *Poesie Ital. Ined.*, ii, p. 139. See also *Poesie Musicali dei Secoli XIV, XV e XVI tratte da Vari Codici per Cura di Antonio Cappelli* (Bologna, 1868).   For the theorists of the fourteenth century, Filippo Villani, *Vite*, p. 46, and Scardeonius, *De Urb. Patav. Antiq.*, in Græv., *Thesaur.*, vi, iii, col. 297.   A full account of the music at the Court of Federigo of Urbino is to be found in Vespas. Fiorent., p. 122.   For the children's chapel (ten children six to eight years old whom F. had educated in his house, and who were taught singing) at the Court of Hercules I, see *Diario Ferrarese*, in Murat., xxiv, col. 359.   Out of Italy it was still hardly allowable for persons of consequence to be musicians; at the Flemish Court of the young Charles V a serious dispute took place on the subject.   See Hubert. Leod., *De Vita Frid. II Palat.*, lib. iii.   Henry VIII of England is an exception, and also the German Emperor Maximilian, who favoured music as well as all other arts.   Joh. Cuspinian, in his life of the Emperor, calls him " Musices singularis amator," and adds, " Quod vel hinc maxime patet, quod nostra ætate musicorum principes omnes, in omni genere musices omnibusque instrumentis in ejus curia, veluti in fertilissimo agro succreverant.   Scriberem catalogum musicorum quos novi, nisi magnitudinem operis vererer."   In consequence of this music was much cultivated at the University of Vienna.   The presence of the musical young Duke Francesco Sforza of Milan contributed to this result.   See Aschbach, *Gesch. der Wiener Universität*, ii, 79 *sqq.* (1877).

A remarkable and comprehensive passage on music is to be found where we should not expect it, in the *Macaroneide*, *Phant.* xx.   It is a comic description of a quartette, from which we see that Spanish and French songs were often sung, that music already had its enemies (1520), and that the chapel of Leo X and the still earlier composer, Josquin des Près, whose principal works are mentioned, were the chief subjects of enthusiasm in the musical world of that time.   The same writer (Folengo) displays in his *Orlandino* (iii, 23, etc.), published under the name Limerno Ritocco, a musical fanaticism of a thoroughly modern sort.

Barth. Facius, *De Vir. Ill.*, p. 12, praises Leonardus Justinianus as a composer who produced love-songs in his youth and religious pieces in his old age.   J. A. Campanus (*Epist.*, i, 4, ed. Mencken) extols the musician Zacarus at Teramo, and says of him, " Inventa pro oraculis habentur."   Thomas of Forlì, " musicien du Pape " in *Burchardi Diarium*, pp. 62 *sqq.* (ed. Leibnitz).

at a very early period, we find not only the organ, but a corresponding string-instrument, the *gravicembalo* or *clavicembalo*. Fragments of these, dating from the beginning of the fourteenth century, have come down to our own days, adorned with paintings from the hands of the greatest masters. Among other instruments the first place was held by the violin, which even then conferred great celebrity on the successful player. At the Court of Leo X, who when

FIG. 189. CONCERT
By Ercole de' Roberti
London, Salting Collection

cardinal had filled his house with singers and musicians, and who enjoyed the reputation of a critic and performer, the Jew Giovan Maria and Jacopo Sanse-condo were among the most famous. The former received from Leo the title of count and a small town;[1] the latter has been taken to be the Apollo in the *Parnassus* of Raphael. In the course of the sixteenth century celebrities in every branch of music appeared in abundance, and Lomazzo (about 1580) names the then most distinguished masters of the art of singing, of the organ, the lute, the lyre, the *viola da gamba*, the harp, the cithern, the horn, and the trumpet,

[1] *Leonis Vita Anonyma*, in Roscoe, ed. Bossi, xii, p. 171. *Cf. Regesta Leonis*, No. 3315. May he not be the violinist in the Palazzo Sciarra? A certain Giovan Maria da Corneto is praised in the *Orlandino*, iii, 27 (Milan, 1584). *Cf.* Pastor, iv, 2, p. 173, note 7.

nd wishes that their portraits might be painted on the instruments themselves.[1]
Such many-sided comparative criticism would have been impossible anywhere
but in Italy, although the same instruments were to be found in other countries.

The number and variety of these instruments is shown by the fact that
collections of them were now made from curiosity. In Venice, which was one
of the most musical cities of Italy,[2] there were several such collections, and when
a sufficient number of performers happened to be on the spot a concert was at

FIG. 190. CONCERT
By a Venetian artist
London, National Gallery

once improvised. In one of these museums there were a large number of
instruments made after ancient pictures and descriptions, but we are not told
if anybody could play them, or how they sounded. It must not be forgotten
that such instruments were often beautifully decorated, and could be arranged
in a manner pleasing to the eye. We thus meet with them in collections of
other rarities and works of art.

The players, apart from the professional performers, were either single

[1] Lomazzo, *Trattato dell' Arte della Pittura*, etc., p. 347. The text, however, does not bear out the last
statement, which perhaps rests on a misunderstanding of the final sentence, " Et insieme vi si possono gratio-
samente rappresentar convitti et simili abbellimenti, che il pittore leggendo i poeti et gli historici può trovare
copiosamente et anco essendo ingenioso et ricco d' invenzione può per se stesso imaginare? " Speaking of
the lyre, he mentions Leonardo da Vinci and Alfonso (Duke?) of Ferrara. The author includes in his work
all the celebrities of the age, among them several Jews. The most complete list of the famous musicians of
the sixteenth century, divided into an earlier and a later generation, is to be found in Rabelais, in the *New
Prologue* to the fourth book. A virtuoso, the blind Francesco of Florence (d. 1390), was crowned at Venice
with a wreath of laurel by the King of Cyprus.

[2] Sansovino, *Venezia*, fol. 138. The same people naturally collected books of music. Sansovino's words
are " è vera cosa che la musica ha la sua propria sede in questa città."

amateurs, or whole orchestras of them, organized into a corporate academy. Many artists in other branches were at home in music, and often masters of th art. People of position were averse to wind-instruments for the same reason which made them distasteful to Alcibiades and Pallas Athene. In good societ singing, either alone or accompanied with the violin, was usual; but quartette of string-instruments were also common,[3] and the *clavicembalo* was liked o account of its varied effects. In singing the solo only was permitted, "for single voice is heard, enjoyed, and judged far better." In other words, a singing, notwithstanding all conventional modesty, is an exhibition of the indi vidual man of society, it is better that each should be seen and heard separately The tender feelings produced in the fair listeners are taken for granted, an elderly people are therefore recommended to abstain from such forms of art even though they excel in them. It was held important that the effect of th song should be enhanced by the impression made on the sight. We hea nothing, however, of the treatment in these circles of musical composition a an independent branch of art. On the other hand, it happened sometimes tha the subject of the song was some terrible event which had befallen the singer himself.[4]

This dilettantism, which pervaded the middle as well as the upper classes, was in Italy both more widely spread and more genuinely artistic than in any other country in Europe. Wherever we meet with a description of social inter course there music and singing are always and expressly mentioned. Hundreds of portraits show us men and women, often several together, playing or holding some musical instrument, and the angelic concerts represented in the ecclesi astical pictures prove how familiar the painters were with the living effects of music. We read of the lute-player Antonio Rota at Padua (d. 1549), who became a rich man by his lessons, and published a handbook to the practice of the lute.[5]

At a time when there was no opera to concentrate and monopolize musical talent this general cultivation of the art must have been something wonderfully varied, intelligent, and original. It is another question how much we should find to satisfy us in these forms of music, could they now be reproduced for us.

---

[1] The Accademia de' Filarmonici at Verona is mentioned by Vasari, xi, 133, in the life of Sanmichele. Lorenzo the Magnificent was in 1480 already the centre of a School of Harmony consisting of fifteen members, among them the famous organist and organ-builder Squarcialupi. See Delecluze, *Florence et ses Vicissitudes*, vol. ii, p. 256, and Reumont, *Lorenzo dei Medici*, i, 177 *sqq.*; ii, 471–473. Marsilio Ficino took part in these exercises, and gives in his letters (*Epist.*, i, 73 ; iii, 52 ; v, 15) remarkable rules as to music. Lorenzo seems to have transmitted his passion for music to his son Leo X. His eldest son Pietro was also musical.

[2] *Il Cortigiano*, fol. 56. *Cf.* fol. 41.

[3] " Quatro viole da arco "—a high and, except in Italy, rare achievement for amateurs.

[4] Bandello, i, *Nov.* 26. The song of Antonio Bologna in the house of Ippolita Bentivoglio. *Cf.* iii, 26. In these delicate days this would be called a profanation of the holiest feelings. (*Cf.* the last song of Britannicus, Tacit., *Annal.*, xiii, 15.) Recitations accompanied by the lute or *viola* are not easy to distinguish, in the accounts left us, from singing properly so called.

[5] Scardeonius, *loc. cit.*

CHAPTER VI

THE POSITION OF WOMEN

To understand the higher forms of social intercourse at this period we must keep before our minds the fact that women stood on a footing of perfect equality with men.[1] We must not suffer ourselves to be misled by the sophistical and often malicious talk about the assumed inferiority of the female sex, which we meet with now and then in the dialogues of this time,[2] nor by such satires as the third of Ariosto,[3] who treats woman as a dangerous grown-up child, whom a man must learn how to manage in spite of the great gulf between them. There is, indeed, a certain amount of truth in what he says. Just because the educated woman was on a level with the man that communion of mind and heart which comes from the sense of mutual dependence and completion could not be developed in marriage at this time, as it has been developed later in the cultivated society of the North.

The education given to women in the upper classes was essentially the same as that given to men. The Italian, at the time of the Renaissance, felt no scruple in putting sons and daughters alike under the same course of literary and even philological instruction (p. 229).[4] Indeed, looking at this ancient culture as the chief treasure of life, he was glad that his girls should have a share in it. We have seen what perfection was attained by the daughters of princely houses in writing and speaking Latin (p. 241).[5] Many others must at least have been able to read it, in order to follow the conversation of the day, which turned

---

[1] For biographies of women see above, p. 158, note 1. *Cf.* the excellent work of Attilio Hortis, *Le Donne Famose, descritte da Giovanni Boccacci* (Trieste, 1877).

[2] For example, in Castiglione, *Il Cortigiano*. In the same strain Francesco Barbaro, *De Re Uxoria*; Poggio, *An Seni sit Uxor ducenda*, in which much evil is said of women; the ridicule of Codrus Urceus, especially his remarkable discourse *An Uxor sit ducenda* (*Opera*, fol. xviii–xxi, 1506), and the sarcasms of many of the epigrammatists. Marcellus Palingenius (vol. i, p. 304) recommends celibacy in various passages (lib. iv, pp. 275 *sqq.*; v, 466–585); as a means of subduing disobedient wives he recommends to married people:

> " Tu verbera misce
> Tergaque nunc duro resonent pulsata bacillo."

Italian writers on the woman's side are Benedetto da Cesena, *De Honore Mulierum* (Venice, 1500), Dardano, *La Defesa della Donna* (Venice, 1554), *Per Donne Romane* (ed. Manfredi, Bologna, 1575). The defence of, or attack on, women, supported by instances of famous or infamous women down to the time of the writer, was also treated by the Jews, partly in Italian and partly in Hebrew; and in connexion with an earlier Jewish literature dating from the thirteenth century we may mention Abr. Sarteano and Eliah Gennazzano, the latter of whom defended the former against the attacks of Abigdor (for their manuscript poems about the year 1500 *cf.* Steinschneider, *Hebr. Bibliogr.*, vi, 48).

[3] Addressed to Annibale Maleguccio, sometimes numbered as the fifth or sixth.

[4] But there was no lack of voices to urge a different education for girls than for boys, and to deplore the activity of women in learned matters.—L. G.]

[5] When the Hungarian Queen Beatrice, a Neapolitan princess, came to Vienna in 1485 she was addressed in Latin, and " arrexit diligentissime aures domina regina sæpe, cum placide audierat, subridendo (Aschbach, *op. cit.*, ii, 10, note).

largely on classical subjects. An active interest was taken by many in Italian poetry, in which, whether prepared or improvised, a large number of Italian women, from the time of the Venetian Cassandra Fedele onward (about the close of the fifteenth century), made themselves famous.[1] One, indeed, Vittoria Colonna, may be called immortal. If any proof were needed of the assertion

FIG. 191. VITTORIA COLONNA
By Girolamo Muziano
Rome, Galleria Colonna
Photo Alinari

made above, it would be found in the manly tone of this poetry. Even the love-sonnets and religious poems are so precise and definite in their character, and so far removed from the tender twilight of sentiment, and from all the dilettantism which we commonly find in the poetry of women, that we should not hesitate to attribute them to male authors, if we had not clear external evidence to prove the contrary.

For with education the individuality of women in the upper classes was developed in the same way as that of men. Till the time of the Reformation the personality of women out of Italy, even of the highest rank, comes forward but little. Exceptions like Isabella of Bavaria, Margaret of Anjou, and Isabella of Castile are the forced result of very unusual circumstances. In Italy throughout the whole of the fifteenth century the wives of the rulers, and still more those of the *condottieri*, have nearly all a distinct, recognizable personality, and take their share of notoriety and glory. To these came gradually to be added a crowd of famous women of the most varied kind (p. 158, note 1); among them those whose distinction consisted in the fact that their beauty, disposition, education, virtue, and piety combined to render them harmonious human beings.[2] There was no question of 'woman's rights' or female emancipation,

[1] The share taken by women in the plastic arts was insignificant. The learned Isotta Nogarola deserves a word of mention. On her intercourse with Guarino see Rosmini, ii, 67 *sqq.*; with Pius II, see Voigt, iii, 515 *sqq.*

[2] It is from this point of view that we must judge of the life of Allessandra de' Bardi in Vespasiano Fiorentino (Mai, *Spicileg. Rom.*, xi, pp. 593 *sqq.*). The author, by the way, is a great "laudator temporis acti," and it must not be forgotten that nearly a hundred years before what he calls the good old time Boccaccio wrote the

simply because the thing itself was a matter of course. The educated woman, no less than the man, strove naturally after a characteristic and complete individuality. The same intellectual and emotional development which perfected the man was demanded for the perfection of the woman. Active literary

work, nevertheless, was not expected from her, and if she were a poet some powerful utterance of feeling, rather than the confidences of the novel or the diary, was looked for. These women had no thought of the public;[1] their function was to influence distinguished men and to moderate male impulse and caprice.

The highest praise which could then be given to the great Italian women was that they had the mind and the courage of men. We have only to observe the thoroughly manly bearing of most of the women in the heroic poems, especially those of Bojardo and Ariosto, to convince ourselves that we have before us the ideal of the time. The title *virago*, which is an equivocal compliment in the present day, then

FIG. 192. CATERINA SFORZA
By Lorenzo di Credi (?)
Forlì, Pinacotheca
Photo Alinari

Decamerone. On the culture and education of the Italian women of that day *cf.* the numerous facts quoted in Gregorovius, *Lucrezia Borgia.* There is a catalogue of the books possessed by Lucrezia in 1502 and 1503 (Gregorovius, ed. 3, i, 310; ii, 167), which may be considered characteristic of the Italian women of the period. We there find a breviary; a little book with the seven Penitential Psalms and some prayers; a parchment book with gold miniature, called *De Coppelle alla Spagnola*; the printed letters of Catherine of Siena; the printed Epistles and Gospels in Italian; a religious book in Spanish; a manuscript collection of Spanish odes, with the proverbs of Domenico Lopez; a printed book, called *Aquila Volante*; the *Mirror of Faith*, printed in Italian; an Italian printed book called *The Supplement of Chronicles*; a printed Dante, with commentary; an Italian book on philosophy; the legends of the saints in Italian; an old book, *De Ventura*; a Donatus; a life of Christ in Spanish; a manuscript Petrarch on duodecimo parchment. A second catalogue of 1516 contains no secular books whatever.

[1] Ant. Galateo, *Epist.* 3, to the young Bona Sforza, the future wife of Sigismund of Poland: "Incipe aliquid de viro sapere, quoniam ad imperandum viris nata es. . . . Ita fac, ut sapientibus viris placeas, ut te prudentes et graves viri admirentur, et vulgi et muliercularum studia et judicia despicias," etc. A remarkable letter in other respects also (Mai, *Spicileg. Rom.*, viii, p. 532).

implied nothing but praise. It was borne in all its glory by Caterina Sforza, wife and afterward widow of Girolamo Riario, whose hereditary possession,

FIG. 193. VENETIAN COURTESANS
By Carpaccio
Venice, Museo Correr

Forlì, she gallantly defended first against his murderers, and then against Cesare Borgia. Though finally vanquished, she retained the admiration of her countrymen and the title " prima donna d'Italia."[1] This heroic vein

[1] She is so called in the *Chron. Venetum*, in Murat., xxiv, col. 121 *sqq.* (in the account of her heroic defence, *ibid.*, col. 121, she is called a virago). *Cf.* Infessura, in Eccard, *Scriptores*, ii, col. 1981, and *Archiv. Stor.*, App. II, p. 250, and Gregorovius, vii, 437, note 1.

can be detected in many of the women of the Renaissance, though none found the same opportunity of showing their heroism to the world. In Isabella Gonzaga this type is clearly recognizable, and not less in Clarice, of the house of Medici, the wife of Filippo Strozzi.[1]

Women of this stamp could listen to novels like those of Bandello without social intercourse suffering from it.[2] The ruling genius of society was not, as now, womanhood, or the respect for certain presuppositions, mysteries, and susceptibilities, but the consciousness of energy, of beauty, and of a social state full of danger and opportunity. And for this reason we find, side by side with the most measured and polished social forms, something our age would call immodesty,[3] forgetting that by which it was corrected and counterbalanced—the powerful characters of the women who were exposed to it.

FIG. 194. THE COURTSHIP
By Paris Bordone
Milan, Brera Gallery
Photo Alinari

That in all the dialogues and treatises together we can find no absolute evidence on these points is only natural, however freely the nature of love and the position and capacities of women were discussed.

---

[1] Contemporary historians speak of her more than womanly intellect and eloquence. *Cf.* Ranke's *Filippo Strozzi*, in *Historisch-biographische Studien*, p. 371, note 2.

[2] Bandello, however, says (i, *Nov.* 30): " poichè ci manca la compagnia delle donne . . . possiamo più liberamente parlare che quando siamo a la presenza loro."—L. G.]

[3] And rightly so, sometimes. How ladies should behave while such tales are telling we learn from *Cortigiano*, lib. iii, cap. 17. That the ladies who were present at his dialogues must have known how to conduct themselves in case of need is shown by the strong passage, lib. ii, cap. 69. What is said of the Donna di Palazzo —the counterpart of the Cortigiano—that she should neither avoid frivolous company nor use unbecoming language is not decisive, since she was far more the servant of the princess than the Cortigiano of the prince. See Bandello, i, *Nov.* 44. Bianca d'Este tells the terrible love-story of her ancestor, Niccolò of Ferrara, and Parisina. The tales put into the mouths of the women in the *Decamerone* may also serve as instances of this indelicacy. Bandello, i, *Nov.* 44; and Landau, *Beitr. z. Gesch. der Ital. Nov.*, p. 102, note 32 (Vienna, 1875).

What seems to have been wanting in this society were the young girls,[1] who even when not brought up in the monasteries were still carefully kept away from it. It is not easy to say whether their absence was the cause of the greater freedom of conversation, or whether they were removed on account of it.

Even the intercourse with courtesans seems to have assumed a more elevated character, reminding us of the position of the *hetairæ* in classical Athens. The famous Roman courtesan Imperia was a woman of intelligence and culture, had learned from a certain Domenico Campana the art of making sonnets, and was not without musical accomplishments.[2] The beautiful Isabella da Luna, of Spanish extraction, who was reckoned amusing company, seems to have been an odd compound of a kind heart with a shockingly foul tongue, which latter sometimes brought her into trouble.[3] At Milan Bandello knew the majestic Caterina di S. Celso,[4] who played and sang and recited superbly. It is clear from all we read on the subject that the distinguished people who visited these women and from time to time lived with them demanded from them a considerable degree of intelligence and instruction, and that the famous courtesans were treated with no slight respect and consideration. Even when relations with them were broken off their good opinion was still desired,[5] which shows that departed passion had left permanent traces behind. But on the whole this intellectual intercourse is not worth mentioning by the side of that sanctioned by the recognized forms of social life, and the traces which it has left in poetry and literature are for the most part of a scandalous nature. We may well be astonished that among the 6800 persons of this class who were to be found in Rome in 1490 [6]—that is, before the appearance of syphilis— scarcely a single woman seems to have been remarkable for any higher gifts.

[1] Sansovino, *Venezia*, fol. 152 *sqq.* How highly the travelled Italians valued the freer intercourse with girls in England and the Netherlands is shown by Bandello, ii, *Nov.* 44; iv, *Nov.* 27. For the Venetian women and the Italian women generally see the work of Yriarte, pp. 50 *sqq.*

[2] Paul. Jovius, *De Rom. Piscibus*, cap. 5; Bandello, iii, *Nov.* 42. Aretino, in the *Ragionamento del Zoppino*, p. 327, says of a courtesan: " She knows by heart all Petrarch and Boccaccio, and many beautiful verses of Virgil, Horace, Ovid, and a thousand other authors."

[3] Bandello, ii, *Nov.* 51; iv, *Nov.* 16.

[4] Bandello, iv, *Nov.* 8.

[5] For a characteristic instance of this see Giraldi, *Hecatommithi*, iv, *Nov.* 7.

[6] Infessura, in Eccard, *Scriptores*, ii, col. 1997. The public women only, not the kept women, are meant. The number, compared with the population of Rome, is certainly enormous, perhaps owing to some clerical error. According to Giraldi, vi, 7, Venice was exceptionally rich " di quella sorte di donne che cortigiane son dette "; see also the epigram of Pasquinus (Gregorovius, viii, 279, note 2); but Rome did not stand behind Venice (Giraldi, *Introduz.*, *Nov.* 2). *Cf.* the notice of the *meretrices* in Rome (1480) who met in a church and were robbed of their jewels and ornaments, in Murat., xxii, 342 *sqq.*, and the account in *Burchardi Diarium*, ed. Leibnitz, pp. 75–77, etc. Landi (*Commentario*, fol. 76) mentions Rome, Naples, and Venice as the chief seats of the *cortigiane*; *ibid.*, 286, the fame of the women of Chiavenna is to be understood ironically. The *Quæstiones Forcianæ*, fol. 9, of the same author give most interesting information on love and love's delights, and the style and position of women in the different cities of Italy. On the other hand, Egnatius (*De Exemp. Ill. Vir.*, Venice, fol. 212b *sqq.*) praises the chastity of the Venetian women, and says that the prostitutes come every year from Germany. Corn. Agr., *De Van. Scientiæ*, cap. 63 (*Opp.*, ed. Lugd., ii, 158), says: " Vidi ego nuper atque legi sub titulo ' Cortosanæ ' Italica lingua editum et Venetiis typis excusum de arte meretricia dialogum, utriusque Veneris omnium flagitiosissimum et dignissimum, qui ipse cum autore suo ardeat." Ambr. Traversari (*Epist.*, viii, 2 *sqq.*) calls the beloved of Niccolò Niccoli " fœmina fidelissima." In the *Lettere dei Principi*, i, 108 (report of Negro, September 1, 1522), the " donne Greche " are described as " fonte di ogni cortesia et amorevolezza." A great authority, especially for Siena, is the *Hermaphroditus* of Panormitanus. The enumeration of the " lenæ lupæque " in Florence (ii, 37) is hardly fictitious; the line there occurs:

" Annaque *Theutonico* tibi si dabit obvia cantu."

Those whom we have mentioned all belong to the period which immediately followed. The mode of life, the morals, and the philosophy of the public women, who with all their sensuality and greed were not always incapable of deeper passions, as well as the hypocrisy and devilish malice shown by some in their later years, are best set forth by Giraldi in the novels which form the introduction to the *Hecatommithi*. Pietro Aretino, in his *Ragionamenti*, gives us rather a picture of his own depraved character than of this unhappy class of women as they really were.

The mistresses of the princes, as has already been pointed out (p. 72), were sung by poets and painted by artists, and in consequence have been personally familiar to their contemporaries and to posterity. We hardly know more than the names of Alice Perrers and Clara Dettin, the mistress of Frederick the Victorious, and of Agnes Sorel have only a half-legendary story. With the monarchs of the age of the Renaissance—Francis I and Henry II—the case is different.

CHAPTER VII

DOMESTIC ECONOMY

FTER treating of the intercourse of society let us glance for a moment at the domestic life of this period. We are commonly disposed to look on the family life of the Italians at this time as hopelessly ruined by the national immorality, and this side of the question will be more fully discussed in the sequel. For the moment we must content ourselves with pointing out that conjugal infidelity has by no means so disastrous an

FIG. 195. VILLA MEDICI AT CAREGGI, NEAR FLORENCE
By Michelozzo
Photo Alinari

influence on family life in Italy as in the North, so long, at least, as certain limits are not overstepped.

The domestic life of the Middle Ages was a product of popular morals, or, if we prefer to put it otherwise, a result of the inborn tendencies of national life, modified by the varied circumstances which affected them. Chivalry at the time of its splendour left domestic economy untouched. The knight wandered from Court to Court, and from one battlefield to another. His homage was given systematically to some other woman than his own wife, and things went how they might at home in the castle.[1] The spirit of the Renaissance first brought order into domestic life, treating it as a work of deliberate contrivance. Intelligent economical views (p. 98) and a rational style of domestic architecture served to promote this end. But the chief cause of the change was the

FIG. 196. VILLA MEDICI, NEAR FIESOLE
Photo Alinari

thoughtful study of all questions relating to social intercourse, to education, to domestic service and organization.

The most precious document on this subject is the treatise on the management of the home by Agnolo Pandolfini (L. B. Alberti).[2] He represents a father speaking to his grown-up sons, and initiating them into his method of administration. We are introduced into a large and wealthy household, which if governed with moderation and reasonable economy promises happiness and prosperity for generations to come. A considerable landed estate, whose produce furnishes the table of the house and serves as the basis of the family fortune, is combined with some industrial pursuit, such as the weaving of wool or silk. The dwelling is solid and the food good. All that has to do with the plan and arrangement of the house is great, durable, and costly, but the daily life within it is as simple as possible. All other expenses, from the largest in

[1] Were these wandering knights really married?

[2] *Trattato del Governo della Famiglia.* See above, p. 145, note 2. Pandolfini died in 1446; L. B. Alberti, by whom the work was really written, in 1472. [Franz Harder points out to me that the treatise was written with reference to Xenophon's Œconomicus, and that among the ancients mentioned on p. 117 of the Turin edition Xenophon particularly is to be understood. *Cf.* especially Chapters 7–10 of the Œconomicus.—L. G.]

which the family honour is at stake down to the pocket-money of the younger sons, stand to one another in a rational, not a conventional, relation. Nothing is considered of so much importance as education, which the head of the house gives not only to the children, but to the whole household. He first develops his wife from a shy girl, brought up in careful seclusion, to the true woman of the house, capable of commanding and guiding the servants. The sons are brought up without any undue severity,[1] carefully watched and counselled,

FIG. 197. VILLA MEDICI WITH GARDENS IN CAFAGGIUOLO
Wall lunette in the Uffizi Gallery, Florence

and controlled "rather by authority than by force." And finally the servants are chosen and treated on such principles that they gladly and faithfully hold by the family.

One feature of this book must be referred to which is by no means peculiar to it, but which treats it with special warmth—the love of the educated Italian

[1] A thorough history of 'flogging' among the Germanic and Latin races treated with some psychological power would be worth volumes of dispatches and negotiations. (A modest beginning has been made by Lichtenberg, *Vermischte Schriften*, v, 276–283.) When, and through what influence, did flogging become a daily practice in the German household? Not till after Walther sang: "Nieman kan mit gerten kindes zuht beherten."

In Italy beating ceased early; Maffeo Vegio (d. 1458) recommends (*De Educ. Liber.*, lib. i, c. 19) moderation in flogging, but adds: "Cædendos magis esse filios quam pestilentissimis blanditiis lætandos." At a later time a child of seven was no longer beaten. The little Roland (*Orlandino*, cap. vii, str. 42) lays down the principle:
"Sol gli asini si ponno bastonare,
Se una tal bestia fussi, patirei."
The German humanists of the Renaissance, like Rudolf Agricola and Erasmus, speak decisively against flogging, which the older schoolmasters regarded as an indispensable means of education. In the biographies of the *Fahrenden Schüler* at the close of the fifteenth century (Platter's *Lebensbeschreibung*, ed. Fechter, Basel, 1840; Butzbach's *Wanderbuch*, ed. Becher, Regensburg, 1869) there are gross examples of the corporal punishment of the time.

for country life.[1] In Northern countries the nobles lived in the country in their castles, and the monks of the higher orders in their well-guarded monasteries, while the wealthiest burghers dwelt from one year's end to another in the cities. But in Italy, so far as the neighbourhood of certain towns at all events was concerned,[2] the security of life and property was so great, and the passion for a country residence was so strong, that men were willing to risk a loss in time of war. Thus arose the villa, the country house

FIG. 198. GARDENS AND STATUARY AT THE BELVEDERE (ABOUT 1550)
By Hendrik van Cleve
Vienna, Art Gallery

of the well-to-do citizen. This precious inheritance of the old Roman world was thus revived as soon as the wealth and culture of the people were sufficiently advanced.

One author finds at his villa a peace and happiness, for an account of which the reader must hear him speak himself:

While every other possession causes work and danger, fear and disappointment, the villa brings a great and honourable advantage; the villa is always true and kind; if you dwell in it at the right time and with love it will not only satisfy you, but add reward to reward. In spring the green trees and the song of the birds will make you joyful and hopeful; in autumn a moderate exertion will bring forth fruit a hundredfold; all through the year melancholy will be banished from you. The

[1] But the taste was not universal. J. A. Campanus (*Epist.*, iv, 4) writes vigorously against country life. He admits: " Ego si rusticus natus non essem, facile tangerer voluptate "; but since he was born a peasant, " quod tibi deliciæ, mihi satietas est."

[2] Giovanni Villani, xi, 93, our principal authority for the building of villas before the middle of the fourteenth century. The villas were more beautiful than the town houses, and great exertions were made by the Florentines to have them so, " onde erano tenuti matti."

villa is the spot where good and honest men love to congregate. Nothing secret, nothing treacherous, is done here; all see all; here is no need of judges or witnesses, for all are kindly and peaceably disposed one to another. Hasten hither, and fly away from the pride of the rich and the dishonour of the bad. O blessed life in the villa, O unknown fortune!

The economical side of the matter is that one and the same property must, if possible, contain everything—corn, wine, oil, pasture-land and woods—and that in such cases the property was paid for well, since nothing needed then to be got from the market. But the higher enjoyment derived from the villa is shown by some words of the introduction:

Round about Florence lie many villas in a transparent atmosphere, amid cheerful scenery, and with a splendid view; there is little fog, and no injurious winds; all is good, and the water pure and healthy. Of the numerous buildings many are like palaces, many like castles, costly and beautiful to behold.

He is speaking of those unrivalled villas of which the greater number were sacrificed, though vainly, by the Florentines themselves in the defence of their city in the year 1529.[1]

In these villas, as in those on the Brenta, on the Lombard hills, at Posilippo, and on the Vomero, social life assumed a freer and more rural character than in the palaces within the city. We meet with charming descriptions of the intercourse of the guests, the hunting-parties, and all the open-air pursuits and amusements.[2] But the noblest achievements of poetry and thought are sometimes also dated from these scenes of rural peace.

---

[1] *Trattato del Governo della Famiglia*, pp. 84, 88 (Torino, 1829).
[2] See above, Part IV, Chapter II. Petrarch was called "Silvanus" on the ground of his dislike of the town and love of the country. *Epist. Fam.*, ed. Fracassetti, ii, 87 *sqq.* Guarino's description of a villa to Gianbattista Candrata, in Rosmini, ii, 13 *sqq.*, 157 *sqq.* Poggio, in a letter to Facius (*De Vir. Ill.*, p. 106): "Sum enim deditior senectutis gratia rei rusticæ quam antea." See also Poggio, *Opp.*, pp. 112 *sqq.* (1513); and Shepherd-Tonelli, i, 255 and 261. Similarly Maffeo Vegio (*De Lib. Educ.*, vi, 4) and B. Platina at the beginning of his dialogue *De Vera Nobilitate.* Politian's descriptions of the country houses of the Medici in Reumont, *Lorenzo dei Medici*, ii, 73, 87. For the Farnesina see Gregorovius, viii, 114.

CHAPTER VIII

THE FESTIVALS

T is by no arbitrary choice that in discussing the social life of this period we are led to treat of the processions and shows which formed part of the popular festivals.[1] The artistic power of which the Italians of the Renaissance gave proof on such occasions [2] was attained only by means of that free intercourse of all classes which formed the basis of Italian society. In Northern Europe the monasteries, the courts, and the burghers had their special feasts and shows as in Italy; but in the one case the form and substance of these displays differed according to the class which took part in them, and in the other an art and culture common to the whole nation stamped them with both a higher and a more popular character. The decorative architecture, which served to aid in these festivals, deserves a chapter to itself in the history of art, although our imagination can only form a picture of it from the descriptions which have been left to us. We are here more especially concerned with the festival as a higher phase in the life of the people, in which its religious, moral, and poetical ideas took visible shape. The Italian festivals in their best form mark the point of transition from real life into the world of art.

The two chief forms of festal display were originally here, as elsewhere in the West, the mystery, or the dramatization of sacred history and legend, and the procession, the motive and character of which was also purely ecclesiastical.

The performances of the mysteries in Italy were from the first more frequent and splendid than elsewhere, and were most favourably affected by the progress of poetry and of the other arts. In the course of time not only did the farce and the secular drama branch off from the mystery, as in other countries of Europe, but the pantomime also, with its accompaniments of singing and dancing, the effect of which depended on the richness and beauty of the spectacle.

The procession in the broad, level, and well-paved streets of the Italian cities,[3] was soon developed into the *trionfo*, or train of masked figures on foot and in chariots, the ecclesiastical character of which gradually gave way to the secular. The processions at the carnival and at the feast of Corpus Christi [4]

---

[1] *Cf.* J. Burckhardt, *Geschichte der Renaissance in Italien*, pp. 320–332 (Stuttgart, 1868).

[2] *Cf.* pp. 313 *sqq.*, where the magnificence of the festivals is shown to have been a hindrance to the higher development of the drama. [3] In comparison with the cities of the North.

[4] The procession at the feast of Corpus Christi was not established at Venice until 1407; Cecchetti, *Venezia a Corte di Roma*, i, 108.

were alike in the pomp and brilliancy with which they were conducted, and set the pattern afterward followed by the royal or princely progresses. Other nations were willing to spend vast sums of money on these shows, but in Italy alone do we find an artistic method of treatment which arranged the procession as a harmonious and significative whole.

What is left of these festivals is but a poor remnant of what once existed. Both religious and secular displays of this kind have largely abandoned the dramatic element—the costumes—partly from dread of ridicule and partly because the cultivated classes, who formerly gave their whole energies to these things, have for several reasons lost their interest in them. Even at the carnival the great processions of masks are out of fashion. What still remains, such as the costumes adopted in imitation of certain religious confraternities, or even the brilliant festival of S. Rosalia at Palermo, shows clearly how far the higher culture of the country has withdrawn from such interests.

The festivals did not reach their full development till after the decisive victory of the modern spirit in the fifteenth century,[1] unless perhaps Florence was here, as in other things, in advance of the rest of Italy. In Florence the several quarters of the city were in early times organized with a view to such exhibitions, which demanded no small expenditure of artistic effort. Of this kind was the representation of hell, with a scaffold and boats in the Arno on May 1, 1304, when the Ponte alla Carraja broke down under the weight of the spectators.[2] That at a later time Florentines used to travel through Italy as directors of festivals (festaiuoli) shows that the art was early perfected at home.[3]

In setting forth the chief points of superiority in the Italian festivals over those of other countries the first that we shall have to remark is the developed sense of individual characteristics—in other words, the capacity to invent a given mask and to act the part with dramatic propriety. Painters and sculptors not merely did their part toward the decoration of the place where the festival was held, but helped in getting up the characters themselves, and prescribed the dress, the paints (p. 364), and the other ornaments to be used. The second fact to be pointed out is the universal familiarity of the people with the poetical basis of the show. The mysteries, indeed, were equally well understood all over Europe, since the Biblical story and the legends of the saints were the common property of Christendom; but in all other respects the advantage was on the side of Italy. For the recitations, whether of religious or secular heroes, she possessed a lyrical poetry so rich and harmonious that none could resist its charm.[4] The majority, too, of the spectators—at least, in the cities—understood the meaning of mythological figures, and could guess without

---

[1] The festivities which took place when Visconti was made Duke of Milan, 1395 (Corio, fol. 274), had, with all their splendour, something of medieval coarseness about them, and the dramatic element was wholly wanting. Notice, too, the relative insignificance of the processions in Pavia during the fourteenth century (*Anonymus de Laudibus Papiæ*, in Murat., xi, col. 34 *sqq*.).

[2] Gio. Villani, viii, 70.

[3] See, for example, Infessura, in Eccard, *Scriptores*, ii, col. 1896; Corio, fols. 417, 421.

[4] The dialogue in the mysteries was chiefly in octaves, the monologue in *terzine*. For the mysteries see J. L. Klein, *Geschichte der Ital. Dramas*, i, 153 *sqq*.

much difficulty at the allegorical and historical, which were drawn from sources familiar to the mass of Italians.

This point needs to be discussed more fully. The Middle Ages were essentially the ages of allegory. Theology and philosophy treated their categories as independent beings,[1] and poetry and art had but little to add in order to give them personality. Here all the countries of the West were on the same

FIG. 199. THE TRIUMPH OF LOVE
After Petrarch. Bronze relief
Paris, Louvre

level. Their world of ideas was rich enough in types and figures, but when these were put into concrete shape the costume and attributes were likely to be unintelligible and unsuited to the popular taste. This, even in Italy, was often the case, and not only so during the whole period of the Renaissance, but down to a still later time. To produce the confusion it was enough if a predicate of the allegorical figures was wrongly translated by an attribute. Even Dante is not wholly free from such errors,[2] and, indeed, he prides himself on the

[1] We have no need to refer to the realism of the schoolmen for proof of this. About the year 970 Bishop Wibold of Cambray recommended to his clergy, instead of dice, a sort of spiritual *bézique*, with fifty-six abstract names represented by as many combinations of cards. *Gesta Episcopor. Cameracens.*, in *Mon. Germ.*, SS. vii, p. 433.

[2] For example, when he found pictures on metaphors. At the gate of Purgatory the central broken step signifies contrition of heart (*Purgatorio*, ix, 97), though the slab through being broken loses its value as a step (?). And again (*Purgatorio*, xviii, 94), the idle in this world have to show their penitence by running in the other, though running could be a symbol of flight.

obscurity of his allegories in general.[1] Petrarch, in his *trionfi*, attempts to giv
clear, if short, descriptions of at all events the figures of Love, of Chastity, o
Death, and of Fame. Others, again, load their allegories with inappropriat
attributes. In the satires of Vinciguerra,[2] for example, Envy is depicted wit
rough, iron teeth, Gluttony as biting its own lips, and with a shock of tanglec
hair, the latter probably to show its indifference to all that is not meat anc
drink. We cannot here discuss the bad influence of these misunderstandings
on the plastic arts. They, like poetry, might think themselves fortunate i
allegory could be expressed by a mythological figure—by a figure which antiquity saved from absurdity—if Mars might stand for war, and Diana [3] for the
love of the chase.

Nevertheless art and poetry had better allegories than these to offer, and
we may assume with regard to such figures of this kind as appeared in the
Italian festivals that the public required them to be clearly and vividly characteristic, since its previous training had fitted it to be a competent critic. Elsewhere, particularly at the Burgundian Court, the most inexpressive figures, and
even mere symbols, were allowed to pass, since to understand, or to seem to
understand, them was a part of aristocratic breeding. On the occasion of the
famous " Oath of the Pheasant " in 1453[4] the beautiful young horsewoman
who appears as " Queen of Pleasure " is the only pleasing allegory. The huge
dishes with automatic or even living figures within them are either mere
curiosities or are intended to convey some clumsy moral lesson. A naked
female statue guarding a live lion was supposed to represent Constantinople
and its future saviour, the Duke of Burgundy. The rest, with the exception
of a pantomime—Jason in Colchis—seems either too recondite to be understood or to have no sense at all. Olivier himself, to whom we owe the description of the scene, appeared costumed as " The Church," in a tower on the back
of an elephant, and sang a long elegy on the victory of the unbelievers.[5]

But although the allegorical element in the poetry, the art, and the festivals
of Italy is superior both in good taste and in unity of conception to what we
find in other countries, yet it is not in these qualities that it is most characteristic
and unique. The decisive point of superiority [6] lay rather in the fact that
besides the personifications of abstract qualities historical representatives of
them were introduced in great number—that both poetry and plastic art were
accustomed to represent famous men and women. The *Divine Comedy*, the

---

[1] *Inferno*, ix, 61; *Purgatorio*, viii, 19. [Pochhammer contests this reading of both passages.—W. G.]

[2] *Poesie Satiriche*, pp. 70 *sqq.* (ed. Milan). Dating from the end of the fourteenth century.

[3] The latter, for example, in the *Venatio* of Cardinal Adriano da Corneto (Strasburg, 1512; often printed).
Ascanio Sforza is there supposed to find consolation for the fall of his house in the pleasures of the chase. See
above, p. 264.

[4] More properly 1454. See Olivier de la Marche, *Mémoires*, chap. 29.

[5] For other French festivals see, for example, Juvenal des Ursins (Paris, 1614), *ad a.* 1389 (entrance of Queen
Isabella); Jean de Troyes, *ad a.* 1461 (often printed) (entrance of Louis XI). Here too we meet with living
statues, machines for raising bodies, and so forth; but the whole is confused and disconnected, and the allegories
are mostly unintelligible. The festivals at Lisbon in 1452, held at the departure of the Infanta Eleonora, the
bride of the Emperor Frederick III, lasted several days and were remarkable for their magnificence. See
Freher-Struve, *Rer. German. Script.*, ii, fol. 51—the report of Nic. Lauckmann.

[6] A great advantage for those poets and artists who knew how to use it.

trionfi of Petrarch, the *Amorosa Visione* of Boccaccio—all of them works constructed on this principle—and the great diffusion of culture which took place under the influence of antiquity had made the nation familiar with this historical element. These figures now appeared at festivals, either individualized, as definite masks, or in groups, as characteristic attendants on some leading allegorical figure. The art of grouping and composition was thus learnt in Italy

FIG. 200. THE TRIUMPH OF DEATH
After Petrarch. Bronze relief
Paris, Louvre

at a time when the most splendid exhibitions in other countries were made up of unintelligible symbolism or unmeaning puerilities.

Let us begin with that kind of festival which is perhaps the oldest of all— the mysteries.[1] They resembled in their main features those performed in the rest of Europe. In the public squares, in the churches, and in the cloisters extensive scaffolds were constructed, the upper storey of which served as a paradise to open and shut at will, and the ground floor often as a hell, while between the two lay the stage properly so called, representing the scene of all the earthly events of the drama. In Italy, as elsewhere, the Biblical or legendary

[1] *Cf.* Bartol. Gambia, *Notizie intorno alle Opere di Feo Belcari* (Milan, 1808); and especially the introduction to the work *Le Rappresentazioni di Feo Belcari ed altre di lui Poesie* (Firenze, 1833). As a parallel, see the introduction of the bibliophile Jacob to his edition of Pathelin (Paris, 1859). *Cf.* d'Ancona, *Origini del Teatro Italiano*, vols. 1 and 2 (Turin, 1891).

play often began with an introductory dialogue between Apostles, Prophets, Sibyls, Virtues, and Fathers of the Church, and sometimes ended with a dance. As a matter of course the half-comic *intermezzi* of secondary characters were not wanting in Italy, yet this feature was hardly so broadly marked as in Northern countries.[1] The artificial means by which figures were made to rise and float in the air—one of the chief delights of these representations—were probably much better understood in Italy than elsewhere; and at Florence in the fourteenth century the hitches in these performances were a stock subject of ridicule.[2] Soon after Brunellesco invented for the feast of the Annunciation in the Piazza S. Felice a marvellous apparatus consisting of a heavenly globe surrounded by two circles of angels, out of which Gabriel flew down in a machine shaped like an almond. Cecca too devised the mechanism for such displays.[3] The spiritual corporations or the quarters of the city which undertook the charge and in part the performance of these plays spared, at all events in the larger towns, no trouble and expense to render them as perfect and artistic as possible. The same was no doubt the case at the great Court festivals, when mysteries were acted as well as pantomimes and secular dramas. The Court of Pietro Riario (p. 124) and that of Ferrara were assuredly not wanting in all that human invention could produce.[4] When we picture to ourselves the theatrical talent and the splendid costumes of the actors, the scenes constructed in the style of the architecture of the period and hung with garlands and tapestry, and in the background the noble buildings of an Italian *piazza* or the slender columns of some great courtyard or cloister, the effect is one of great brilliance. But just as the secular drama suffered from this passion for display so the higher poetical development of the mystery was arrested by the same cause. In the texts which are left we find for the most part the poorest dramatic groundwork, relieved now and then by a fine lyrical or rhetorical passage, but no trace of the grand symbolic enthusiasm which distinguishes the *Autos Sagramentales* of Calderon.

In the smaller towns, where the scenic display was less, the effect of these spiritual plays on the character of the spectators may have been greater. We read [5] that one of the great preachers of repentance of whom more will be said later on, Roberto da Lecce, closed his Lenten sermons during the plague of 1448, at Perugia, with a representation of the Passion. The piece followed the New Testament closely. The actors were few, but the whole people wept aloud.

---

[1] It is true that a mystery at Siena on the subject of the Massacre of the Innocents closed with a scene in which the disconsolate mothers seized one another by the hair. Della Valle, *Lettere Sanesi*, iii, p. 53. It was one of the chief aims of Feo Belcari (d. 1484), of whom we have spoken, to free the mysteries from these monstrosities.

[2] Franco Sacchetti, *Nov.* 72.

[3] Vasari, iii, 232 *sqq.*, *Vita di Brunellesco*; v, 36 *sqq.*, *Vita del Cecca*. *Cf.* v, 32, *Vita di Don Bartolommeo*.

[4] *Archiv. Stor.*, App. II, p. 310. The mystery of the Annunciation at Ferrara, on the occasion of the wedding of Alfonso, with fireworks and flying apparatus. For an account of the representation of Susanna, John the Baptist, and a legend at the house of Cardinal Riario see Corio, fol. 417. For the mystery of Constantine the Great in the Papal Palace at the carnival of 1484 see Jac. Volaterranus, in Murat., xxiii, col. 194. The chief actor was a Genoese born and educated at Constantinople.

[5] Graziani, *Cronaca di Perugia*, *Archiv. Stor.*, xiv, i, p. 598. At the Crucifixion a figure was kept ready and put in the place of the actor.

It is true that on such occasions emotional stimulants were resorted to which were borrowed from the crudest realism. We are reminded of the pictures of Matteo da Siena, or of the groups of clay figures by Guido Mazzoni, when we read that the actor who took the part of Christ appeared covered with wales and apparently sweating blood, and even bleeding from a wound in the side.[1]

The special occasions on which these mysteries were performed, apart from the great festivals of the Church, from princely weddings, and the like, were of various kinds. When, for example, S. Bernardino of Siena was canonized by the Pope (1450) a sort of dramatic imitation of the ceremony took place (*rappresentazione*), probably on the great square of his native city, and for two days there was feasting with meat and drink for all comers.[2] We are told that a learned monk celebrated his promotion to the degree of Doctor of Theology by giving a representation of the legend about the patron saint of the city.[3] Charles VIII had scarcely entered Italy before he was welcomed at Turin by the widowed Duchess Bianca of Savoy with a sort of half-religious pantomime,[4] in which a pastoral scene first symbolized the Law of Nature, and then a

FIG. 201. FORTUNA
By Giovanni Bellini
Venice, Accademia

---

[1] For this see Graziani, *loc. cit.*, and *Pii II Comment.*, lib. viii, pp. 383 and 386. The poetry of the fifteenth century sometimes shows the same coarseness. A *canzone* of Andrea da Basso traces in detail the corruption of the corpse of a hard-hearted fair one. In a monkish drama of the twelfth century King Herod was put on the stage with the worms eating him (*Carmina Burana*, pp. 80 *sqq.*). Many of the German dramas of the seventeenth century offer parallel instances.

[2] Allegretto, *Diari Sanesi*, in Murat., xxii, col. 767.

[3] Matarazzo, *Archiv. Stor.*, xvi, ii, p. 36. The monk had previously undertaken a voyage to Rome to make the necessary studies for the festival.

[4] Extracts from the *Vergier d'Honneur*, in Roscoe, *Leo X*, ed. Bossi, i, p. 20; iii, p. 263.

procession of patriarchs the Law of Grace. Afterward followed the story of Lancelot of the Lake, and that " of Athens." And no sooner had the King reached Chieri than he was received with another pantomime, in which a woman in childbed was shown, surrounded by distinguished visitors.

If any Church festival was held by universal consent to call for exceptional efforts it was the feast of Corpus Christi, which in Spain (p. 401) gave rise to a special class of poetry. We possess a splendid description of the manner in which that feast was celebrated at Viterbo by Pius II in 1482.[1] The procession itself, which advanced from a vast and gorgeous tent in front of S. Francesco along the main street to the cathedral, was the least part of the ceremony. The cardinals and wealthy prelates had divided the whole distance into parts, over which they severally presided, and which they decorated with curtains, tapestry, and garlands.[2] Each of them had also erected a stage of his own, on which, as the procession passed by, short historical and allegorical scenes were represented. It is not clear from the account whether all the characters were living beings or some merely draped figures;[3] the expense was certainly very great. There was a suffering Christ amid singing cherubs, the Last Supper with a figure of St Thomas Aquinas, the combat between the Archangel Michael and the devils, fountains of wine and orchestras of angels, the grave of Christ with the scene of the Resurrection, and finally, on the square before the cathedral, the tomb of the Virgin. It opened after High Mass and the Benediction, and the Mother of God ascended singing to Paradise, where she was crowned by her Son and led into the presence of the Eternal Father.

Among these representations in the public street that given by the Cardinal Vice-Chancellor Roderigo Borgia, afterward Pope Alexander VI, was remarkable for its splendour and obscure symbolism.[4] It offers an early instance of the fondness for salvos of artillery [5] which was characteristic of the house of Borgia.

The account is briefer which Pius II gives us of the procession held the same year in Rome on the arrival of the skull of St Andrew from Greece. There too Roderigo Borgia distinguished himself by his magnificence; but this festival had a more secular character than the other, as, besides the customary choirs of angels, other masks were exhibited, as well as " strong men," who seemed to have performed various feats of muscular prowess.

---

[1] *Pii II Comment.*, lib. viii, pp. 382 *sqq.* Another gorgeous celebration of the " Corpus Domini " is mentioned by Bursellis, *Annal. Bonon.*, in Murat., xxiii, col. 911, for the year 1492. The representations were from the Old and New Testaments.

[2] On such occasions we read, " Nulla di muro si potea vedere."

[3] The same is true of many such descriptions.

[4] Five kings with an armed retinue, and a savage who fought with a (tamed?) lion; the latter, perhaps, with an allusion to the name of the Pope—Sylvius. [According to Croce (*Arch. Stor. Napolet.*, xiv, 660) it was not a real lion, but an artificial one, made of straw and wood.—L. G.]

[5] Instances under Sixtus IV, Jac. Volaterranus, in Murat., xxiii, col. 135 (" bómbardorum et sclopulorum crepitus "), 139. At the accession of Alexander VI there were great salvos of artillery. Fireworks, a beautiful invention due to Italy, belong, like festive decorations generally, rather to the history of art than to our present work. So too the brilliant illuminations we read of in connexion with many festivals, and the hunting-trophies and table ornaments. (See p. 315. The elevation of Julius II to the Papal throne was celebrated at Venice by three days' illumination. Brosch, *Julius II*, p. 325, note 17.)

Such representations as were wholly or chiefly secular in their character were arranged, especially at the more important princely Courts, mainly with a view to splendid and striking effects. The subjects were mythological or allegorical, and the interpretation commonly lay on the surface. Extravagances, indeed, were not wanting—gigantic animals from which a crowd of masked figures suddenly emerged, as at Siena [1] in 1465, when at a public reception a ballet of

FIG. 202. HOLY RELICS PROCESSION IN VENICE
Part of one of Gentile Bellini's compositions
Venice, Accademia
Photo Anderson, Rome

twelve persons came out of a golden wolf; living table ornaments, not always, however, showing the tasteless exaggeration of the Burgundian Court (p. 404) —and the like. Most of them showed some artistic or poetical feeling. The mixture of pantomime and the drama at the Court of Ferrara has been already referred to in the treating of poetry (p. 315). The entertainments given in 1473 by Cardinal Pietro Riario at Rome when Leonora of Aragon, the destined bride of Prince Hercules of Ferrara, was passing through the city were famous far beyond the limits of Italy.[2] The plays acted were mysteries on some

[1] Allegretto, in Murat., xxiii, col. 772. See besides col. 770, for the reception of Pius II in 1459. A Paradise, or choir of angels, was represented, out of which came an angel and sang to the Pope, "in modo che il Papa si commosse a lagrime per gran tenerezza da si dolci parole."

[2] See the authorities quoted in Favre, *Mélanges d'Hist. Lit.*, i, 138; Corio, fol. 417 *sqq.* The menu fills almost two closely printed pages. "Among other dishes a mountain was brought in, out of which stepped a living man, with signs of astonishment to find himself amid this festive splendour; he repeated some verses and then disappeared" (Gregorovius, vii, 241). Infessura, in Eccard, *Scriptores*, ii, col. 1896; *Strozzii Poetæ*, fol. 193 *sqq.* A word or two may here be added on eating and drinking. Leonardo Aretino (*Epist.*, lib. iii, *Ep.* 18)

ecclesiastical subject, the pantomimes, on the contrary, were mythological There were represented Orpheus with the beasts, Perseus and Andromeda, Ceres drawn by dragons, Bacchus and Ariadne by panthers, and finally the education of Achilles. Then followed a ballet of the famous lovers of ancient times, with a troop of nymphs, which was interrupted by an attack of predatory centaurs, who in their turn were vanquished and put to flight by Hercules.

FIG. 203. FESTAL CHARIOT FROM THE "TRIUMPH OF VENUS"

Ferrara, Palazzo Schifanoja
Photo Anderson, Rome

The fact, in itself a trifle, may be mentioned, as characteristic of the taste of the time, that the human beings who at all the festivals appeared as statues in niches or on pillars and triumphal arches, and then showed themselves to be alive by singing or speaking, wore their natural complexion and a natural costume, and thus the sense of incongruity was removed; while in the house of Riario there was exhibited a living child, gilt from head to foot, who showered water round him from a spring.[1]

Brilliant pantomimes of the same kind were given at Bologna, at the marriage of Annibale Bentivoglio with Lucrezia d'Este.[2] Instead of the orchestra, choral songs were sung, while the fairest of Diana's nymphs flew over to the Juno Pronuba, and while Venus walked with a lion—which in this case was a disguised man—among a troop of savages. The decorations were a faithful representation

complains that he had to spend so much for his wedding-feast, garments and so forth, that on the same day he had concluded a *matrimonium* and squandered a *patrimonium*. Ermolao Barbaro describes, in a letter to Pietro Cara, the bill of fare at a wedding-feast at Trivulzio's (*Angeli Politiani Epist.*, lib. iii). The list of meats and drinks in the appendix to Landi's *Commentario* (above) is of special interest. Landi speaks of the great trouble he had taken over it, collecting it from five hundred writers. The passage is too long to be quoted (we there read: "Li antropofagi furono i primi che mangiassero carne humana"). Poggio (*Opera*, fol. 14 *sqq.*, 1513) discusses the question "Uter alteri gratias debeat pro convivio impenso, isne qui vocatus est ad convivium an qui vocavit?" Platina wrote a treatise *De Arte Coquinaria*, said to have been printed several times, and quoted under various titles, but which, according to his own account (*Dissert. Vossiane*, i, 253 *sqq.*), contains more warnings against excess than instructions on the art in question.

[1] Vasari, ix, p. 37, *Vita di Puntormo*, tells how a child, during such a festival at Florence in 1513 died from the effects of the exertion—or shall we say of the gilding? The poor boy had to represent the Golden Age!

[2] Phil. Beroaldi, *Nuptiæ Bentivolorum*, in the *Orationes Ph. B.*, c. 3 *sqq.* (Paris, 1492). The description of the other festivities at this wedding is very remarkable.

of a forest. At Venice in 1491 the princesses of the house of Este [1] were met and welcomed by the Bucentaur, and entertained by boat-races and a splendid pantomime called *Meleager* in the court of the ducal palace. At Milan Leonardo da Vinci [2] directed the festivals of the Duke and of some

leading citizens. One of his machines, which must have rivalled that of Brunellesco (p. 406), represented the heavenly bodies with all their movements on a colossal scale. Whenever a planet approached Isabella, the bride of the young Duke, the divinity whose name it bore stepped forth from the globe [3] and sang some verses written by the Court poet Bellincioni (1489).[4] At another festival (1493) the model of the equestrian statue of Francesco Sforza appeared with other objects under a triumphal arch in the square before the castle. We read in Vasari of the ingenious automata which Leonardo invented to welcome the French kings as masters of Milan. Even in the smaller

FIG. 204. MARCUS AURELIUS TRIUMPHING
Rome, Museo dei Conservatori

cities great efforts were sometimes made on these occasions. When Duke

[1] M. Anton. Sabellici, *Epist.*, lib. iii, fol. 17. Beatrice describes the festival herself in letters to her husband (il Moro), which E. Motta has published in the *Giorn. Stor. della Lett. Ital.*, vii, 386 *sqq.*

[2] Amoretti, *Memorie, etc., su Lionardo da Vinci*, pp. 38 *sqq.*

[3] To what extent astrology influenced even the festivals of this century is shown by the introduction of the planets (not described with sufficient clearness) at the reception of the ducal brides at Ferrara. *Diario Ferrarese*, in Murat., xxiv, col. 248, *ad a.* 1473; col. 282, *ad a.* 1491. So, too, at Mantua, *Archiv. Stor.*, App. II, p. 233.

[4] Burckhardt gives the date as 1489, but Solmi (*Archiv. Stor. Lomb.*, pp. 31, 76) fixes it at January 13, 1490, and on pp. 80 *sqq.* gives, concerning the feast, a piece of information hitherto unknown.—W. G.]

Borso came in 1453 to Reggio [1] to receive the homage of the city he was met at the gate by a great machine, on which S. Prospero, the patron saint of the town, appeared to float, shaded by a *baldachino* held by angels, while below him was a revolving disk with eight singing cherubs, two of whom received from the saint the sceptre and keys of the city, which they then delivered to the Duke, while saints and angels held forth in his praise. A chariot drawn by concealed

...NA PACE TERRIS RESTITVTA CELIQVE IANVA BONIS OMNIBVS

FIG. 205. THE TRIUMPH OF FAITH
Woodcut from part of one of Titian's compositions

horses now advanced, bearing an empty throne, behind which stood a figure of Justice attended by a genius. At the corners of the chariot sat four grey-headed lawgivers, encircled by angels with banners; by its side rode standard-bearers in complete armour. It need hardly be added that the goddess and the genius did not suffer the Duke to pass by without an address. A second car, drawn by a unicorn, bore a Caritas with a burning torch; between the two came the classical spectacle of a car in the form of a ship, moved by men concealed within it. The whole procession now advanced before the Duke. In front of the church of S. Pietro a halt was again made. The saint, attended by two angels, descended in an aureole from the façade, placed a wreath of laurel on the head of the Duke, and then floated back to his former position.[2]

[1] *Annal. Estens.*, in Murat., xx, col. 468 *sqq.* The description is unclear and printed from an incorrect transcript.

[2] We read that the ropes of the machine used for this purpose were made to imitate garlands.

The clergy provided another allegory of a purely religious kind. Idolatry and Faith stood on two lofty pillars, and after Faith, represented by a beautiful girl, had uttered her welcome the other column fell to pieces with the lay figure upon it. Farther on Borso was met by Cæsar with seven beautiful women, who were presented to him as the Seven Virtues, which he was exhorted to pursue. At last the cathedral was reached, but after the service the

FIG. 206. THE TRIUMPH OF FAITH
Woodcut from part of one of Titian's compositions

Duke again took his seat on a lofty golden throne, and a second time received the homage of some of the masks already mentioned. To conclude all, three angels flew down from an adjacent building, and amid songs of joy delivered to him branches of palm as symbols of peace.

Let us now take a glance at those festivals of which the chief feature was the procession itself.

There is no doubt that from an early period of the Middle Ages the religious processions gave rise to the use of masks. Little angels accompanied the Sacrament or the sacred pictures and relics on their way through the streets; or characters in the Passion—such as Christ with the Cross, the thieves and the soldiers, or the faithful women—were represented for public edification. But the great feasts of the Church were from an early time accompanied by a civic

413

procession, and the *naïveté* of the Middle Ages found nothing unfitting in the many secular elements which it contained. We may mention especially the naval car (*carrus navalis*), which had been inherited from pagan times,[1] and which, as an instance already quoted shows, was admissible at festivals of very

FIG. 207. TRIUMPHAL PROCESSION OF CÆSAR (FIRST PICTURE)
By Mantegna
Hampton Court

various kinds, and has left its name permanently on one of them in particular—the carnival. Such ships, decorated with all possible splendour, delighted the eyes of spectators long after the original meaning of them was forgotten. When Isabella of England met her bridegroom, the Emperor Frederick II, at Cologne she was met by a number of such chariots drawn by invisible horses and filled with a crowd of priests who welcomed her with music and singing.

[1] Strictly the ship of Isis, which entered the water on March 5 as a symbol that navigation was reopened. For analogies in the German religion see Jac. Grimm, *Deutsche Mythologie*.

414

But the religious processions were not only mingled with secular accessories of all kinds, but were often replaced by processions of clerical masks. Their origin is perhaps to be found in the parties of actors who wound their way through the streets of the city to the place where they were about to act the

FIG. 208. TRIUMPHAL PROCESSION OF CÆSAR (LAST PICTURE)
By Mantegna
Hampton Court

mystery; but it is possible that at an early period the clerical procession may have constituted itself as a distinct species. Dante [1] describes the *trionfo* of Beatrice, with the twenty-four Elders of the Apocalypse, with the four mystical Beasts, with the three Christian and four Cardinal Virtues, and with St Luke, St Paul, and other Apostles, in a way which almost forces us to conclude that such processions actually occurred before his time. We are chiefly led to this

---

[1] *Purgatorio*, xxix, 43 to the end, and xxx at the beginning. According to v, 115, the chariot is more splendid than the triumphal chariot of Scipio, of Augustus, and even of the Sun-god.

conclusion by the chariot on which Beatrice drives, and which in the miraculous forest of the vision would have been unnecessary or rather out of place. It is possible, on the other hand, that Dante looked on the chariot as a symbol of victory and triumph, and that his poem rather served to give rise to these processions, the form of which was borrowed from the triumphs of the Roman Emperors. However this may be, poetry and theology continued to make free use of the symbol. Savonarola [1] in his *Triumph of the Cross* represents Christ on a Chariot of Victory, above His head the shining sphere of the Trinity, in His left hand the Cross, in His right the Old and New Testaments; below Him the Virgin Mary; on both sides the Martyrs and Doctors of the Church

FIG. 209. TRIUMPHAL PROCESSION OF ALFONSO I
Part of the triumphal arch at the Castel Nuovo, in Naples

with open books; behind Him all the multitude of the saved; and in the distance the countless host of His enemies—emperors, princes, philosophers, heretics— all vanquished, their idols broken and their books burned. A great picture of Titian, which is known only as a woodcut, has a good deal in common with this description. The ninth and tenth of Sabellico's (p. 83) thirteen elegies on the Mother of God contain a minute account of her triumph, richly adorned with allegories, and especially interesting from that matter-of-fact air which also characterizes the realistic painting of the fifteenth century.

Nevertheless, the secular *trionfi* were far more frequent than the religious. They were modelled on the procession of the Roman Imperator as it was known from the old reliefs and from the writings of ancient authors.[2] The historical conceptions then prevalent in Italy, with which these shows were closely connected, have been already discussed (p. 151).

We now and then read of the actual triumphal entrance of a victorious general, which was organized as far as possible on the ancient pattern, even against the will of the hero himself. Francesco Sforza had the courage (1450)

[1] Ranke, *Gesch. der Roman. und German. Völker*, p. 95, ed. 2; P. Villari, *Savonarola*; Schnitzer, *Savonarola*, ii, pp. 463 *sqq.*

[2] Fazio degli Uberti, *Dittamondo* (lib. ii, cap. 3), treats specially " del modo del triumphare."

to refuse the triumphal chariot which had been prepared for his return to Milan, on the ground that such things were monarchical superstitions.[1] Alfonso the Great, on his entrance into Naples (1443), declined the wreath of laurel,[2] which Napoleon did not disdain to wear at his coronation in Notre-Dame. For the rest, Alfonso's procession, which passed by a breach in the wall through the city to the cathedral, was a strange mixture of antique, allegorical, and purely comic elements. The car, drawn by four white horses, on which he sat enthroned, was lofty and covered with gilding; twenty patricians carried the poles of the canopy of cloth of gold which shaded his head. The part of the procession which the Florentines then present in Naples had undertaken was composed of elegant young cavaliers, skilfully brandishing their lances, of a chariot with the figure of Fortune, and of seven Virtues on horseback. The goddess herself,[3] in accordance with the inexorable logic of allegory, to which even the painters at that time conformed, wore hair only on the front part of her head, while the back part was bald, and the genius who sat on the lower steps of the car, and who symbolized the fugitive character of Fortune, had his feet immersed (?) in a basin of water. Then followed, equipped by the same Florentines, a troop of horsemen in the costumes of various nations, dressed as foreign princes and nobles, and then, crowned with laurel and standing above a revolving globe, a Julius Cæsar,[4] who explained to the King in Italian verse the meaning of the allegories and then took his place in the procession. Sixty Florentines, all in purple and scarlet, closed this splendid display of what their home could achieve. Then a band of Catalans advanced on foot, with lay figures of horses fastened on to them before and behind, and engaged in a mock combat with a body of Turks, as though in derision of the Florentine sentimentalism. Last of all came a gigantic tower, the door of which was guarded by an angel with a drawn sword; on it stood four Virtues, each of whom addressed the King with a song. The rest of the show had nothing specially characteristic about it.

At the entrance of Louis XII into Milan in 1507 [5] we find, besides the inevitable chariot with Virtues, a living group representing Jupiter, Mars, and a figure of Italy caught in a net. After which came a car laden with trophies and so forth.

And when there were in reality no triumphs to celebrate the poets found a compensation for themselves and their patrons. Petrarch and Boccaccio had

---

[1] Corio, fol. 401: " dicendo tali cose essere superstitioni de' Re." Cf. Cagnola, Archiv. Stor., iii, p. 127, who says that the Duke declined from modesty.

[2] See above, pp. 231 sqq.; cf. p. 31, note 1. Triumphus Alfonsi, as appendix to the Dicta et Facta of Panormita, pp. 129-139, 256 sqq. (ed. 1538). A dislike to excessive display on such occasions was shown by the gallant Comneni. Cf. Cinnamus, Epitome Rer. ab Comnenis Gestarum., i, 5; vi, 1.

[3] The position assigned to Fortune is characteristic of the naïveté of the Renaissance. At the entrance of Massimiliano Sforza into Milan (1512) she stood as the chief figure of a triumphal arch above Fama, Speranza, Audacia, and Penitenza, all represented by living persons. Cf. Prato, Archiv. Stor., iii, p. 305.

[4] The entrance of Borso d' Este into Reggio, described above (p. 412), shows the impression which Alfonso's triumph had made in all Italy. On the entrance of Cesare Borgia into Rome in 1500 see Gregorovius, vii, 439.

[5] Prato, Archiv. Stor., iii, 260 sqq. The author says expressly, " le quali cose da li triumfanti Romani se soliano anticamente usare."

described the representation of every sort of fame as attendants each of an allegorical figure (p. 405); the celebrities of past ages were now made attendants of the prince. The poetess Cleofe Gabrielli of Gubbio paid this honour to Borso of Ferrara.[1] She gave him seven queens—the seven liberal arts—as his handmaids, with whom he mounted a chariot; further, a crowd of heroes, distinguished by names written on their foreheads; then followed all the famous poets; and after them the gods driving in their chariots. There is, in fact, at this time simply no end to the mythological and allegorical charioteering, and the most important work of art of Borso's time—the frescoes in the Palazzo Schifanoja—shows us a whole frieze filled with these motives.[2] Raphael, when he had to paint the Camera della Segnatura, found this mode of artistic thought completely vulgarized and worn out. The new and final consecration which he gave to it will remain a wonder to all ages.

FIG. 210. THE TRIUMPH OF FEDERIGO OF URBINO
By Piero della Francesca
Florence, Uffizi

The triumphal processions, strictly speaking, of victorious generals formed the exception. But all the festive processions, whether they celebrated any special event or were mainly held for their own sakes, assumed more or less the character and nearly always the name of a *trionfo*. It is a wonder that funerals were not also treated in the same way.[3]

It was the practice, both at the carnival and on other occasions, to represent the triumphs of ancient Roman commanders, such as that of Paulus Æmilius under Lorenzo the Magnificent at Florence, and that of Camillus on the visit

[1] Her three *capitoli* in *terzine*, *Anecd. Lit.*, iv, 461 *sqq.*

[2] Old paintings of similar scenes are by no means rare, and no doubt often represent masquerades actually performed. The wealthy classes soon became accustomed to drive in chariots at every public solemnity. We read that Annibale Bentivoglio, eldest son of the ruler of Bologna, returned to the palace after presiding as umpire at the regular military exercises, " cum triumpho more romano." Bursellis, *loc. cit.*, col. 909, *ad a.* 1490.

[3] The remarkable funeral of Malatesta Baglione, poisoned at Perugia in 1437 (Graziani, *Archiv. Stor.*, xvi, i, p. 413), reminds us of the splendour of an Etruscan funeral. The knights in mourning, however, and other features of the ceremony, were in accordance with the customs of the nobility throughout Europe. See, for example, the funeral of Bertrand du Guesclin, in Juvénal des Ursins, *ad a.* 1389. See also Graziani, *loc. cit.*, p. 360.

of Leo X. Both were conducted by the painter Francesco Granacci.[1] In Rome the first complete exhibition of this kind was the triumph of Augustus after the victory over Cleopatra,[2] under Paul II, where, besides the comic and mythological masks, which, as a matter of fact, were not wanting in the ancient triumphs, all the other requisites were to be found—kings in chains, tablets with decrees of the Senate and people, a Senate clothed in the ancient costume, prætors, ædiles, and quæstors, four chariots filled with singing masks, and, doubtless, cars laden

with trophies. Other processions rather aimed at setting forth, in a general way, the universal empire of ancient Rome; and in answer to the very real danger which threatened Europe from the side of the Turks a cavalcade of camels bearing masks representing Ottoman prisoners appeared before the people. Later, at the carnival of 1500, Cesare Borgia, with a bold allusion to himself, celebrated the triumph of Julius Cæsar, with a procession of eleven magnificent chariots,[3] doubtless to the scan-

FIG. 211. THE TRIUMPH OF THE WIFE OF FEDERIGO OF URBINO
By Piero della Francesca
Florence, Uffizi

dal of the pilgrims who had come for the Jubilee. Two *trionfi*, famous for their taste and beauty, were given by rival companies in Florence on the election of Leo X to the Papacy.[4] One of them represented the Three Ages of Man, the other the Four Ages of the World, ingeniously set forth in five scenes of Roman history and in two allegories of the Golden Age of Saturn and of its final return. The imagination displayed in the adornment of the chariots when the great Florentine artists undertook the work made the scene so impressive that such representations became in time a permanent element in the popular life. Hitherto the subject cities had been satisfied merely to present their symbolical gifts—costly stuffs and wax candles—on the day when they annually did homage. The

[1] Vasari, ix, p. 218, *Vita di Granacci.* On the triumphs and processions in Florence see Reumont, *Lorenzo dei Medici*, ii, 433.

[2] Mich. Cannesius, *Vita Pauli II*, in Murat., iii, ii, col. 118 *sqq.*

[3] Tommasi, *Vita di Cesare Borgia*, p. 251. Gregorovius, *Rom.*, vii, p. 441.

[4] Vasari, ix, pp. 34 *sqq.*, *Vita di Puntormo.* A most important passage of its kind.

guild of merchants now built ten chariots, to which others were afterward
to be added, not so much to carry as to symbolize the tribute, and Andrea
del Sarto, who painted some of them, no doubt did his work to perfection.[1]
These cars, whether used to hold tribute or trophies, now formed a part of
all such celebrations, even when there was not much money to be laid out

FIG. 212. DRAWING OF A TRIUMPH, WITH VIEW OF THE CITY OF FLORENCE
By Salviati
Rome, Galleria Nazionale
Photo G. Grote'sche Verlagsbuchhandlung, Berlin

The Sienese announced, in 1477, the alliance between Ferrante and Sixtus IV,
with which they themselves were associated, by driving a chariot round the
city, with "one clad as the goddess of peace standing on a hauberk and
other arms." [2]

At the Venetian festivals the processions—not on land, but on water—were
marvellous in their fantastic splendour. The sailing of the Bucentaur to meet
the Princess of Ferrara in 1491 (p. 411) seems to have been something belonging

[1] Vasari, viii, p. 264, *Vita di Andrea del Sarto.*
[2] Allegretto, in Murat., xxiii, col. 783. It was reckoned a bad omen that one of the wheels broke.

o fairyland.[1] Countless vessels with garlands and hangings, filled with the richly dressed youth of the city, moved in front; genii with attributes symbolizing the various gods floated on machines hung in the air; below stood others grouped as tritons and nymphs; the air was filled with music, sweet odours, and the fluttering of embroidered banners. The Bucentaur was followed by such a crowd of boats of every sort that for a mile all round (*octo stadia*) the water could not be seen. With regard to the rest of the festivities,

FIG. 213. SINGER WITH LUTE
Florentine copper engraving, 1470–80

besides the pantomime mentioned above we may notice as something new a boat-race of fifty powerful girls. In the sixteenth century the nobility were divided into corporations with a view to these festivals,[2] whose most noteworthy feature was some extraordinary machine placed on a ship. So, for instance, in 1541, at the festival of the "Sempiterni," a round "universe" floated along the Grand Canal, and a splendid ball was given inside it. The carnival too in this city was famous for its dances, processions, and exhibitions of every kind. The Square of St Mark was found to give space enough not only for tournaments (p. 384), but for *trionfi* similar to those common on the mainland. At

[1] *M. Anton. Sabellici Epist.*, lib. iii, letter to M. Anton. Barbavarus. He says: "Vetus est mos civitatis in illustrium hospitum adventu eam navim auro et purpura insternere."
[2] Sansovino, *Venezia*, fol. 151 *sqq.* The names of these corporations were Pavoni, Accessi, Eterni, Reali, and Sempiterni. The academies probably had their origin in these guilds.

421

a festival held on the conclusion of peace [1] the pious brotherhoods (*scuole*) took each its part in the procession. There, among golden chandeliers with red candles, among crowds of musicians and winged boys with golden bowls and horns of plenty, was seen a car in which Noah and David sat together enthroned; then came Abigail, leading a camel laden with treasures, and a second car with a group of political figures—Italy sitting between Venice and Liguria, the last two with their coats of arms, the former with a stork, the symbol of unity—and on a raised step three female symbolical figures with the arms of the allied princes. This was followed by a great globe with the constellations, as it seems, round it. The princes themselves, or rather their bodily representatives, appeared on other chariots with their servants and their coats of arms if we have rightly interpreted our author. [2] There was also music at these and all other similar processions.

The carnival properly so called, apart from these great triumphal marches, had nowhere, perhaps, in the fifteenth century so varied a character as in Rome. [3] There were races of every kind—of horses, asses, buffaloes, old men, young men, Jews, and so on. Paul II entertained the people in crowds before the Palazzo di Venezia, in which he lived. The games in the Piazza Navona, which had probably never altogether ceased since classical times, were remarkable for their warlike splendour. We read of a sham fight of cavalry and a review of all the citizens in arms. The greatest freedom existed with regard to the use of masks, which were sometimes allowed for several months together. [4] Sixtus IV ventured in the most populous part of the city—at the Campofiore and near the Banchi—to make his way through crowds of masks, though he declined to receive them as visitors in the Vatican. Under Innocent VIII a discreditable usage which had already appeared among the cardinals attained its height. In the carnival of 1491 they sent one another chariots full of spendid masks, of singers and buffoons, chanting scandalous verses. They were accompanied by men on horseback. [5] Apart from the carnival, the Romans seem to have been the first to discover the effect of a great procession by torchlight. When Pius II came back from the Congress of Mantua in 1459 [6] the people waited on him with a squadron of horsemen bearing torches, who rode in shining circles before his palace. Sixtus IV, however, thought it better to decline a nocturnal visit of the people, who proposed to wait on him with torches and olive-branches. [7]

[1] April 12, 1495, peace festival with Pope and Emperor. Cf. *M. Anton. Sabellici Epist.*, lib. v, fol. 28, last letter to M. Ant. Barbavarus.

[2] " Terræ globum socialibus signis circunquaque figuratum," and " quinis pegmatibus, quorum singula fœderatorum regum, principumque suas habuere effigies et cum his ministros signaque in auro affabre cælata."

[3] Infessura, in Eccard, *Scriptores*, ii, col. 1093, 2000; Mich. Cannesius, *Vita Pauli II*, in Murat., iii, ii, col. 1012; Platina, *Vitæ Pontiff.*, p. 318; Jac. Volaterranus, in Murat., xxiii, col. 163, 194; Paul. Jovius, *Elogia*, under " Juliano Cæsarino." Elsewhere, too, there were races for women, *Diario Ferrarese*, in Murat., xxiv, col. 384: *cf.* Gregorovius, vi, 690 *sqq.*; vii, 219, 616 *sqq.*

[4] Once under Alexander VI from October till Lent. See Tommasi, *loc. cit.*, p. 322, 1502, for the wedding of Lucrezia Borgia.

[5] Baluz., *Miscell.*, iv, 517 (*cf.* Gregorovius, vii, 288 *sqq.*).   [6] *Pii II Comment.*, lib. iv, p. 211.

[7] Nantiporto, in Murat., iii, ii, col. 1080. They wished to thank him for a peace which he had concluded, but found the gates of the palace closed and troops posted in all the open places.

FIG. 214. THE TRIUMPH OF CHASTITY
By Francesco di Giorgio (?)
Mrs Wantage, Lockinge House, Berks.

But the Florentine carnival surpassed the Roman in a certain class of pro
cessions, which have left their mark even in literature.[1] Among a crowd o
masks on foot and on horseback appeared some huge, fantastic chariot, an
upon it an allegorical figure or group of figures with the proper accompani
ments, such as Jealousy with four spectacled faces on one head; the fou
temperaments (p. 303) with the planets belonging to them; the three Fates
Prudence enthroned above Hope and Fear, which lay bound before her; th

FIG. 215. RURAL CONCERT
By Giorgione
Paris, Louvre

four Elements, Ages, Winds, Seasons, and so on; as well as the famous chariot
of Death with the coffins, which presently opened. Sometimes we meet with
a splendid scene from classical mythology—Bacchus and Ariadne, Paris and
Helen, and others. Or else a chorus of figures forming some single class or
category, as the beggars, the hunters and nymphs, the lost souls who in their
lifetime were hard-hearted women, the hermits, the astrologers, the vagabonds,
the devils, the sellers of various kinds of wares, and even on one occasion
il popolo, the people as such, who all reviled one another in their songs. The
songs, which still remain and have been collected, give the explanation of the
masquerade sometimes in a pathetic, sometimes in a humorous, and sometimes in an excessively indecent tone. Some of the worst in this respect are

[1] " Tutti i trionfi, carri, mascherate, o canti carnascialeschi " (Cosmopoli, 1750). Machiavelli, *Opere
Minori*, p. 505 ; Vasari, vii, pp. 115 *sqq.*, *Vita di Piero di Cosimo* to whom a chief part in the development of
these festivities is ascribed. *Cf.* B. Loos, pp. 12 *sqq.*, and Reumont, *Lorenzo dei Medici*, ii, 443 *sqq.*, where the
authorities are collected which show that the carnival was soon restrained. *Cf. ibid.*, ii, p. 24.
424

ttributed to Lorenzo the Magnificent, probably because the real author did
ot venture to declare himself. However this may be, we must certainly
scribe to him the beautiful song which accompanied the masque of Bacchus
nd Ariadne, whose refrain still echoes to us from the fifteenth century, like
regretful presentiment of the brief splendour of the Renaissance itself :

> Quanto è bella giovinezza,
> Che si fugge tuttavia!
> Chi vuol esser lieto, sia:
> Di doman non c' è certezza.

PART VI
MORALITY AND RELIGION

CHAPTER I

MORALITY

THE relation of the various peoples of the earth to the supreme interests of life, to God, virtue, and immortality, may be investigated up to a certain point, but can never be compared to one another with absolute strictness and certainty. The more plainly in these matters our evidence seems to speak, the more carefully must we refrain from unqualified assumptions and rash generalizations.

This remark is especially true with regard to our judgment on questions of morality. It may be possible to indicate many contrasts and shades of difference among different nations, but to strike the balance of the whole is not given to human insight. The ultimate truth with respect to the character, the conscience, and the guilt of a people remains for ever a secret; if only for the reason that its defects have another side, where they reappear as peculiarities or even as virtues. We must leave those who find a pleasure in passing sweeping censures on whole nations to do so as they like. The peoples of Europe can maltreat, but happily not judge, one another. A great nation, interwoven by its civilization, its achievements, and its fortunes with the whole life of the modern world, can afford to ignore both its advocates and its accusers. It lives on with or without the approval of theorists.

Accordingly what here follows is no judgment, but rather a string of marginal notes, suggested by a study of the Italian Renaissance extending over some years. The value to be attached to them is all the more qualified as they mostly touch on the life of the upper classes, with respect to which we are far better informed in Italy than in any other country in Europe at that period. But though both fame and infamy sound louder here than elsewhere, we are not helped thereby in forming an adequate moral estimate of the people.

What eye can pierce the depths in which the character and fate of nations are determined?—in which that which is inborn and that which has been experienced combine to form a new whole and a fresh nature?—in which even those intellectual capacities, which at first sight we should take to be most original, are in fact evolved late and slowly? Who can tell if the Italian before the thirteenth century possessed that flexible activity and certainty in his whole being—that play of power in shaping whatever subject he dealt with in word r in form—which was peculiar to him later? And if no answer can be found to these questions how can we possibly judge of the infinite and infinitely intricate channels through which character and intellect are incessantly pouring their influence one upon the other. A tribunal there is for each one of us, whose voice is our conscience; but let us have done with these generalities about nations. For the people that seems to be most sick the cure may be at hand; and one that appears to be healthy may bear within it the ripening germs of death, which the hour of danger will bring forth from their hiding-place.

At the beginning of the sixteenth century, when the civilization of the Renaissance had reached its highest pitch, and at the same time the political ruin of the nation seemed inevitable, there were not wanting serious thinkers who saw a connexion between this ruin and the prevalent immorality. It was not one of those methodistical moralists who in every age think themselves called to declaim against the wickedness of the time, but it was Machiavelli, who, in one of his most well-considered works,[1] said openly: " We Italians are irreligious and corrupt above others." Another man had perhaps said, " We are individually highly developed; we have outgrown the limits of morality and religion which were natural to us in our undeveloped state, and we despise outward law, because our rulers are illegitimate, and their judges and officers wicked men." Machiavelli adds, " because the Church and her representatives set us the worst example."

Shall we add also, " because the influence exercised by antiquity was in this respect unfavourable "? The statement can only be received with many qualifications. It may possibly be true of the humanists (pp. 272 *sqq.*), especially as regards the profligacy of their lives. Of the rest it may perhaps be said with some approach to accuracy that after they became familiar with antiquity they substituted for holiness—the Christian ideal of life—the cultus of historical greatness (see Part II, Chapter III). We can understand, therefore, how easily they would be tempted to consider those faults and vices to be matters of indifference, in spite of which their heroes were great. They were probably scarcely conscious of this themselves, for if we are summoned to quote any statement of doctrine on this subject we are again forced to appeal to humanists like Paolo Giovio, who excuses the perjury of Giangaleazzo Visconti, through which he was enabled to found an empire, by the example of Julius Cæsar.[2] The great Florentine historians and statesmen never stoop to these slavish quotations, and what seems antique in their deeds and their judgments is so because the nature of their political life necessarily fostered in them a mode of thought which has some analogy with that of antiquity.

Nevertheless, it cannot be denied that Italy at the beginning of the sixteenth century found itself in the midst of a grave moral crisis, out of which the best men saw hardly any escape.

[1] *Discorsi*, lib. i, c. 12. Also c. 55: Italy is more corrupt than all other countries; then come the French and Spaniards.

[2] Paul. Jovius, *Viri Illustres*, Jo. Gal. Vicecomes. *Cf.* pp. 31 *sqq.* and notes.

Let us begin by saying a few words about that moral force which was the the strongest bulwark against evil. The highly gifted men of that day though to find it in the sentiment of honour. This is that enigmatic mixture of con science and egoism which often survives in the modern man after he has los whether by his own fault or not, faith, love, and hope. This sense of honou is compatible with much selfishness and great vices, and may be the victim o astonishing illusions; yet, nevertheless, all the noble elements that are left i the wreck of a character may gather round it, and from this fountain may draw new strength. It has become, in a far wider sense than is commonly believed a decisive test of conduct in the minds of the cultivated Europeans of our ow day, and many of those who yet hold faithfully by religion and morality ar unconsciously guided by this feeling in the gravest decisions of their lives.[1]

It lies without the limits of our task to show how the men of antiquity als experienced this feeling in a peculiar form, and how, afterward, in the Middl Ages, a special sense of honour became the mark of a particular class. No can we here dispute with those who hold that conscience, rather than honour is the motive power. It would, indeed, be better and nobler if it were so; bu since it must be granted that even our worthier resolutions result from " conscience more or less dimmed by selfishness," it is better to call the mixtur by its right name.[2] It is certainly not always easy, in treating of the Italian o this period, to distinguish this sense of honour from the passion for fame into which, indeed, it easily passes. Yet the two sentiments are essentiall different.

There is no lack of witnesses on this subject. One who speaks plainly may here be quoted as a representative of the rest. We read in the *Aphorisms* o Guicciardini: [3]

> He who esteems honour highly succeeds in all that he undertakes, since he fear neither trouble, danger, nor expense; I have found it so in my own case, and may say it and write it; vain and dead are the deeds of men which have not this as thei motive.

It is necessary to add that, from what is known of the life of the writer, he can here be only speaking of honour, and not of fame. Rabelais has put the matter more clearly than perhaps any Italian. We quote him, indeed, un willingly in these pages. What the great, baroque Frenchman gives us is a picture of what the Renaissance would be without form and without beauty.[4] But his description of an ideal state of things in the Thelemite monastery is decisive as historical evidence. In speaking of his gentlemen and ladies of the Order of Free Will,[5] he tells us as follows:

[1] On the part filled by the sense of honour in the modern world see Prévost-Paradol, *La France Nouvelle*, liv. iii, chap. 2.

[2] *Cf.* what Darwin said of blushing in *The Expression of the Emotions in Man and Animals*, and of the relations between shame and conscience.

[3] Franc. Guicciardini, *Ricordi Politici e Civili*, n. 118 (*Opere Inedite*, vol. i).

[4] His closest counterpart is Merlinus Coccajus (Teofilo Folengo), whose *Opus Macaronicorum* Rabelais certainly knew, and quotes more than once (*Pantagruel*, liv. ii, chap. 1 and chap. 7 at the end). It is possible that Merlinus Coccajus may have given the impulse which resulted in Pantagruel and Gargantua.

[5] *Gargantua*, liv. i, chap. 57.

En leur reigle n'estoit que ceste clause: Fay ce que vouldras. Parce que gens liberes, bien nayz,[1] bien instruictz, conversans en compaignies honnestes, ont par nature un instinct et aguillon qui toujours les poulse à faitz vertueux, et retire de vice; lequel ilz nommoyent honneur.

This is that same faith in the goodness of human nature which inspired the men of the second half of the eighteenth century and helped to prepare the way for the French Revolution. Among the Italians too each man appeals to this noble instinct within him, and though with regard to the people as a whole—chiefly in consequence of the national disasters—judgments of a more pessimistic sort became prevalent, the importance of this sense of honour must still be rated highly. If the boundless development of individuality, stronger than the will of the individual, be the work of a historical Providence, not less so is the opposing force which then manifested itself in Italy. How often, and against what passionate attacks of selfishness, it won the day we cannot tell, and therefore no human judgment can estimate with certainty the absolute moral value of the nation.

A force which we must constantly take into account in judging of the morality of the more highly developed Italian of this period is that of the imagination. It gives to his virtues and vices a peculiar colour, and under its influence his unbridled egoism shows itself in its most terrible shape.

The force of his imagination explains, for example, the fact that he was the first gambler on a large scale in modern times. Pictures of future wealth and enjoyment rose in such lifelike colours before his eyes that he was ready to hazard everything to reach them. The Mohammedan nations would doubtless have anticipated him in this respect had not the Koran, from the beginning, set up the prohibition against gambling as a chief safeguard of public morals, and directed the imagination of its followers to the search after buried treasures. In Italy the passion for play reached an intensity which often threatened or altogether broke up the existence of the gambler. Florence had already, at the end of the fourteenth century, its Casanova—a certain Buonaccorso Pitti,[2] who in the course of his incessant journeys as merchant, political agent, diplomatist, and professional gambler won and lost sums so enormous that none but princes like the Dukes of Brabant, Bavaria, and Savoy were able to compete with him. That great lottery-bank which was called the Court of Rome accustomed people to a need of excitement, which found its satisfaction in games of hazard during the intervals between one intrigue and another. We read, for example, how Franceschetto Cybò in two games with Cardinal Raffaello Riario lost no less than fourteen thousand ducats, and afterward complained to the Pope that his opponent had cheated him.[3] Italy has since that time been the home of the lottery.

[1] That is, well born in the higher sense, since Rabelais, son of the innkeeper of Chinon, has here no motive for assigning any special privilege to the nobility. The preaching of the Gospel, which is spoken of in the inscription at the entrance to the monastery, would fit in badly with the rest of the life of the inmates; it must be understood in a negative sense, as implying defiance of the Roman Church.

[2] See extracts from his diary in Delécluze, *Florence et ses Vicissitudes*, vol. 2.

[3] Infessura, in Eccard, *Scriptores*, ii, col. 1992. On Franceschetto Cybò see above, p. 126.

It was to the imagination of the Italians that the peculiar character of their vengeance was due. The sense of justice was, indeed, one and the same throughout Europe, and any violation of it, so long as no punishment was inflicted, must have been felt in the same manner. But other nations, though they found it no easier to forgive, nevertheless forgot more easily, while the Italian imagination kept the picture of the wrong alive with frightful vividness.[1] The fact that according to the popular morality the avenging of blood is a duty—a duty often performed in a way to make us shudder—gives to this passion a peculiar and still firmer basis. The Government and the tribunals recognize its existence and justification, and only attempt to keep it within certain limits. Even among the peasantry we read of Thyestean banquets and mutual assassination on the widest scale. Let us look at an instance.[2]

In the district of Acquapendente three boys were watching cattle, and one of them said: "Let us find out the way how people are hung." While one was sitting on the shoulders of the other and the third, after fastening the rope round the neck of the first, was tying it to an oak, a wolf came, and the two who were free ran away and left the other hanging. Afterward they found him dead, and buried him. On the Sunday his father came to bring him bread, and one of the two confessed what had happened, and showed him the grave. The old man then killed him with a knife, cut him up, brought away the liver, and entertained the boy's father with it at home. After dinner he told him whose liver it was. Hereupon began a series of reciprocal murders between the two families, and within a month thirty-six persons were killed, women as well as men.

And such *vendette*, handed down from father to son, and extending to friends and distant relations, were not limited to the lower classes, but reached to the highest. The chronicles and novels of the period are full of such instances, especially of vengeance taken for the violation of women. The classic land for these feuds was Romagna, where the *vendetta* was intertwined with intrigues and party divisions of every conceivable sort. The popular legends present an awful picture of the savagery into which this brave and energetic people had relapsed. We are told, for instance, of a nobleman at Ravenna who had got all his enemies together in a tower, and might have burned them; instead of which he let them out, embraced them, and entertained them sumptuously; whereupon shame drove them mad, and they conspired against him.[3] Pious and saintly monks exhorted unceasingly to reconciliation, but they can scarcely have done more than restrain to a certain extent the feuds already established; their influence hardly prevented the growth of new ones. The novelists sometimes describe to us this effect of religion—how sentiments of generosity and forgiveness were suddenly awakened, and then again paralysed by the force of what had once been done and could never be undone. The Pope himself was not always lucky as a peacemaker.

---

[1] This opinion of Stendhal (*La Chartreuse de Parme*, ed. Delahaye, p. 355) seems to me to rest on profound psychological observation.   [2] Graziani, *Cronaca di Perugia*, for the year 1437 (*Archiv. Stor.*, xvi, i, p. 415).
[3] Giraldi, *Hecatommithi*, i, Nov. 7.

Pope Paul II desired that the quarrel between Antonio Caffarello and the family of Alberino should cease, and ordered Giovanni Alberino and Antonio Caffarello to come before him, and bade them kiss one another, and promised them a fine of two thousand ducats in case they renewed this strife, and two days after Antonio was stabbed by the same Giacomo Alberino, son of Giovanni, who had wounded him once before; and the Pope was full of anger, and confiscated the goods of Alberino, and destroyed his houses, and banished father and son from Rome.[1]

The oaths and ceremonies by which reconciled enemies attempted to guard themselves against a relapse are sometimes utterly horrible. When the parties of the " Nove " and the " Popolari " met and kissed one another by twos in the cathedral at Siena on Christmas Eve 1494 [2] an oath was read by which all salvation in time and eternity was denied to the future violator of the treaty— " an oath more astonishing and dreadful than had ever yet been heard." The last consolations of religion in the hour of death were to turn to the damnation of the man who should break it. It is clear, however, that such a ceremony rather represents the despairing mood of the mediators than offers any real guarantee of peace, inasmuch as the truest reconciliation is just that one which has least need of it.

This personal need of vengeance felt by the cultivated and highly placed Italian, resting on the solid basis of an analogous popular custom, naturally displays itself under a thousand different aspects, and receives the unqualified approval of public opinion, as reflected in the works of the novelists.[3] All are at one on the point that, in the case of those injuries and insults for which Italian justice offered no redress, and all the more in the case of those against which no human law can ever adequately provide, each man is free to take the law into his own hands. Only there must be art in the vengeance, and the satisfaction must be compounded of the material injury and moral humiliation of the offender. A mere brutal, clumsy triumph of force was held by public opinion to be no satisfaction. The whole man with his sense of fame and of scorn, not only his fist, must be victorious.

The Italian of that time shrank, it is true, from no dissimulation in order to attain his ends, but was wholly free from hypocrisy in matters of principle. In these he attempted to deceive neither himself nor others. Accordingly revenge was declared with perfect frankness to be a necessity of human nature. Cool-headed people declared that it was most worthy of praise when it was disengaged from passion, and worked simply from motives of expedience, " in order that other men may learn to leave us unharmed." [4] Yet such instances must have formed only a small minority in comparison with those in which passion sought an outlet. This sort of revenge differs clearly from the avenging of blood, which has been already spoken of; while the latter keeps more or less within the limits of retaliation—the *ius talionis*—the former necessarily

---

[1] Infessura, in Eccard, *Scriptores*, ii, col. 1892, for the year 1464.

[2] Allegretto, *Diari Sanesi*, in Murat., xxiii, col. 837. Allegretto was himself present when the oath was taken, and had no doubt of its efficacy.

[3] Those who leave vengeance to God are ridiculed by Pulci, *Morgante*, canto xxi, str. 83 *sqq.*, 104 *sqq.*

[4] Guicciardini, *Ricordi, loc. cit.*, n. 74.

goes much farther, not only requiring the sanction of the sense of justice, but craving admiration, and even striving to get the laugh on its own side.

Here lies the reason why men were willing to wait so long for their revenge. A *bella vendetta* demanded as a rule a combination of circumstances for which it was necessary to wait patiently. The gradual ripening of such opportunities is described by the novelists with heartfelt delight.

There is no need to discuss the morality of actions in which plaintiff and judge are one and the same person. If this Italian thirst for vengeance is to be palliated at all it must be by proving the existence of a corresponding national virtue—namely, gratitude. The same force of imagination which retains and magnifies wrong once suffered might be expected also to keep alive the memory of kindness received.[1] It is not possible, however, to prove this with regard to the nation as a whole, though traces of it may be seen in the Italian character of to-day. The gratitude shown by the inferior classes for kind treatment, and the good memory of the upper for politeness in social life, are instances of this.

This connexion between the imagination and the moral qualities of the Italian repeats itself continually. If, nevertheless, we find more cold calculation in cases where the Northerner rather follows his impulses, the reason is that individual development in Italy was not only more marked and earlier in point of time, but also far more frequent. Where this is the case in other countries the results are also analogous. We find, for example, that the early emancipation of the young from domestic and paternal authority is common to North America with Italy. Later on, in the more generous natures, a tie of freer affection grows up between parents and children.

It is, in fact, a matter of extreme difficulty to judge fairly of other nations in the sphere of character and feeling. In these respects a people may be developed highly, and yet in a manner so strange that a foreigner is utterly unable to understand it. Perhaps all the nations of the West are in this point equally favoured.

But where the imagination has exercised the most powerful and despotic influence on morals is in the illicit intercourse of the two sexes. It is well known that prostitution was freely practised in the Middle Ages before the appearance of syphilis. A discussion, however, on these questions does not belong to our present work. What seems characteristic of Italy at this time is that here marriage and its rights were more often and more deliberately trampled under foot than anywhere else. The girls of the higher classes were carefully secluded, and of them we do not speak. All passion was directed to the married women.

Under these circumstances it is remarkable that, so far as we know, there was no diminution in the number of marriages, and that family life by no means underwent that disorganization which a similar state of things would have produced in the North. Men wished to live as they pleased, but by no means

[1] Thus Cardanus (*De Propria Vita*, cap. 13) describes himself as very revengeful, but also as " verax, memor beneficiorum, amans justitiæ."

to renounce the family, even when they were not sure that it was all their own. Nor did the race sink, either physically or mentally, on this account; for that apparent intellectual decline which showed itself toward the middle of the sixteenth century may be certainly accounted for by political and ecclesiastical causes, even if we are not to assume that the circle of achievements possible to the Renaissance had been completed. Notwithstanding their profligacy, the Italians continued to be, physically and mentally, one of the healthiest and

FIG. 216. DANCING PAIR AND LOVE SCENE
Florentine copper engraving, 1470–80

best-born populations in Europe,[1] and have retained this position, with improved morals, down to our own time.

When we come to look more closely at the ethics of love at the time of the Renaissance we are struck by a remarkable contrast. The novelists and comic poets give us to understand that love consists only in sensual enjoyment, and that to win this all means, tragic or comic, are not only permitted, but are interesting in proportion to their audacity and unscrupulousness. But if we turn to the best of the lyric poets and writers of dialogues we find in them a deep and spiritual passion of the noblest kind, whose last and highest expression is a revival of the ancient belief in an original unity of souls in the Divine Being. And both modes of feeling were then genuine, and could co-exist in the same

[1] It is true that when the Spanish rule was fully established the population fell off to a certain extent. Had this fact been due to the demoralization of the people it would have appeared much earlier.

individual. It is not exactly a matter of glory, but it is a fact that in the cultivated man of modern times this sentiment can be not merely unconsciously
present in both its highest and lowest stages, but may thus manifest itself
openly, and even artistically. The modern man, like the man of antiquity, is in
this respect too a microcosm, which the medieval man was not and could not be.

To begin with the morality of the novelists. They treat chiefly, as we have
said, of married women, and consequently of adultery.

The opinion mentioned above (p. 389) of the equality of the two sexes is
of great importance in relation to this subject. The highly developed and
cultivated woman disposes of herself with a freedom unknown in Northern
countries; and her unfaithfulness does not break up her life in the same terrible
manner, so long as no outward consequence follow from it. The husband's
claim on her fidelity has not that firm foundation which it acquires in the
North through the poetry and passion of courtship and betrothal. After the
briefest acquaintance with her future husband the young wife quits the convent
or the paternal roof to enter upon a world in which her character begins to
develop rapidly. The rights of the husband are for this reason conditional,
and even the man who regards them in the light of a *jus quæsitum* thinks only
of the outward conditions of the contract, not of the affections. The beautiful
young wife of an old man sends back the presents and letters of a youthful
lover in the firm resolve to keep her honour (*honesta*). " But she rejoices in
the love of the youth for the sake of his great excellence; and she perceives that
a noble woman may love a man of merit without loss to her honour." [1] But
the way is short from such a distinction to a complete surrender.

The latter seems, indeed, as good as justified, when there is unfaithfulness
on the part of the husband. The woman, conscious of her own dignity, feels
this not only as a pain, but also as a humiliation and deceit, and sets to work,
often with the calmest consciousness of what she is about, to devise the vengeance which the husband deserves. Her tact must decide as to the measure
of punishment which is suited to the particular case. The deepest wound,
for example, may prepare the way for a reconciliation and a peaceful life in the
future, if only it remain secret. The novelists, who themselves undergo such
experiences or invent them according to the spirit of the age, are full of admiration when the vengeance is skilfully adapted to the particular case—in fact,
when it is a work of art. As a matter of course the husband never at bottom
recognizes this right of retaliation, and submits to it only from fear or prudence.
Where these motives are absent, where his wife's unfaithfulness exposes him
or may expose him to the derision of outsiders, the affair becomes tragical, and
not seldom ends in murder or other vengeance of a violent sort. It is characteristic of the real motive from which these deeds arise that not only the
husbands, but the brothers [2] and the father of the woman feel themselves not

---

[1] Giraldi, *Hecatommithi*, iii, *Nov.* 2. In the same strain, *Cortigiano*, lib. iii, cap. 57.

[2] A shocking instance of vengeance taken by a brother at Perugia in 1455 is to be found in the chronicle of
Graziani (*Archiv. Stor.*, xvi, p. 629). The brother forces the gallant to tear out the sister's eyes, and then
beats him from the place. It is true that the family was a branch of the Oddi, and the lover only a cordwainer.

only justified in taking vengeance, but bound to take it.   Jealousy, therefore, has nothing to do with the matter, moral reprobation but little; the real reason is the wish to spoil the triumph of others.   Bandello says: [1]

> Nowadays we see a woman poison her husband to gratify her lusts, thinking that a widow may do whatever she desires.   Another, fearing the discovery of an illicit *amour*, has her husband murdered by her lover.   And though fathers, brothers, and husbands arise to extirpate the shame with poison, with the sword, and by every other means, women still continue to follow their passions, careless of their honour and their lives.

Another time, in a milder strain, he exclaims :

> Would that we were not daily forced to hear that one man has murdered his wife because he suspected her of infidelity; that another has killed his daughter on account of a secret marriage; that a third has caused his sister to be murdered because she would not marry as he wished!   It is great cruelty that we claim the right to do whatever we list and will not suffer women to do the same.   If they do anything which does not please us there we are at once with cords and daggers and poison.   What folly it is of men to suppose their own and their house's honour depends on the appetite of a woman!

The tragedy in which such affairs commonly ended was so well known that the novelist looked on the threatened gallant as a dead man, even while he went about alive and merry.   The physician and lute-player Antonio Bologna [2] had made a secret marriage with the widowed Duchess of Amalfi, of the house of Aragon.   Soon afterward her brother succeeded in securing both her and her children, and murdered them in a castle.   Antonio, ignorant of their fate, and still cherishing the hope of seeing them again, was staying at Milan, closely watched by hired assassins, and one day in the society of Ippolita Sforza sang to the lute the story of his misfortunes.   A friend of the house, Delio, " told the story up to this point to Scipione Atellano, and added that he would make it the subject of a novel, as he was sure that Antonio would be murdered."   The manner in which this took place, almost under the eyes of Delio and Atellano, is thrillingly described by Bandello (i, Nov. 26).

Nevertheless, the novelists habitually show a sympathy for all the ingenious, comic, and cunning features which may happen to attend adultery.   They describe with delight how the lover manages to hide himself in the house, all the means and devices by which he communicates with his mistress, the boxes with cushions and sweetmeats in which he can be hidden and carried out of danger.   The deceived husband is described sometimes as a fool to be laughed at, sometimes as a bloodthirsty avenger of his honour; there is no third situation except when the woman is painted as wicked and cruel, and the husband or lover is the innocent victim.   It may be remarked, however, that narratives of the latter kind are not, strictly speaking, novels, but rather warning examples taken from real life. [3]

[1] Bandello, i, *Nov.* 9 and 26.   Sometimes the wife's confessor is bribed by the husband and betrays the adultery.

[2] See above, p. 388, and note 4.

[3] As instance, Bandello, i, *Nov.* 4.

435

When in the course of the sixteenth century Italian life fell more and more under Spanish influence the violence of the means to which jealousy had recourse perhaps increased. But this new phase must be distinguished from the punishment of infidelity which existed before, and which was founded in the spirit of the Renaissance itself. As the influence of Spain declined these excesses of jealousy declined also, till toward the close of the seventeenth century they had wholly disappeared, and their place was taken by that indifference which regarded the *cicisbeo* as an indispensable figure in every household, and took no offence at one or two supernumerary lovers (*patiti*).

But who can undertake to compare the vast sum of wickedness which all these facts imply with what happened in other countries? Was the marriage-tie, for instance, really more sacred in France during the fifteenth century than in Italy? The *fabliaux* and farces would lead us to doubt it, and rather incline us to think that unfaithfulness was equally common, though its tragic consequences were less frequent, because the individual was less developed and his claims were less consciously felt than in Italy. More evidence, however, in favour of the Germanic peoples lies in the fact of the social freedom enjoyed among them by girls and women, which impressed Italian travellers so pleasantly in England and in the Netherlands (p. 394, note 1). And yet we must not attach too much importance to this fact. Unfaithfulness was doubtless very frequent, and in certain cases led to a sanguinary vengeance. We have only to remember how the Northern princes of that time dealt with their wives on the first suspicion of infidelity.

But it was not merely the sensual desire, not merely the vulgar appetite of the ordinary man, which trespassed upon forbidden ground among the Italians of that day, but also the passion of the best and noblest; and this not only because the unmarried girl did not appear in society, but also because the man, in proportion to the completeness of his own nature, felt himself most strongly attracted by the woman whom marriage had developed. These are the men who struck the loftiest notes of lyrical poetry, and who have attempted in their treatises and dialogues to give us an idealized image of the devouring passion—*l'amor divino*. When they complain of the cruelty of the winged god they are not only thinking of the coyness or hard-heartedness of the beloved one, but also of the unlawfulness of the passion itself. They seek to raise themselves above this painful consciousness by that spiritualization of love which found a support in the Platonic doctrine of the soul and of which Pietro Bembo is the most famous representative. His thoughts on this subject are set forth by himself in the third book of the *Asolani*, and indirectly by Castiglione, who puts in his mouth the splendid speech with which the fourth book of the *Cortigiano* concludes; neither of these writers was a Stoic in his conduct, but at that time it meant something to be at once a famous and a good man, and this praise must be accorded to both of them; their contemporaries took what these men said to be a true expression of their feeling, and we have not the right to despise it as affectation. Those who take the trouble to study the speech in the *Cortigiano* will see how poor an idea of it can be given by an xtract. There were then living in Italy several distinguished women who owed their celebrity chiefly to relations of this kind, such as Giulia Gonzaga, Veronica da Coreggio, and, above all, Vittoria Colonna. The land of profligates and scoffers respected these women and this sort of love—and what more can be said in their favour? We cannot tell how far vanity had to do with the matter, how far Vittoria was flattered to hear round her the sublimated utterances of hopeless love from the most famous men in Italy. If the thing was here and there a fashion, it was still no trifling praise for Vittoria that she, at least, never went out of fashion, and in her latest years produced the most profound impressions. It was long before other countries had anything similar to show.[1]

In the imagination, then, which governed the people more than any other, lies one general reason why the course of every passion was violent, and why the means used for the gratification of passion were often criminal. There is a violence which cannot control itself because it is born of weakness; but in Italy what we find is the corruption of powerful natures. Sometimes this corruption assumes a colossal shape, and crime seems to acquire almost a personal existence of its own.

The restraints of which men were conscious were but few. Each individual, even among the lowest of the people, felt himself inwardly emancipated from the control of the State and its police, whose title to respect was illegitimate, and itself founded on violence; and no man believed any longer in the justice of the law. When a murder was committed the sympathies of the people, before the circumstances of the case were known, ranged themselves instinctively on the side of the murderer.[2] A proud, manly bearing before and at the execution excited such admiration that the narrator often forgets to tell us for what offence the criminal was put to death.[3] But when we add to this inward contempt of law and to the countless grudges and enmities which called for satisfaction the impunity which crime enjoyed during times of political disturbance we can only wonder that the State and society were not utterly dissolved. Crises of this kind occurred at Naples during the transition from the Aragonese to the French and Spanish rule, and at Milan on the repeated expulsions and returns of the Sforzas; at such times those men who have never in their hearts recognized the bonds of law and society come forward and give free play to their instincts of murder and rapine. Let us take, by way of example, a picture drawn from a humbler sphere.

When the Duchy of Milan was suffering from the disorders which followed the death of Giangaleazzo Sforza, about the year 1480 all safety came to

[1] It is remarkable that Burckhardt makes no mention of the practice of sodomy, which was so prevalent in Renaissance Italy. S. Barnardino da Siena raged vehemently against this vice in his sermons, as did other preachers of repentance. See Schnitzer, *Savonarola*, i, pp. 272 *sqq.*—W. G.]

[2] "Piaccia al Signore Iddio che non si ritrovi," say the women in Giraldi (iii, *Nov.* 10) when they are told that the deed may cost the murderer his head.

[3] This is the case, for example, with Gioviano Pontano (*De Fortitudine*, lib. ii). His heroic Ascolans, who spend their last night in singing and dancing, the Abruzzian mother, who cheers up her son on his way to the gallows, etc., belong probably to brigand families, but he forgets to say so.

an end in the provincial cities. This was the case in Parma,[1] where the Milanese Governor, terrified by threats of murder, and after vainly offering rewards for the discovery of the offenders, consented to throw open the gaols and let loose the most abandoned criminals. Burglary, the demolition of houses, shameless offences against decency, public assassination and murders, especially of Jews, were events of everyday occurrence. At first the authors of these deeds prowled about singly and masked; soon large gangs of armed men went to work every night without disguise. Threatening letters, satires, and scandalous jests circulated freely; and a sonnet in ridicule of the Government seems to have roused its indignation far more than the frightful condition of the city. In many churches the sacred vessels with the Host were stolen, and this fact is characteristic of the temper which prompted these outrages. It is impossible to say what would happen now in any country of the world if the Government and police ceased to act, and yet hindered by their presence the establishment of a provisional authority; but what then occurred in Italy wears a character of its own through the great share which personal hatred and revenge had in it. The impression, indeed, which Italy at this period makes on us is that even in quiet times great crimes were commoner than in other countries. We may, it is true, be misled by the fact that we have far fuller details on such matters here than elsewhere, and that the same force of imagination which gives a special character to crimes actually committed causes much to be invented which never really happened. The amount of violence was perhaps as great elsewhere. It is hard to say for certain whether in 1500 men were any safer, whether human life was after all better protected, in powerful, wealthy Germany, with its robber-knights, extortionate beggars, and daring highwaymen. But one thing is certain, that premeditated crimes, committed professionally and for hire by third parties, occurred in Italy with great and appalling frequency.

So far as regards brigandage, Italy, especially in the more fortunate provinces, such as Tuscany, was certainly not more, and probably less, troubled than the countries of the North. But the figures which do meet us are characteristic of the country. It would be hard, for instance, to find elsewhere the case of a priest gradually driven by passion from one excess to another, till at last he came to head a band of robbers. That age offers us this example among others.[2] On August 12, 1495, the priest Don Niccolò de' Pelegati of Figarolo was shut up in an iron cage outside the tower of S. Giuliano at Ferrara. He had twice celebrated his first Mass; the first time he had the same day committed murder, but afterward received absolution at Rome; he then killed four people and married two wives, with whom he travelled about. He afterward took part in many assassinations, violated women, carried others away by force, plundered far and wide, and infested the territory of Ferrara with a band of

---

[1] *Diarium Parmense*, in Murat., xxii, col. 330–349 *passim*; the sonnet, col. 340. [In the new edition of Muratori, under the title of *Cronica Gestorum in Partibus Lombardiae et Reliquis Italiae*, ed. A. Bonazzi, pp. 63 *sqq.* (1904); the sonnet, p. 71.—W. G.]

[2] *Diario Ferrarese*, in Murat., xxiv, col. 312. We are reminded of the gang led by a priest which for some time before 1837 infested Western Lombardy.

followers in uniform, extorting food and shelter by every sort of violence. When we think of what all this implies, the mass of guilt on the head of this one man is something tremendous. The clergy and monks had many privileges and little supervision, and among them were doubtless plenty of murderers and other malefactors—but hardly a second Pelegati. It is another matter, though by no means creditable, when ruined characters sheltered themselves in the cowl in order to escape the arm of the law, like the corsair whom Massuccio knew in a convent at Naples.[1] What the real truth was with regard to Pope John XXIII in this respect is not known with certainty.[2]

The age of the famous brigand chief did not begin till later, in the seventeenth century, when the political strife of Guelph and Ghibelline, of Frenchman and Spaniard, no longer agitated the country. The robber then took the place of the partisan.

In certain districts of Italy where civilization had made little progress the country people were disposed to murder any stranger who fell into their hands. This was especially the case in the more remote parts of the kingdom of Naples, where the barbarism dated probably from the days of the Roman *latifundia*, and when the stranger and the enemy (*hospes* and *hostis*) were in all good faith held to be one and the same. These people were far from being irreligious. A herdsman once appeared in great trouble at the confessional, avowing that while making cheese during Lent a few drops of milk had found their way into his mouth. The confessor, skilled in the customs of the country, discovered in the course of his examination that the penitent and his friends were in the practice of robbing and murdering travellers, but that, through the force of habit, this usage gave rise to no twinges of conscience within them.[3] We have already mentioned (p. 348, note 7) to what a degree of barbarism the peasants elsewhere could sink in times of political confusion.

A worse symptom than brigandage of the morality of that time was the frequency of paid assassination. In that respect Naples was admitted to stand at the head of all the cities of Italy. " Nothing," says Pontano,[4] " is cheaper here than human life." But other districts could also show a terrible list of these crimes. It is hard, of course, to classify them according to the motives by which they were prompted, since political expediency, personal hatred, fear, and revenge all play into one another. It is no small honour to the Florentines, the most highly developed people of Italy, that offences of this kind occurred more rarely among them than anywhere else,[5] perhaps because there was a

---

[1] Massuccio, *Nov.* 29. As a matter of course the man has luck in his *amours*.

[2] If he appeared as a corsair in the war between the two lines of Anjou for the possession of Naples he may have done so as a political partisan, and this, according to the notions of the time, implied no dishonour. The Archbishop Paolo Fregoso of Genoa in the second half of the fifteenth century probably allowed himself quite as much freedom, or more. Contemporaries and later writers—for example, Aretino and Poggio—record much worse things of John. Gregorovius, vi, p. 600.

[3] Poggio, *Facetiæ*, fol. 164.

[4] Jov. Pontan., *Antonius*: " Nec est quod Neapoli quam hominis vita minoris vendatur." It is true he thinks it was not so under the house of Anjou, " sicam ab iis [the Aragonese] accepimus." The state of things about 1534 is described by Benvenuto Cellini, i, 70.

[5] Absolute proof of this cannot be given, but few murders are recorded, and the imagination of the Florentine writers at the best period is not filled with the suspicion of them.

justice at hand for legitimate grievances which was recognized by all, or because
the higher culture of the individual gave him different views as to the right
of men to interfere with the decrees of Fate. In Florence, if anywhere, men
were able to feel the incalculable consequences of a deed of blood, and to
understand how insecure the author of a so-called profitable crime is of any
true and lasting gain. After the fall of Florentine liberty assassination,
especially by hired agents, seems to have rapidly increased, and continued till
the Government of Cosimo I had attained such strength that the police
were at last able to repress it.

Elsewhere in Italy paid crimes were probably more or less frequent in proportion to the existence of powerful and solvent buyers. It is impossible to
make any statistical estimate of their number, but if only a fraction of the deaths
which public report attributed to violence were really murders the crime must
have been terribly frequent. The worst example of all was set by princes and
Governments, who without the faintest scruple reckoned murder as one of the
instruments of their power. And this without being in the same category
with Cesare Borgia. The Sforzas, the Aragonese monarchs, the Republic of
Venice,[2] and, later on, the agents of Charles V resorted to it whenever it suited
their purpose. The imagination of the people at last became so accustomed
to facts of this kind that the death of any powerful man was seldom or never
attributed to natural causes.[3] There were certainly absurd notions current
with regard to the effects of various poisons. There may be some truth in the
story of that terrible white powder used by the Borgias, which did its work
at the end of a definite period (p. 132), and it is possible that it was really a
velenum atterminatum which the Prince of Salerno handed to the Cardinal of
Aragon with the words: " In a few days you will die, because your father,
King Ferrante, wished to trample upon us all."[4] But the poisoned letter which
Caterina Riario sent to Pope Alexander VI[5] would hardly have caused his death
even if he had read it; and when Alfonso the Great was warned by his physicians
not to read in the Livy which Cosimo de' Medici had presented to him he told
them with justice not to talk like fools.[6] Nor can that poison with which
the secretary of Piccinino wished to anoint the Sedan chair of Pius II[7] have
affected any other organ than the imagination. The proportion which mineral
and vegetable poisons bore to one another cannot be ascertained precisely.
The poison with which the painter Rosso Fiorentino destroyed himself (1541)

---

[1] See on this point the report of Fedeli, in Alberi, *Relazioni*, serie ii, vol. i, pp. 353 *sqq.*

[2] M. Brosch (*Hist. Ztschr.*, Bd. 27, pp. 295 *sqq.*) has collected from the Venetian archives five proposals,
approved by the Council, to poison the Sultan (1471-1504), as well as evidence of the plan to murder Charles VIII
(1495) and of the order given to the Proveditor at Faenza to have Cesare Borgia put to death (1504).

[[3] Dr Geiger adds several conjectural statements and references on this subject. It may be remarked that
the suspicion of poisoning, which I believe to be now generally unfounded, is often expressed in certain parts
of Italy with regard to any death not at once to be accounted for.—S. G. C. M.]

[4] Infessura, in Eccard, *Scriptores*, ii, col. 1956.

[5] *Chron. Venetum*, in Murat., xxiv, col. 131. In Northern countries still more wonderful things were believed
as to the art of poisoning in Italy. See Juvénal des Ursins, *ad a.* 1382 (ed. Buchon, p. 336), for the lancet of the
poisoner whom Charles of Durazzo took into his service; whoever looked at it steadily died.

[6] Petr. Crinitus, *De Honesta Disciplina*, lib. xviii, cap. 9.

[7] *Pii II Comment.*, lib. xi, p. 562. Joh. Ant. Campanus, *Vita Pii II*, in Murat., iii, ii, col. 988.

was evidently a powerful acid,[1] which it would have been impossible to administer to another person without his knowledge. The secret use of weapons, especially of the dagger, in the service of powerful individuals was habitual in Milan, Naples, and other cities. Indeed, among the crowds of armed retainers who were necessary for the personal safety of the great, and who lived in idleness, it was natural that outbreaks of this mania for blood should from time to time occur. Many a deed of horror would never have been committed had not the master known that he needed but to give a sign to one or other of his followers.

Among the means used for the secret destruction of others—so far, that is, as the intention goes—we find magic,[2] practised, however, sparingly. Where *maleficii, malie*, and so forth are mentioned they appear rather as a means of heaping up additional terror on the head of some hated enemy. At the Courts of France and England in the fourteenth and fifteenth centuries magic, practised with a view to the death of an opponent, plays a far more important part than in Italy.

In this country, finally, where individuality of every sort attained its highest development we find instances of that ideal and absolute wickedness which delights in crimes for their own sake, and not as means to an end, or at any rate as means to ends for which our psychology has no measure.

Among these appalling figures we may first notice certain of the *condottieri*,[3] such as Braccio di Montone, Tiberto Brandolino, and that Werner von Urslingen whose silver hauberk bore the inscription: " The enemy of God, of pity, and of mercy." This class of men offers us some of the earliest instances of criminals deliberately repudiating every moral restraint. Yet we shall be more reserved in our judgment of them when we remember that the worst part of their guilt—in the estimate of those who record it—lay in their defiance of spiritual threats and penalties, and that to this fact is due that air of horror with which they are represented as surrounded. In the case of Braccio the hatred of the Church went so far that he was infuriated at the sight of monks at their Psalms, and had thrown them down from the top

---

[1] Vasari, ix, 82, *Vita di Rosso.* In the case of unhappy marriages it is hard to say whether there were more real or imaginary instances of poisoning. *Cf.* Bandello, ii, *Nov.* 5 and 54; ii, *Nov.* 40, is more serious. In one and the same city of Western Lombardy, the name of which is not given, lived two poisoners. A husband, wishing to convince himself of the genuineness of his wife's despair, made her drink what she believed to be poison, but which was really coloured water, whereupon they were reconciled. In the family of Cardanus alone four cases of poisoning occurred (*De Propria Vita*, cap. 30, 50). Even at a banquet given at the coronation of a Pope each cardinal brought his own cup-bearer with him, and his own wine, " probably because they knew from experience that otherwise they would run the risk of being poisoned." And this usage was general at Rome, and practised " sine injuria invitantis! " Blas Ortiz, *Itinerar. Hadriani VI*, in Baluz., *Miscell.*, ed. Mansi, i, 380.

[2] For the magic arts used against Leonello of Ferrara see *Diario Ferrarese*, in Murat., xxiv, col. 194, *ad a.* 1445. When the sentence was read in the public square to the author, a certain Benato, a man in other respects of bad character, a noise was heard in the air and the earth shook, so that many people fled away or fell to the ground; this happened because Benato " havea chiamato e scongiurato il diavolo." What Guicciardini (lib. i) says of the wicked arts practised by Lodovico il Moro against his nephew Giangaleazzo rests on his own responsibility. On magic see below, Chapter IV.

[3] Ezzelino da Romano might be put first were it not that he rather acted under the influence of ambitious motives and astrological delusions.

of a tower;[1] but at the same time " he was loyal to his soldiers and a great general." As a rule, the crimes of the *condottieri* were committed for the sake of some definite advantage, and must be attributed to a position in which men could not fail to be demoralized. Even their apparently gratuitous cruelty had commonly a purpose, if it were only to strike terror. The barbarities of the house of Aragon, as we have seen, were mainly due to fear and to the desire for vengeance. The thirst for blood on its own account, the devilish delight in destruction, is most clearly exemplified in the case of the Spaniard Cesare Borgia, whose cruelties were certainly out of all proportion to the end which he had in view (pp. 132 *sqq.*). In Sigismondo Malatesta, tyrant of Rimini (pp. 50, 235), the same disinterested love of evil may also be detected. It is not only the Court of Rome,[2] but the verdict of history, which convicts him of murder, rape, adultery, incest, sacrilege, perjury, and treason, committed not once, but often. The most shocking crime of all—the unnatural attempt on his own son Roberto, who frustrated it with his drawn dagger[3]—may have been the result not merely of moral corruption, but perhaps of some magical or astrological superstition. The same conjecture has been made to account for the rape of the Bishop of Fano[4] by Pierluigi Farnese of Parma, son of Paul III.

If we now attempt to sum up the principal features in the Italian character of that time, as we know it from a study of the life of the upper classes, we shall obtain something like the following result. The fundamental vice of this character was at the same time a condition of its greatness—namely, excessive individualism. The individual first inwardly casts off the authority of a state which, as a fact, is in most cases tyrannical and illegitimate, and what he thinks and does is, rightly or wrongly, now called treason. The sight of victorious egoism in others drives him to defend his own right by his own arm. And while thinking to restore his inward equilibrium he falls, through the vengeance which he executes, into the hands of the Powers of Darkness. His love, too, turns mostly for satisfaction to another individuality equally developed—namely, to his neighbour's wife. In face of all objective facts, of laws and restraints of whatever kind, he retains the feeling of his own sovereignty, and in each single instance forms his decision independently, according as honour or interest, passion or calculation, revenge or renunciation, gain the upper hand in his own mind.

If, therefore, egoism in its wider as well as in its narrower sense is the root and fountain of all evil, the more highly developed Italian was for this reason more inclined to wickedness than the member of other nations of that time. But this individual development did not come upon him through any fault

---

[1] *Giornali Napoletani*, in Murat., xxi, col. 1092, *ad a.* 1425. According to the narrative this deed seems to have been committed out of mere pleasure in cruelty. Braccio, it is true, believed neither in God nor in the saints, and despised and neglected all the precepts and ceremonies of the Church.

[2] *Pii II Comment.*, lib. vii, p. 338.

[3] Jov. Pontan., *De Immanitate*, cap. 17, where he relates how Malatesta got his own daughter with child—and so forth.

[4] Varchi, *Stor. Fiorent.*, at the end. (When the work is published without expurgations, as in the Milanese edition.)

of his own, but rather through an historical necessity. It did not come upon him alone, but also, and chiefly by means of Italian culture, upon the other nations of Europe, and has constituted since then the higher atmosphere which they breathe. In itself it is neither good nor bad, but necessary; within it has grown up a modern standard of good and evil—a sense of moral responsibility —which is essentially different from that which was familiar to the Middle Ages.

But the Italian of the Renaissance had to bear the first mighty surging of a new age. Through his gifts and his passions he has become the most characteristic representative of all the heights and all the depths of his time. By the side of profound corruption appeared human personalities of the noblest harmony and an artistic splendour which shed upon the life of man a lustre which neither antiquity nor medievalism either could or would bestow upon it.

CHAPTER II

RELIGION IN DAILY LIFE

HE morality of a people stands in the closest connexion with its consciousness of God—that is to say, with its firmer or weaker faith in the divine government of the world, whether this faith looks on the world as destined to happiness or to misery and speedy destruction.[1] The infidelity then prevalent in Italy is notorious, and whoever takes the trouble to look about for proofs will find them by the hundred. Our present task, here as elsewhere, is to separate and discriminate, refraining from an absolute and final verdict.

The belief in God at earlier times had its source and chief support in Christianity and the outward symbol of Christianity, the Church. When the Church became corrupt men ought to have drawn a distinction, and kept their religion in spite of all. But this is more easily said than done. It is not every people which is calm enough, or dull enough, to tolerate a lasting contradiction between a principle and its outward expression. But history does not record a heavier responsibility than that which rests upon the decaying Church. She set up as absolute truth and by the most violent means a doctrine which she had distorted to serve her own aggrandizement. Safe in the sense of her inviolability, she abandoned herself to the most scandalous profligacy, and, in order to maintain herself in this state, she levelled mortal blows against the conscience and the intellect of nations, and drove multitudes of the noblest spirits, whom she had inwardly estranged, into the arms of unbelief and despair.

Here we are met by the question: Why did not Italy, intellectually so great, react more energetically against the hierarchy; why did she not accomplish a reformation like that which occurred in Germany, and accomplish it at an earlier date?

A plausible answer has been given to this question. The Italian mind, we are told, never went farther than the denial of the hierarchy, while the origin and the vigour of the German Reformation was due to its positive religious doctrines, most of all to the doctrines of justification by faith and of the inefficacy of good works.

It is certain that these doctrines only worked upon Italy through Germany, and this not till the power of Spain was sufficiently great to root them out

---

[1] On which point feeling differs according to the place and the people. The Renaissance prevailed in times and cities where the tendency was to enjoy life heartily. The general darkening of the spirits of thoughtful men did not begin to show itself till the time of the foreign supremacy in the sixteenth century.

without difficulty, partly by itself, and partly by means of the Papacy and its instruments.[1] Nevertheless, in the earlier religious movements of Italy, from the mystics of the thirteenth century down to Savonarola, there was a large amount of positive religious doctrine which, like the very definite Christianity of the Huguenots, failed to achieve success only because circumstances were against it. Mighty events like the Reformation elude, as respects their details, their outbreak, and their development, the deductions of the philosophers, however clearly the necessity of them as a whole may be demonstrated. The movements of the human spirit, its sudden flashes, its expansions, and its pauses, must for ever remain a mystery to our eyes, since we can but know this or that of the forces at work in it, never all of them together.

The feeling of the upper and middle classes in Italy with regard to the Church at the time when the Renaissance culminated was compounded of deep and contemptuous aversion, of acquiescence in the outward ecclesiastical customs which entered into daily life, and of a sense of dependence on Sacraments and ceremonies. The great personal influence of religious preachers may be added as a fact characteristic of Italy.

That hostility to the hierarchy, which displays itself more especially from the time of Dante onward in Italian literature and history, has been fully treated by several writers. We have already (p. 229) said something of the attitude of public opinion with regard to the Papacy. Those who wish for the strongest evidence which the best authorities offer us can find it in the famous passages of Machiavelli's *Discorsi* and in the unmutilated edition of Guicciardini. Outside the Roman Curia some respect seems to have been felt for the best men among the bishops,[2] and for many of the parochial clergy. On the other hand, the mere holders of benefices, the canons, and the monks were held in almost universal suspicion, and were often the objects of the most scandalous aspersions, extending to the whole of their order.

It has been said that the monks were made the scapegoats for the whole clergy, for the reason that none but they could be ridiculed without danger.[3] But this is certainly incorrect. They are introduced so frequently in the novels and comedies because these forms of literature need fixed and well-known types where the imagination of the reader can easily fill up an outline. Besides which, the novelists do not as a fact spare the secular clergy.[4] In the third place we

[1] What is termed the spirit of the Counter-Reformation was developed in Spain some time before the Reformation itself, chiefly through the sharp surveillance and partial reorganization of the Church under Ferdinand and Isabella. The principal authority on this subject is Gomez, *Life of Cardinal Ximenes*, in Rob. Belus, *Rer. Hispan. Scriptores* (3 vols., 1581).

[2] It is to be noticed that the novelists and satirists scarcely ever mention the bishops, although they might, under altered names, have attacked them like the rest. They do so, however—for example, in Bandello, ii, *Nov.* 45; yet in ii, 40, he describes a virtuous bishop. Gioviano Pontano in the *Charon* introduces the ghost of a luxurious bishop with a " duck's walk."

[3] Foscolo, *Discorso sul Testo del "Decamerone,"* " Ma dei preti in dignità niuno poteva far motto senza pericolo; onde ogni frate fu l' irco delle iniquità d' Israele," etc. Timotheus Maffeus dedicates a book against the monks to Pope Nicholas V; Facius, *De Vir. Ill.*, p. 24. There are specially strong passages against the monks and clergy in the work of Palingenius already mentioned, iv, 289; v, 184 *sqq.*, 586 *sqq.*

[4] Bandello prefaces ii, *Nov.* 1, with the statement that the vice of avarice was more discreditable to priests than to any other class of men, since they had no families to provide for. On this ground he justifies the

have abundant proof in the rest of Italian literature that men could speak boldly enough about the Papacy and the Court of Rome. In works of imagination we cannot expect to find criticism of this kind. Fourthly the monks, when attacked, were sometimes able to take a terrible vengeance.

It is nevertheless true that the monks were the most unpopular class of all, and that they were reckoned a living proof of the worthlessness of conventual life, of the whole ecclesiastical organization, of the system of dogma, and of religion altogether, according as men pleased, rightly or wrongly, to draw their conclusions. We may also assume that Italy retained a clearer recollection of the origin of the two great mendicant orders than other countries, and had not forgotten that they were the chief agents in the reaction [1] against what is called the heresy of the thirteenth century—that is to say, against an early and vigorous movement of the modern Italian spirit. And that spiritual police which was permanently entrusted to the Dominicans certainly never excited any other feeling than secret hatred and contempt.

After reading the *Decamerone* and the novels of Franco Sacchetti we might imagine that the vocabulary of abuse directed at the monks and nuns was exhausted. But toward the time of the Reformation this abuse became still fiercer. To say nothing of Aretino, who in the *Ragionamenti* uses conventual life merely as a pretext for giving free play to his own poisonous nature, we may quote one author as typical of the rest—Massuccio, in the first ten of his fifty novels. They are written in a tone of the deepest indignation, and with the purpose to make the indignation general; and are dedicated to men in the highest position, such as King Ferrante and Prince Alfonso of Naples. Many of the stories are old, and some of them familiar to readers of Boccaccio. But others reflect, with a frightful realism, the actual state of things at Naples. The way in which the priests befool and plunder the people by means of spurious miracles, added to their own scandalous lives, is enough to drive any thoughtful observer to despair. We read of the Minorite friars who travelled to collect alms: " They cheat, steal, and fornicate, and when they are at the end of their resources they set up as saints and work miracles, one displaying the cloak of St Vincent, another the handwriting [2] of S. Bernardino, a third the bridle of Capistrano's donkey." Others " bring with them confederates who pretend to be blind or afflicted with some mortal disease, and after touching the hem of the monk's cowl, or the relics which he carried, are healed before the eyes of the multitude. All then shout '*Misericordia*,' the bells are rung, and the miracle is recorded in a solemn protocol." Or else a monk in the pulpit is denounced as a liar by another who stands below among the audience; the accuser is immediately possessed by the devil, and then healed by the preacher. The whole thing was a prearranged comedy, in which, however, the principal with his assistant made so much money that he was able to buy a bishopric

disgraceful attack made on a parsonage by two soldiers or brigands at the orders of a young gentleman, on which occasion a sheep was stolen from the stingy and gouty old priest. A single story of this kind illustrates the ideas in which men lived and acted better than all the dissertations in the world.

[1] Giov. Villani, iii, 29, says this clearly a century later.

[2] *L'Ordine*. Probably the tablet with the inscription " I. H. S." is meant.

from a cardinal, on which the two confederates lived comfortably to the end of their days. Massuccio makes no great distinction between Franciscans and Dominicans, finding the one worth as much as the other. "And yet the foolish people lets itself be drawn into their hatreds and divisions, and quarrels about them in public places,[1] and calls itself *franceschino* or *domenichino*." The nuns are the exclusive property of the monks. Those of the former who have anything to do with the laity are prosecuted and put in prison, while others are wedded in due form to the monks, with the accompaniments of Mass, a marriage-contract, and a liberal indulgence in food and wine. "I myself," says the author, "have been there not once, but several times, and seen it all with my own eyes. The nuns afterward bring forth pretty little monks or else use means to hinder that result. And if anyone charges me with falsehood let him search the nunneries well, and he will find there as many little bones as in Bethlehem at Herod's time."[2] These things and the like are among the secrets of monastic life. The monks are by no means too strict with one another in the confessional, and impose a *Paternoster* in cases where they would refuse all absolution to a layman as if he were a heretic. "Therefore may the earth open and swallow up the wretches alive, with those who protect them !" In another place Massuccio, speaking of the fact that the influence of the monks depends chiefly on the dread of another world, utters the following remarkable wish: "The best punishment for them would be for God to abolish Purgatory; they would then receive no more alms, and would be forced to go back to their spades."

If men were free to write in the time of Ferrante, and to him, in this strain the reason is perhaps to be found in the fact that the King himself had been incensed by a false miracle which had been palmed off on him.[3] An attempt had been made to urge him to a persecution of the Jews, like that carried out in Spain and imitated by the Popes,[4] by producing a tablet with an inscription bearing the name of St Cataldus, said to have been buried at Tarentum, and afterward dug up again. When he discovered the fraud the monks defied him. He had also managed to detect and expose a pretended instance of fasting, as his father Alfonso had done before him.[5] The Court, certainly, was no accomplice in maintaining these blind superstitions.[6]

We have been quoting from an author who wrote in earnest, and who by

[1] He adds (*Nov.* 10, ed. Settembrini, p. 132), "and in the *seggi*"—that is, the clubs into which the Neapolitan nobility was divided. The rivalry of the two orders is often ridiculed—for example, Bandello, iii, *Nov.* 14.

[2] *Nov.* 6, ed. Settembrini, p. 83, where it is remarked that in the Index of 1564 a book is mentioned, *Matrimonio delli Preti e delle Monache*.

[3] For what follows see Jov. Pontan., *De Sermone*, lib. ii, cap. 17, and Bandello, i, *Nov.* 32. The fury of brother Franciscus, who attempted to work upon the King by a vision of St Cataldus, was so great at his failure, and the talk on the subject so universal, "ut Italia ferme omnis ipse in primis Romanus pontifex de tabulæ hujus fuerit inventione sollicitus atque anxius."

[4] Alexander VI and Julius II, whose cruel measures, however, did not appear to the Venetian ambassadors Giustiniani and Soderini as anything but a means of extorting money. *Cf.* M. Brosch, *Hist. Ztschr.*, Bd. 37.

[5] Panormita, *De Dictis et Factis Alfonsi*, lib. ii. Æneas Sylvius in his commentary to it (*Opp.*, p. 79, ed. 1651) tells of the detection of a pretended faster, who was said to have eaten nothing for four years.

[6] For which reason they could be openly denounced in the neighbourhood of the Court. See Jov. Pontan., *Antonius* and *Charon*. One of the stories is the same as in Massuccio, *Nov.* 2.

no means stands alone in his judgment. All the Italian literature of that time is full of ridicule and invective aimed at the begging friars.[1] It can hardly have been doubted that the Renaissance would soon have destroyed these two orders had it not been for the German Reformation and the Counter-Reformation which that provoked. Their saints and popular preachers could hardly have saved them. It would only have been necessary to come to an understanding at a favourable moment with a Pope like Leo X, who despised the mendicant orders. If the spirit of the age found them ridiculous or repulsive they could no longer be anything but an embarrassment to the Church. And who can say what fate was in store for the Papacy itself if the Reformation had not saved it?

The influence which the Father Inquisitor of a Dominican monastery was able habitually to exercise in the city where it was situated was in the latter part of the fifteenth century just considerable enough to hamper and irritate cultivated people, but not strong enough to extort any lasting fear or obedience.[2] It was no longer possible to punish men for their thoughts, as it once was (pp. 284 sqq.), and those whose tongues wagged most impudently against the clergy could easily keep clear of heretical doctrine. Except when some powerful party had an end to serve, as in the case of Savonarola, or when there was a question of the use of magical arts, as was often the case in the cities of North Italy, we seldom read at this time of men being burnt at the stake. The Inquisitors were in some instances satisfied with the most superficial retractation, in others it even happened that the victim was saved out of their hands on the way to the place of execution. In Bologna (1452) the priest Niccolò da Verona had been publicly degraded on a wooden scaffold in front of S. Domenico as a wizard and profaner of the Sacraments, and was about to be led away to the stake when he was set free by a gang of armed men, sent by Achille Malvezzi, a noted friend of heretics and violater of nuns. The legate, Cardinal Bessarion, was only able to catch and hang one of the party; Malvezzi lived on in peace.[3]

It deserves to be noticed that the higher monastic orders—the Benedictines, with their many branches—were, notwithstanding their great wealth and easy lives, far less disliked than the mendicant friars. For ten novels which treat of *frati*, hardly one can be found in which a *monaco* is the subject and the victim. It was no small advantage to this order that it was founded earlier, and not as an instrument of police, and that it did not interfere with private life. It contained men of learning, wit, and piety, but the average has been described by a member of it, Firenzuola,[4] who says:

[1] See for one example the eighth canto of the *Macaroneide*.

[2] The story in Vasari—see p. 120, *Vita di Sandro Botticelli*—shows that the Inquisition was sometimes treated jocularly. It is true that the *vicario* here mentioned may have been the archbishop's deputy instead of the Inquisitor's.

[3] Bursellis, *Ann. Bonon.*, in Murat., xxiii, col. 886; *cf.* 896. Malvezzi died 1468; his *beneficium* passed to his nephew.

[4] See pp. 340 sqq. He was abbot at Vallombrosa. The passage, of which we give a free translation, is to be found in the *Opere*, vol. ii, p. 209, in the tenth novel. See an inviting description of the comfortable life of the Carthusians in the *Commentario d'Italia*, fol. 32 sqq., quoted at p. 337.

These well-fed gentlemen with the capacious cowls do not pass their time in barefooted journeys and in sermons, but sit in elegant slippers with their hands crossed over their paunches, in charming cells wainscotted with cyprus-wood. And when they are obliged to quit the house they ride comfortably, as if for their amusement, on mules and sleek, quiet horses. They do not overstrain their minds with the study of many books, for fear lest knowledge might put the pride of Lucifer in the place of monkish simplicity.

Those who are familiar with the literature of the time will see that we have only brought forward what is absolutely necessary for the understanding of the subject.[1] That the reputation attaching to the monks and the secular clergy must have shattered the faith of multitudes in all that is sacred is of course obvious.

And some of the judgments which we read are terrible; we will quote one of them in conclusion, which is but little known. The historian Guicciardini, who was for many years in the service of the Medicean Popes, says (1529) in his *Aphorisms*[2]:

No man is more disgusted than I am with the ambition, the avarice, and the profligacy of the priests, not only because each of these vices is hateful in itself, but because each and all of them are most unbecoming in those who declare themselves to be men in special relations with God, and also because they are vices so opposed to one another that they can only coexist in very singular natures. Nevertheless my position at the Court of several Popes forced me to desire their greatness for the sake of my own interest. But had it been for this I should have loved Martin Luther as myself, not in order to free myself from the laws which Christianity, as generally understood and explained, lays upon us, but in order to see this swarm of scoundrels [*questa caterva di scellerati*] put back into their proper place, so that they may be forced to live either without vices or without power.[3]

The same Guicciardini is of opinion that we are in the dark as to all that is supernatural, that philosophers and theologians have nothing but nonsense to tell us about it, that miracles occur in every religion and prove the truth of none in particular, and that all of them may be explained as unknown phenomena of nature. The faith which moves mountains, then common among the followers of Savonarola, is mentioned by Guicciardini as a curious fact, but without any bitter remark.

Notwithstanding this hostile public opinion, the clergy and the monks had the great advantage that the people were used to them, and that their existence was interwoven with the everyday existence of all. This is the advantage which every old and powerful institution possesses. Everybody had some cowled or frocked relative, some prospect of assistance or future gain from the treasure of the Church; and in the centre of Italy stood the Court of Rome, where men sometimes became rich in a moment. Yet it must never be forgotten that all this did not hinder people from writing and speaking freely. The authors of

---

[1] Pius II was on principle in favour of the abolition of the celibacy of the clergy. One of his favourite sentences was " Sacredotibus magna ratione sublatus nuptias majori restituendas videri." Platina, *Vitæ Pontiff.*, p. 311. [Platina, however, is not entirely trustworthy.—W. G.]

[2] Ricordi, n. 28, in the *Opere Ined.*, vol. i.   [3] Ricordi, n. i, 123, 125.

the most scandalous satires were themselves mostly monks or beneficed priests. Poggio, who wrote the *Facetiæ*, was a clergyman; Francesco Berni, the satirist, held a canonry; Teofilo Folengo, the author of the *Orlandino*, was a Benedictine, certainly by no means a faithful one; Matteo Bandello, who held up his own order to ridicule, was a Dominican, and nephew of a General of this order. Were they encouraged to write by the sense that they ran no risk? Or did they feel an inward need to clear themselves personally from the infamy which attached to their order? Or were they moved by that selfish pessimism which takes for its maxim, " It will last our time "? Perhaps all of these motives were more or less at work. In the case of Folengo the unmistakable influence of Lutheranism must be added.[1]

The sense of dependence on rites and Sacraments, which we have already touched upon in speaking of the Papacy (p. 121), is not surprising among that part of the people which still believed in the Church. Among those who were more emancipated it testifies to the strength of youthful impressions, and to the magical force of traditional symbols. The universal desire of dying men for priestly absolution shows that the last remnants of the dread of hell had not, even in the case of one like Vitellozzo, been altogether extinguished. It would hardly be possible to find a more instructive instance than this. The doctrine taught by the Church of the " character *indelibilis* " of the priesthood, independently of the personality of the priest, had so far borne fruit that it was possible to loathe the individual and still desire his spiritual gifts. It is true, nevertheless, that there were defiant natures like Galeotto of Mirandola,[2] who died unabsolved in 1499, after living for sixteen years under the ban of the Church. All this time the city lay under an interdict on his account, so that no Mass was celebrated and no Christian burial took place.

A splendid contrast to all this is offered by the power exercised over the nation by its great Preachers of Repentance. Other countries of Europe were from time to time moved by the words of saintly monks, but only superficially, in comparison with the periodical upheaval of the Italian conscience. The only man, in fact, who produced a similar effect in Germany during the fifteenth century was an Italian, born in the Abruzzi, named Giovanni Capistrano.[3] Those natures which bear within them this religious vocation and this commanding earnestness wore then in Northern countries an intuitive and mystical aspect. In the South they were practical and expansive, and shared in the national gift of language and oratorical skill. The North produced an *Imitation of Christ*, which worked silently, at first only within the walls of the monastery, but worked for the ages; the South produced men who made on their fellows a mighty but passing impression.

This impression consisted chiefly in the awakening of the conscience. The

---

[1] See the *Orlandino*, cap. vi, str. 40 *sqq.*; cap. vii, str. 57; cap. viii, str. 3 *sqq.*, especially 75.

[2] *Diario Ferrarese*, in Murat., xxiv, col. 362.

[3] He had with him a German and a Slavonian interpreter. St Bernard had to use the same means when he preached in the Rhineland.

FIG. 217. ST BERNARDINE PREACHING BEFORE THE TOWN HALL IN SIENA
By Sano di Pietro
Siena, Cathedral (chapter-house)
Photo Alinari

sermons were moral exhortations, free from abstract notions and full of practical application, rendered more impressive by the saintly and ascetic character of the preacher, and by the miracles which, even against his will, the inflamed

imagination of the people attributed to him.[1] The most powerful argument used was not the threat of hell and Purgatory, but rather the living results of the *maledizione*, the temporal ruin wrought on the individual by the curse which clings to wrongdoing. The grieving of Christ and the saints has its consequences in this life. And only thus could men sunk in passion and guilt be brought to repentance and amendment—which was the chief object of these sermons.

Among these preachers were Bernardino da Siena, and his two pupils, Alberto da Sarteano and Jacopo della Marca, Giovanni Capistrano, Roberto da Lecce (p. 406), and, finally, Girolamo Savonarola. No prejudice of the day was stronger than that against the mendicant friar, and this they overcame. They were criticized and ridiculed by a scornful humanism;[2] but when they raised their voices no one gave heed to the humanists. The thing was no novelty, and the scoffing Florentines had already in the fourteenth century learned to caricature it whenever it appeared in the pulpit.[3] But no sooner did Savonarola come forward than he carried the people so triumphantly with him that soon all their beloved art and culture melted away in the furnace which he lighted. Even the grossest profanation done to the cause by hypocritical monks, who got up an effect in the audience by means of confederates (p. 446), could not bring the thing itself into discredit. Men kept on laughing at the ordinary monkish sermons, with their spurious miracles

FIG. 218. STATUE OF ST
BERNARDINE
By L. Vecchietta
Narni, S. Bernardino

[1] Capistrano, for instance, contented himself with making the sign of the Cross over the thousands of sick persons brought to him, and with blessing them in the name of the Trinity and of his master S. Bernardino, after which some of them not unnaturally got well. The Brescian chronicle puts it in this way: " He worked fine miracles, yet not so many as were told of him " (Murat., xxi).

[2] So, for example, Poggio, *De Avaritia*, in the *Opera*, fol. 2. He says they had an easy matter of it, since they said the same thing in every city, and sent the people away stupid than they came. Poggio elsewhere (*Epist.*, ed. Tonelli, i, 281) speaks of Albert of Sarteano as *doctus* and *perhumanus*. Filelfo defended Bernardino da Siena and a certain Nicolaus, probably out of opposition to Poggio (*Sat.*, ii, 3; vi, 5) rather than from liking for the preachers. Filelfo was a correspondent of Albert of Sarteano. He also praises Roberto da Lecce in some respects, but blames him for not using suitable gestures and expressions, for looking miserable when he ought to look cheerful, and for weeping too much and thus offending the ears and tastes of his audience. Filelfo, *Epist.*, fol. 96b (Venet., 1502).

[3] Franco Sacchetti, *Nov.* 73. Preachers who fail are a constant subject of ridicule in all the novels.

nd manufactured relics;[1] but did not cease to honour the great and
enuine prophets. These are a true Italian specialty of the fifteenth
century.

The order—generally that of St Francis, and more particularly the so-called
Observantines—sent them out according as they were wanted. This was
commonly the case when there was some important public or private feud in
city, or some alarming outbreak of violence, immorality, or disease. When
once the reputation of a preacher was made the cities were all anxious to hear
him, even without any special occasion. He went wherever his superiors sent
him. A special form of this work was the preaching of a crusade against the
Turks;[2] but here we have to speak more particularly of the exhortations to
repentance.

The order of these, when they were treated methodically, seems to have
followed the customary list of the deadly sins. The more pressing the occasion
is, however, the more directly does the preacher make for his main point.
He begins perhaps in one of the great churches of the order, or in the cathedral.
Soon the largest *piazza* is too small for the crowds which throng from every
side to hear him, and he himself can hardly move without risking his life.[3]
The sermon is commonly followed by a great procession; but the first magistrates of the city, who take him in their midst, can hardly save him from
the multitude of women who throng to kiss his hands and feet and cut off
fragments from his cowl.[4]

The most immediate consequences which follow from the preacher's denun-
ciations of usury, luxury, and scandalous fashions are the openings of the
gaols—which meant no more than the discharge of the poorer creditors—
and the burning of various instruments of luxury and amusement, whether
innocent or not. Among these are dice, cards, games of all kinds, written
incantations,[5] masks, musical instruments, song-books, false hair, and so
forth. All these would then be gracefully arranged on a scaffold (*talamo*),
a figure of the devil fastened to the top, and then the whole set on fire
(*cf.* p. 364).

Then came the turn of the more hardened consciences. Men who had
long never been near the confessional now acknowledged their sins. Ill-gotten
gains were restored, and insults which might have borne fruit in blood retracted.

---

[1] *Cf.* the well-known story in the *Decamerone*, vi, *Nov.* 10.

[2] In which case the sermons took a special colour. See Malipiero, *Ann. Venet.*, *Archiv. Stor.*, vii, i, p. 18;
Chron. Venetum, in Murat., xxiv, col. 114; *Storia Bresciana*, in Murat., xxi, col. 898. Absolution was freely
promised to those who took part in or contributed money for the crusade.

[3] *Storia Bresciana*, in Murat., xxi, col. 865 *sqq.* On the first day 10,000 persons were present, 2000 of them
strangers.

[4] Allegretto, *Diari Sanesi*, in Murat., xxiii, col. 819 *sqq.* (July 13 to 18, 1446); the preacher was Pietro dell'
Osservanza di S. Francesco.

[5] Infessura (in Eccard, *Scriptores*, ii, col. 1874) says: " Canti, brevi, sorti." The first may refer to song-
books, which actually were burnt by Savonarola. But Graziani (*Cron. di Perugia*, *Archiv. Stor.*, xvi, i, p. 314)
says on a similar occasion, *brieve incanti*, when we must without doubt read *brevi e incanti*, and perhaps the same
emendation is desirable in Infessura [the critical edition of Tommasini reads it as *canti*.—W. G.], whose *sorti*
point to some instrument of superstition, perhaps a pack of cards for fortune-telling. Similarly after the
introduction of printing collections were made of all the attainable copies of Martial, which were then burnt.
Bandello, iii, *Nov.* 10.

Orators like Bernardino da Siena [1] entered diligently into all the details of th daily life of men, and the moral laws which are involved in it. Few theologian nowadays would feel tempted to give a morning sermon " on contracts restitutions, the public debt [*monte*], and the portioning of daughters," lik that which he once delivered in the cathedral at Florence. Imprudent speaker easily fell into the mistake of attacking particular classes, professions, o offices with such energy that the enraged hearers proceeded to violence agains those whom the preacher had denounced.[2] A sermon which Bernardino once preached in Rome (1424) had another consequence besides a bonfire o vanities on the Capitol: " after this," [3] we read, " the witch Finicella wa burnt, because by her diabolical arts she had killed many children and bewitched many other persons; and all Rome went to see the sight."

But the most important aim of the preacher was, as has been already said to reconcile enemies and persuade them to give up thoughts of vengeance Probably this end was seldom attained till toward the close of a course o sermons, when the tide of penitence flooded the city, and when the air re- sounded [4] with the cry of the whole people: " *Misericordia!* " Then followed those solemn embracings and treaties of peace which even previous bloodshed on both sides could not hinder. Banished men were recalled to the city to take part in these sacred transactions. It appears that these *paci* were on the whole faithfully observed, even after the mood which prompted them was over; and then the memory of the monk was blessed from generation to generation. But there were sometimes terrible crises like those in the families della Valle and della Croce in Rome (1482), where even the great Roberto da Lecce raised his voice in vain.[5] Shortly before Holy Week he had preached to immense crowds in the square before the Minerva. But on the night before Maunday Thursday a terrible combat took place in front of the Palazzo della Valle, near the Ghetto. In the morning Pope Sixtus gave orders for its destruction, and then performed the customary ceremonies of the day. On Good Friday Roberto preached again with a crucifix in his hand; but he and his hearers could do nothing but weep.

Violent natures, which had fallen into contradiction with themselves, often resolved to enter a convent under the impression made by these men. Among such were not only brigands and criminals of every sort, but soldiers without

---

[1] See his remarkable biography in Vespas. Fiorent., pp. 244 *sqq.*, and that by Æneas Sylvius, *De Vir. Ill.*, p. 24. In the latter we read: " Is quoque in tabella pictum nomen Jesus deferebat, hominibusque adorandum ostendebat multumque suadebat ante ostia domorum hoc nomen depingi."

[2] Allegretto, *loc. cit.*, col. 823. A preacher excited the people against the judges (if instead of *giudici* we are not to read *giudei*), upon which they narrowly escaped being burnt in their houses. The opposite party threatened the life of the preacher in return.

[3] Infessura, *loc. cit.* In the date of the witch's death there seems to be a clerical error. How the same saint caused an ill-famed wood near Arezzo to be cut down is told in Vasari, iii, 148, *Vita di Parri Spinelli.* Often, no doubt, the penitential zeal of the hearers went no further than such outward sacrifices.

[4] " Pareva che l' aria si fendesse," we read in *Storia Bresciana*, in Murat., xxi, 867.

[5] Jac. Volaterranus, in Murat., xxiii, col. 166 *sqq.* It is not expressly said that he interfered with this feud, but it can hardly be doubted that he did so. Once (1445), when Jacopo della Marca had but just quitted Perugia after an extraordinary success, a frightful *vendetta* broke out in the family of the Ranieri. *Cf.* Graziani, *loc. cit.*, pp. 565 *sqq.* We may here remark that Perugia was visited by these preachers remarkably often ; *cf.* pp. 597, 626, 631, 637, 647.

employment.[1] This resolve was stimulated by their admiration of the holy man, and by the desire to copy at least his outward position.

The concluding sermon is a general benediction, summed up in the words: " la pace sia con voi! " Throngs of hearers accompany the preacher to the next city, and there listen for a second time to the whole course of sermons.

The enormous influence exercised by these preachers made it important, both for the clergy and for the Government, at least not to have them as opponents; one means to this end was to permit only monks,[2] or priests who had received at all events the lesser consecration, to enter the pulpit, so that the order or corporation to which they belonged was, to some extent, responsible for them. But it was not easy to make the rule absolute, since the Church and pulpit had long been used as a means of publicity in many ways, judicial, educational, and other, and since even sermons were sometimes delivered by humanists and other laymen (pp. 239 sqq.). There existed, too, in Italy a dubious class of persons,[3] who were neither monks nor priests, and who yet had renounced the world—that is to say, the numerous class of hermits who appeared from time to time in the pulpit on their own authority, and often carried the people with them. A case of this kind occurred at Milan in 1516, after the second French conquest, certainly at a time when public order was much disturbed. A Tuscan hermit, Hieronymus of Siena, possibly an adherent of Savonarola, maintained his place for months together in the pulpit of the cathedral, denounced the hierarchy with great violence, caused a new chandelier and a new altar to be set up in the church, worked miracles, and abandoned the field only after a long and desperate struggle.[4] During the decades in which the fate of Italy was decided the spirit of prophecy was unusually active, and nowhere where it displayed itself was it confined to any one particular class. We know with what a tone of true prophetic defiance the hermits came forward before the sack of Rome (p. 138). In default of any eloquence of their own these men made use of messengers with symbols of one kind or another, like the ascetic near Siena (1429), who sent a " little hermit "—that is,

---

[1] Capistrano admitted fifty soldiers after one sermon, *Storia Bresciana*, *loc. cit.* Graziani, *loc. cit.*, pp. 565 *sqq.* Æneas Sylvius (*De Vir. Ill.*, p. 25), when a young man, was once so affected by a sermon of S. Bernardino as to be on the point of joining his order. We read in Graziani of a convert quitting the order; he married, " e fu maggiore ribaldo, che non era prima."

[2] That there was no want of disputes between the famous Observantine preachers and their Dominican rivals is shown by the quarrel about the blood of Christ, which was said to have fallen from the Cross to the earth (1462). See Voigt, *Enea Silvio*, iii, 591 *sqq.* Fra Jacopo della Marca, who would not yield to the Dominican Inquisitor, is criticized by Pius II in his detailed account (*Comment.*, lib. xi, p. 511) with delicate irony: " Pauperiem pati, et famem et sitim et corporis cruciatum et mortem pro Christi nomine nonnulli possunt; jacturam nominis vel minimam ferre recusant tanquam sua deficiente fama Dei quoque gloria pereat."

[3] Their reputation oscillated even then between two extremes. They must be distinguished from the hermit-monks. The line was not always clearly drawn in this respect. The Spoletans, who travelled about working miracles, took St Anthony and St Paul as their patrons, the latter on account of the snakes which they carried with them. We read of the money they got from the peasantry even in the thirteenth century by a sort of clerical conjuring. Their horses were trained to kneel down at the name of St Anthony. They pretended to collect for hospitals (Massuccio, *Nov.* 18; Bandello, iii, *Nov.* 7). Firenzuola in his *Asino d' Oro* makes them play the part of the begging priests in Apuleius.

[4] Prato, *Archiv. Stor.*, iii, p. 357; Burigozzo, *ibid.*, pp. 431 *sqq.*

a pupil—into the terrified city with a skull upon a pole, to which was attache
a paper with a threatening text from the Bible.[1]

Nor did the monks themselves scruple to attack princes, Governments, th
clergy, or even their own order. A direct exhortation to overthrow a despoti
house, like that uttered by Jacopo Bussolaro at Pavia in the fourteenth century,
hardly occurs again in the following period; but there is no want of courageou
reproofs addressed even to the Pope in his own chapel (p. 244, note 3), and o
naïve political advice given in the presence of rulers who by no means hel
themselves in need of it.[3] In the Piazza del Castello at Milan a blind preache
from the Incoronata—consequently an Augustinian—ventured in 1494 t
exhort Lodovico il Moro from the pulpit: " My lord, beware of showing th
French the way, else you will repent it." [4] There were further propheti
monks, who, without exactly preaching political sermons, drew such appallin
pictures of the future that the hearers almost lost their senses. After the electio
of Leo X in 1513 a whole association of these men, twelve Franciscan monk
in all, journeyed through the various districts of Italy, of which one or othe
was assigned to each preacher. The one who appeared in Florence,[5] Fr
Francesco di Montepulciano, struck terror into the whole people. The alarm
was not diminished by the exaggerated reports of his prophecies which reache
those who were too far off to hear him. After one of his sermons he suddenl
died " of pain in the chest." The people thronged in such numbers to kis
the feet of the corpse that it had to be secretly buried in the night. But th
newly awakened spirit of prophecy, which seized upon even women an
peasants, could not be controlled without great difficulty.

In order to restore to the people their cheerful humour, the Medici—Giuliano
Leo's brother, and Lorenzo—gave on St John's Day 1514 those splendid festivals
tournaments, processions, and hunting-parties which were attended by many dis
tinguished persons from Rome, and among them, though disguised, by no fewer tha
six cardinals.

But the greatest of the prophets and apostles had been already burnt i
Florence in 1498—Fra Giorolamo Savonarola of Ferrara. We must content
ourselves with saying a few words respecting him.[6]

[1] Allegretto, in Murat., xxiii, col. 856 sqq. The quotation was: " Ecce venio cito et velociter. Estote
parati."

[2] Matteo Villani, viii, cap. 2 sqq. He first preached against tyranny in general, and then, when the ruling
house of the Beccaria tried to have him murdered, he began to preach a change of Government and constitution,
and forced the Beccaria to fly from Pavia (1357). See Petrarch, Epist. Fam., xix, 18, and A. Hortis, Scritti
Inediti di F. P., pp. 174-181.

[3] Sometimes at critical moments the ruling house itself used the services of monks to exhort the people to
loyalty. For an instance of this kind at Ferrara see Sanudo (in Murat., xxii, col. 1218). A preacher from
Bologna reminded the people of the benefits they had received from the house of Este, and of the fate that
awaited them at the hands of the victorious Venetians.

[4] Prato, Archiv. Stor., iii, p. 251. Other fanatical anti-French preachers, who appeared after the expulsion
of the French, are mentioned by Burigozzo, ibid., pp. 443, 449, 485; ad a. 1523, 1526, 1529.

[5] Jac. Pitti, Stor. Fiorent., lib. ii, p. 112.

[6] Perrens, Jérôme Savonarole, 2 vols. Perhaps the most systematic and sober of all the many works on the
subject. P. Villari, La Storia di Girol. Savonarola (2 vols., 8vo, Firenze, Lemonnier). The view taken by the
latter writer differs considerably from that maintained in the text. Cf. Protest. Realenzyklopädie, xxiv, p. 451,
also J. Schnitzer, Savonarola (2 vols., Munich, 1924). Cf. also Ranke in Historisch-biographische Studien, pp. 181-
358 (Leipzig, 1878). On Genaz. see Villani, i, 57 sqq.; ii, 343 sqq.; Reumont, Lor. dei Medici, ii, 522-526, 533 sqq.

The instrument by means of which he transformed and ruled the city of
Florence (1494–98) was his eloquence. Of this the meagre reports that are left

FIG. 219. SAVONAROLA AS PETER THE MARTYR
By Fra Bartolommeo
Florence, Accademia

to us, which were taken down mostly on the spot, give us evidently a very imperfect notion. It was not that he possessed any striking outward advantages,
for voice, accent, and rhetorical skill constituted precisely his weakest side; and

those who required the preacher to be a stylist went to his rival, Fra Mariano da Genazzano. The eloquence of Savonarola was the expression of a lofty and commanding personality, the like of which was not seen again till the time of Luther. He himself held his own influence to be the result of a divine illumination, and could therefore without presumption assign a very high place to the office of the preacher, who, in the great hierarchy of spirits, occupied the next place below the angels.

This man, whose nature seemed made of fire, worked another and greater

FIG. 220. SAVONAROLA IN THE PULPIT
From the *Compendio di Rivelazione* (1496)

miracle than any of his oratorical triumphs. His own Dominican monastery of S. Marco, and then all the Dominican monasteries of Tuscany, became like-minded with himself, and undertook voluntarily the work of inward reform. When we reflect what the monasteries then were, and what measureless difficulty attends the least change where monks are concerned, we are doubly astonished at so complete a revolution. While the reform was still in progress large numbers of Savonarola's followers entered the order, and thereby greatly facilitated his plans. Sons of the first houses in Florence entered S. Marco as novices.

This reform of the order in a particular province was the first step to a national Church, in which, had the reformer himself lived longer, it must infallibly have ended. Savonarola, indeed, desired the regeneration of the whole Church, and near the end of his career sent pressing exhortations to the great Powers urging them to call together a Council. But in Tuscany his order and party were the only organs of his spirit—the salt of the earth—while the neighbouring provinces remained in their old condition. Fancy and sceticism tended more and more to produce in him a state of mind to which Florence appeared as the scene of the kingdom of God upon earth.

The prophecies, whose partial fulfilment conferred on Savonarola a super-natural credit, were the means by which the ever-active Italian imagination

FIG. 221. MAN AT THE PARTING-WAY BETWEEN HEAVEN AND HELL
From an edition of Savonarola's sermon on holy dying

seized control of the soundest and most cautious natures. At first the Fran-ciscans of the Osservanza, trusting in the reputation which had been bequeathed to them by S. Bernardino da Siena, fancied that they could compete with the great Dominican. They put one of their own men into the cathedral pulpit, and outbid the Jeremiads of Savonarola by still more terrible warnings, till Pietro de' Medici, who then still ruled over Florence, forced them both to be silent. Soon after, when Charles VIII came into Italy and the Medici were expelled, as Savonarola had clearly foretold, he alone was believed in.

It must be frankly confessed that he never judged his own premonition and visions critically, as he did those of others. In the funeral oration of Pico della Mirandola he deals somewhat harshly with his dead friend. Since Pico, notwithstanding an inner voice which came from God, would not enter the order he had himself prayed to God to chasten him for his disobedience. He certainly had not desired his death, and alms and prayers had obtained the favour that Pico's soul was safe in Purgatory. With regard to a comforting vision which Pico had upon his sick-bed, in which the Virgin appeared and promised him that he should not die, Savonarola confessed that he had long regarded it as a deceit of the devil, till it was revealed to him that the Madonna meant the second and eternal death.[1] If these things and the like are proof of presumption it must be admitted that this great soul at all events paid a bitter penalty for his fault. In his last days Savonarola seems to have recognized the vanity of his visions and prophecies. And yet enough inward peace was left him to enable him to meet death like a Christian. His partisans held to his doctrine and predictions for thirty years longer.

He only undertook the reorganization of the State for the reason that otherwise his enemies would have got the government into their own hands. It is unfair to judge him by the semi-democratic constitution (p. 104, note 1) of the beginning of 1495. Nor is it either better or worse than other Florentine constitutions.[2]

He was at bottom the most unsuitable man who could be found for such a work. His ideal was a theocracy in which all men were to bow in blessed humility before the Unseen, and all conflicts of passion were not even to be able to arise. His whole mind is written in that inscription on the Palazzo della Signorina, the substance of which was his maxim [3] as early as 1495, and which was solemnly renewed by his partisans in 1527: "Jesus Christus Rex populi Florentini S. P. Q. decreto creatus." He stood in no more relation to mundane affairs and their actual conditions than any other inhabitant of a monastery. Man, according to him, has only to attend to those things which make directly for his salvation.

This temper comes out clearly in his opinions on ancient literature:

> The only good thing which we owe to Plato and Aristotle is that they brought forward many arguments which we can use against the heretics. Yet they and other philosophers are now in hell. An old woman knows more about the Faith than Plato. It would be good for religion if many books that seem useful were destroyed. When there were not so many books and not so many arguments [*ragioni naturali*] and disputes religion grew more quickly than it has done since.

He wished to limit the classical instruction of the schools to Homer, Virgil, and Cicero, and to supply the rest from Jerome and Augustine. Not only Ovid and Catullus, but Terence and Tibullus, were to be banished. This may

---

[1] Sermons on Haggai; close of Sermon 6.

[2] Savonarola was perhaps the only man who could have made the subject cities free and kept Tuscany together. But he never seems to have thought of doing so. Pisa he hated like a genuine Florentine.

[3] A remarkable contrast to the Sienese, who in 1483 solemnly dedicated their distracted city to the Madonna. Allegretto, in Murat., xxiii, col. 815

be no more than the expression of a nervous morality, but elsewhere in a special work he admits that science as a whole is harmful. He holds that only a few people should have to do with it, in order that the tradition of human knowledge may not perish, and particularly that there may be no want of intellectual athletes to confute the sophisms of the heretics. For all others, grammar, morals, and religious teaching (*litteræ sacræ*) suffice. Culture and education would thus return wholly into the charge of the monks, and as, in his opinion, the " most learned and the most pious " are to rule over the states and empires, these rulers should also be monks. Whether he really foresaw this conclusion we need not inquire.

A more childish method of reasoning cannot be imagined. The simple reflection that the new-born antiquity and the boundless enlargement of human thought and knowledge which was due to it might give splendid confirmation to a religion able to adapt itself thereto seems never even to have occurred to the good man. He wanted to forbid what he could not deal with by any other means. In fact, he was anything but liberal, and was ready, for example, to send the astrologers to the same stake at which he afterward himself died.[1]

How mighty must have been the soul which dwelt side by side with this narrow intellect! And what a flame must have glowed within him

FIG. 222. THE TRIUMPH OF DEATH
From an edition of Savonarola's sermon on holy dying

before he could constrain the Florentines, possessed as they were by the passion for culture, to surrender themselves to a man who could thus reason!

How much of their heart and their worldliness they were ready to sacrifice for his sake is shown by those famous bonfires by the side of which all the *talami* of Bernardino da Siena and others were certainly of small account.

All this could not, however, be effected without the agency of a tyrannical police. He did not shrink from the most vexatious interferences with the much-prized freedom of Italian private life, using the espionage of servants on their masters as a means of carrying out his moral reforms. That transformation of public and private life which the iron Calvin was but just able to effect at Geneva with the aid of a permanent state of siege necessarily proved

[1] He says of the " impii astrologi ": " non è da disputar [con loro] altrimenti che col fuoco."

461

impossible at Florence, and the attempt served only to drive the enemies of Savonarola to a more implacable hostility. Among his most unpopular measures may be mentioned those organized parties of boys [1] who forced their way into the houses and laid violent hands on any objects which seemed suitable for the bonfire. As it happened they were sometimes sent away with a beating: they were afterward attended, in order to keep up the figment of a pious "rising generation," by a bodyguard of grown-up persons.

On the last day of the carnival in 1497, and on the same day the year after, the great *auto-da-fé* took place in the Piazza della Signoria. In the centre of it rose a great pyramidal flight of stairs like the *rogus* on which the Roman Emperors were commonly burned. On the lowest tier were arranged false beards, masks, and carnival disguises; above came volumes of the Latin and Italian poets, among others Boccaccio, the *Morgante* of Pulci, and Petrarch, partly in the form of valuable printed parchments and illuminated manuscripts; then women's ornaments and toilette articles, scents, mirrors, veils, and false hair; higher up lutes, harps, chess-boards, playing-cards; and finally, on the two uppermost tiers, paintings only, especially of female beauties, partly fancy-pictures, bearing the classical names of Lucretia, Cleopatra, or Faustina, partly portraits of the beautiful Bencina, Lena Morella, Bina, and Maria de' Lenzi; all the pictures of Bartolommeo della Porta, who brought them of his own accord; and, as it seems, some female heads—masterpieces of ancient sculptors. On the first occasion a Venetian merchant who happened to be present offered the Signoria twenty-two thousand gold florins for the objects on the pyramid; but the only answer he received was that his portrait too was taken and burned along with the rest. When the pile was lighted the Signoria appeared on the balcony, and the air echoed with song, the sound of trumpets, and the pealing of bells. The people then adjourned to the Piazza di S. Marco, where they danced round in three concentric circles. The innermost was composed of monks of the monastery, alternating with boys dressed as angels; then came young laymen and ecclesiastics; and on the outside old men, citizens, and priests, the latter crowned with wreaths of olive.[2]

All the ridicule of his victorious enemies, who in truth had no lack of justification or of talent for ridicule, was unable to discredit the memory of Savonarola. The more tragic the fortunes of Italy became, the brighter grew the halo which in the recollection of the survivors surrounded the figure of the great monk and prophet. Though his predictions may not have been confirmed in detail, the great and general calamity which he foretold was fulfilled with appalling truth.

Great, however, as the influence of all these preachers may have been, and brilliantly as Savonarola justified the claim of the monks to this office,[3] nevertheless the order as a whole could not escape the contempt and condemnation

[1 Schnitzer (*Savonarola*, i, pp. 271 *sqq.*) defends the organized parties of children and holds that the indictments were very exaggerated. The battle raged chiefly around the sodomy and gambling prevalent in Florence.—W. G.]

[2 See Villari on this point.]

[3 See the passage in the fourteenth sermon on Ezekiel, in Perrens, *op. cit.*, i, 30, note.]

of the people. Italy showed that she could give her enthusiasm only to individuals.

If, apart from all that concerns the priests and the monks, we attempt to measure the strength of the old faith, it will be found great or small according

FIG. 223. THE BURNING OF SAVONAROLA
Copy after the original painting (about 1500) by an unknown master
Florence, Museo di S. Marco

to the light in which it is considered. We have spoken already of the need felt for the Sacraments as something indispensable (pp. 121, 450). Let us now glance for a moment at the position of faith and worship in daily life. Both were determined partly by the habits of the people and partly by the policy and example of the rulers.

All that has to do with penitence and the attainment of salvation by means of good works was in much the same stage of development or corruption as in the North of Europe, both among the peasantry and among the poorer inhabitants of the cities. The instructed classes were here and there influenced by the same motives. Those sides of popular Catholicism which had their origin in the old pagan ways of addressing, rewarding, and reconciling the gods have fixed themselves ineradicably in the consciousness of the people. The eighth eclogue of Battista Mantovano,[1] which has been already quoted elsewhere, contains the prayer of a peasant to the Madonna in which she is called upon as the special patroness of all rustic and agricultural interests. And what conceptions they were which the people formed of their protectress in heaven! What was in the mind of the Florentine woman [2] who gave *ex voto* a keg of wax to the Annunziata, because her lover, a monk, had gradually emptied a barrel of wine without her absent husband finding it out! Then too, as still in our own days, different departments of human life were presided over by their respective patrons. The attempt has often been made to explain a number of the commonest rites of the Catholic Church as remnants of pagan ceremonies, and no one doubts that many local and popular usages which are associated with religious festivals are forgotten fragments of the old pre-Christian faiths of Europe. In Italy, on the contrary, we find instances in which the affiliation of the new faith with the old seems consciously recognized. So, for example, the custom of setting out food for the dead four days before the feast of the Chair of St Peter—that is to say, on February 18, the date of the ancient Feralia.[3] Many other practices of this kind may then have prevailed and have since then been extirpated. Perhaps the paradox is only apparent if we say that the popular faith in Italy had a solid foundation just in proportion as it was pagan.

The extent to which this form of belief prevailed in the upper classes can to a certain point be shown in detail. It had, as we have said in speaking of the influence of the clergy, the power of custom and early impressions on its side. The love for ecclesiastical pomp and display helped to confirm it, and now and then there came one of those epidemics of revivalism which few even among the scoffers and the sceptics were able to withstand.

But in questions of this kind it is perilous to grasp too hastily at absolute results. We might fancy, for example, that the feeling of educated men toward the relics of the saints would be a key by which some chambers of their religious consciousness might be opened. And, in fact, some difference of degree may be demonstrable, though by no means as clearly as might be wished. The Government of Venice in the fifteenth century seems to have fully shared in the reverence felt throughout the rest of Europe for the remains of the bodies

[1] With the title *De Rusticorum Religione*. See above, p. 348.

[2] Franco Sacchetti, *Nov.* 109, where there is more of the same kind.

[3] Bapt. Mantuan., *De Sacris Diebus*, lib. ii, exclaims:

> "Ista superstitio, ducens a Manibus ortum
> Tartareis, sancta de religione facessat
> Christigenûm! vivis epulas date, sacra sepultis."

A century earlier, when the army of John XXII entered the Marches to attack the Ghibellines, the pretext was avowedly *eresia* and *idolatria*. Recanati, which surrendered voluntarily, was nevertheless burnt, "because idols had been worshipped there"—in reality as a revenge for those whom the citizens had killed. Giov. Villani, ix, 139, 141. Under Pius II we read of an obstinate sun-worshipper, born at Urbino. Æneas Sylvius, *Opera*, p. 289; *Hist. Rer. ubique Gestar.*, c. 12. More wonderful still was what happened in the Forum in Rome under Leo X (more properly in the interregnum between Hadrian and Leo. June 1522, Gregorovius, viii, 388). To stay the plague a bull was solemnly offered up with pagan rites. Paul. Jovius, *Hist.*, xxi, 8.

f the saints (p. 95). Even strangers who lived in Venice found it well to dapt themselves to this superstition.[1] If we can judge of scholarly Padua

FIG. 224. THE FISHERMAN GIVING ST MARK'S RING TO THE DOGE
By Paris Bordone
Venice, Accademia

from the testimony of its topographer, Michele Savonarola (p. 157), things must have been much the same there. With a mixture of pride and pious awe Michele tells us how in times of great danger the saints were heard to sigh at

[1] See Sabellico, *De Situ Venetæ Urbis*. He mentions the names of the saints, after the manner of many philologists, without the addition of *sanctus* or *divus*, but speaks frequently of different relics, and in the most respectful tone, and even boasts that he kissed several of them.

night along the streets of the city, how the hair and nails on the corpse of a holy nun in S. Chiara kept on continually growing, and how the same corpse when any disaster was impending, used to make a noise and lift up the arms. When he sets to work to describe the chapel of St Anthony in the Santo the writer loses himself in ejaculations and fantastic dreams. In Milan the people at least showed a fanatical devotion to relics; and when once, in 1517, the monks of S. Simpliciano were careless enough to expose six holy corpses during certain alterations of the high altar, which event was followed by heavy floods of rain, the people [2] attributed the visitation to this sacrilege, and gave the monks a sound beating whenever they met them in the street. In other parts of Italy, and even in the case of the Popes themselves, the sincerity of this feeling is much more dubious, though here too a positive conclusion is hardly attainable. It is well known amid what general enthusiasm Pius II solemnly deposited the head of the Apostle Andrew, which had been brought from Greece, and then from Santa Maura, in the church of St Peter (1462); but we gather from his own narrative that he only did it from a kind of shame, as so many princes were competing for the relic. It was not till afterward that the idea struck him of making Rome the common refuge for all the remains of the saints which had been driven from their own churches.[3] Under Sixtus IV the population of the city was still more zealous in this cause than the Pope himself, and the magistracy (1483) complained bitterly that Sixtus had sent to Louis XI, the dying King of France, some specimens of the Lateran relics.[4] A courageous voice was raised about this time at Bologna, advising the sale of the skull of St Dominic to the King of Spain, and the application of the money to some useful public object.[5] But those who had the least reverence of all for the relics were the Florentines. Between the decision to honour their saint, S. Zanobi, with a new sarcophagus and the final execution of the project by Ghiberti nineteen years elapsed (1409-28), and then it happened only by chance, because the master had executed a smaller order of the same kind with great skill.[6]

Perhaps through being tricked by a cunning Neapolitan abbess (1352), who sent them a spurious arm of the patroness of the cathedral, Santa Reparata, made of wood and plaster, they began to get tired of relics.[7] Or perhaps it would be truer to say that their æsthetic sense turned them away in disgust from dismembered corpses and mouldy clothes. Or perhaps their feeling was

[1] *De Laudibus Patavii*, in Murat., xxiv, col. 1149-1151.

[2] Prato, *Archiv. Stor.*, iii, pp. 408 *sqq.* Though he is by no means a freethinker, he still protests against the causal nexus.

[3] *Pii II Comment.*, lib. viii, pp. 352 *sqq.* "Verebatur Pontifex, ne in honore tanti apostoli diminute agere videretur," etc.

[4] Jac. Volaterranus, in Murat., xxiii, col. 187. The Pope excused himself on the ground of Louis's great services to the Church, and by the example of other Popes—for example, St Gregory, who had done the like. Louis was able to pay his devotion to the relic, but died after all. The catacombs were at that time forgotten, yet even Savonarola (*loc. cit.*, col. 1150) says of Rome: "Velut ager Aceldama Sanctorum habita est,"

[5] Bursellis, *Annal. Bonon.*, in Murat., xxiii, col. 905. It was one of the sixteen patricians, Bartol. della Volta. d. 1485 or 1486.

[6] Vasari, iii, 111 *sqq.*, note, *Vita di Ghiberti*. [The above interpretation of the remissness of the Florentines is, however, in this case unjustified, as Sauer has shown in the *Lit. Rundschau*, No. 9, 1911.—W. G.]

[7] Matteo Villani, iii, 15 and 16.

ther due to that sense for glory which thought Dante and Petrarch worthier
of a splendid grave than all the twelve Apostles put together. It is probable
that throughout Italy, apart from Venice and from Rome, the condition of
which latter city was exceptional, the worship of relics had been long giving
way to the adoration of the Madonna,[1] at all events to a greater extent than
elsewhere in Europe; and in this fact lies indirect evidence of an early development of the æsthetic sense.

FIG. 225. THE MIRACLE OF THE TRUE CROSS
By Gentile Bellini
Venice, Accademia

It may be questioned whether in the North, where the vastest cathedrals
are nearly all dedicated to Our Lady, and where an extensive branch of Latin
and indigenous poetry sang the praises of the Mother of God, a greater devotion
to her was possible. In Italy, however, the number of miraculous pictures of
the Virgin was far greater, and the part they played in the daily life of the
people much more important. Every town of any size contained a quantity of
them, from the ancient, or ostensibly ancient, paintings by St Luke down to the
works of contemporaries, who not seldom lived to see the miracles wrought by

---

[1] We must make a further distinction between the Italian cultus of the bodies of historical saints of recent
date and the Northern practice of collecting bones and relics of a sacred antiquity. Such remains were preserved
in great abundance in the Lateran, which for that reason was of special importance for pilgrims. But on the
tombs of St Dominic and St Anthony of Padua rested not only the halo of sanctity, but the splendour of historical
fame.

their own handiwork. The work of art was in these cases by no means as harm‑
less as Battista Mantovano [1] thinks; sometimes it suddenly acquired a magic
virtue. The popular craving for the miraculous, especially strong in women,
may have been fully satisfied by these pictures, and for this reason the relics bee‑
less regarded. It cannot be said with certainty how far the respect for genuine
relics suffered from the ridicule which the novelists aimed at the spurious. [2]

The attitude of the educated classes toward Mariolatry is more clearly
recognizable than toward the worship of images. One cannot but be struck
with the fact that in Italian literature Dante's *Paradise* [3] is the last poem in honour
of the Virgin, while among the people hymns in her praise have been constantly
produced down to our own day. The names of Sannazaro and Sabellico [4] and
other writers of Latin poems prove little on the other side, since the object with
which they wrote was chiefly literary. The poems written in Italian in the
fifteenth [5] and at the beginning of the sixteenth century, in which we meet
with genuine religious feeling, such as the hymns of Lorenzo the Magnificent
and the sonnets of Vittoria Colonna and of Michelangelo, might have been just
as well composed by Protestants. Besides the lyrical expression of faith in
God we chiefly notice in them the sense of sin, the consciousness of deliverance
through the death of Christ, the longing for a better world. The intercession
of the Mother of God is mentioned only by the way. [6] The same phenomenon
is repeated in the classical literature of the French at the time of Louis XIV.
Not till the time of the Counter-Reformation did Mariolatry reappear in the
higher Italian poetry. Meanwhile the plastic arts had certainly done their
utmost to glorify the Madonna. It may be added that the worship of the
saints among the educated classes often took an essentially pagan form (p. 262).

We might thus critically examine the various sides of Italian Catholicism
at this period, and so establish with a certain degree of probability the attitude
of the instructed classes toward popular faith. Yet an absolute and positive
result cannot be reached. We meet with contrasts hard to explain. While
architects, painters, and sculptors were working with restless activity in and

---

[1] The remarkable judgment in his *De Sacris Diebus*, the work of his later years, refers both to sacred and
profane art (lib. i). Among the Jews, he says, there was a good reason for prohibiting all graven images, else
they would have relapsed into the idolatry or devil-worship of the nations around them:

> " Nunc autem, postquam penitus natura Satanum
> Cognita, et antiqua sine majestate relicta est,
> Nulla ferunt nobis statuæ discrimina, nullos
> Fert pictura dolos; jam sunt innoxia signa;
> Sunt modo virtutum testes monimentaque laudum
> Marmora, et æternæ decora immortalia famæ."

[2] Battista Mantovano complains of certain *nebulones* (*De Sacris Diebus*, lib. v) who would not believe in the
genuineness of the Sacred Blood at Mantua. The same criticism which called in question the *Donation of
Constantine* was also, though indirectly, hostile to the belief in relics.

[3] Especially the famous prayer of St Bernard, *Paradiso*, xxxiii, 1: " Vergine madre, figlia del tuo figlio."

[4] Perhaps we may add Pius II, whose elegy on the Virgin is printed in the *Opera*, p. 964, and who from his
youth believed himself to be under her special protection. Jac. Card. Papiens., *De Mort. Pii, Opp.*, p. 656.

[5] That is, at the time when Sixtus IV was so zealous for the Immaculate Conception. *Extravag. Commun.*,
lib. iii, tit. xii. He founded, too, the feast of the Presentation of the Virgin in the Temple, and the feasts of
St Anne and St Joseph. See Trithem., *Ann. Hirsaug.*, ii, p. 518.

[6] The few frigid sonnets of Vittoria on the Madonna are most instructive in this respect (n. 85 *sqq.*, ed.
P. Visconti, Rome, 1840).

FIG. 226. MADONNA AND SAINTS
By Mantegna
Dresden, Art Gallery

for the churches, we hear at the beginning of the sixteenth century the bitterest complaints of the neglect of public worship and of these churches themselves.

> Templa ruunt, passim sordent altaria, cultus
> Paulatim divinus abit.[1]

---

[1] Bapt. Mantuan., *De Sacris Diebus*, lib. v, and especially the speech of the younger Pico, which was intended for the Lateran Council, in Roscoe, *Leo X*, ed. Bossi, viii, p. 115. *Cf.* p. 137, note 4.

It is well known how Luther was scandalized by the irreverence with which the priests in Rome said Mass. And at the same time the feasts of the Church were celebrated with a taste and magnificence of which Northern countries had no conception. It looks as if this most imaginative of nations was easily tempted to neglect everyday things, and as easily captivated by anything extraordinary.

It is to this excess of imagination that we must attribute the epidemic religious revivals, upon which we shall again say a few words. They must be clearly distinguished from the excitement called forth by the great preachers. They were rather due to general public calamities, or to the dread of such.

In the Middle Ages all Europe was from time to time flooded by these great tides, which carried away whole peoples in their waves. The Crusades and the Flagellant revival are instances. Italy took part in both of these movements. The first great companies of Flagellants appeared, immediately after the fall of Ezzelino and his house, in the neighbourhood of the same Perugia [1] which has been already mentioned (p. 454, note 5) as the headquarters of the revivalist preachers. Then followed the Flagellants of 1310 and 1334,[2] and then the great pilgrimage without scourging in 1399, which Corio has recorded.[3] It is not impossible that the Jubilees were founded partly in order to regulate and render harmless this sinister passion for vagabondage which seized on whole populations at times of religious excitement. The great sanctuaries of Italy, such as Loreto and others, had meantime become famous, and no doubt diverted a certain part of this enthusiasm.[4]

But terrible crises had still at a much later time the power to reawaken the glow of medieval penitence, and the conscience-stricken people, often still further appalled by signs and wonders, sought to move the pity of heaven by wailings and scourgings, by fasts, processions, and moral enactments. So it was at Bologna when the plague came in 1457,[5] so in 1496 at a time of internal discord at Siena,[6] to mention two only out of countless instances. No more moving scene can be imagined than that we read of at Milan in 1529, when famine, plague, and war conspired with Spanish extortion to reduce the city to the lowest depths of despair.[7] It chanced that the monk who had the ear of

---

[1] *Monach. Paduani Chron.*, lib. iii, at the beginning, in Murat., xiv. We read there of this revival: " Invasit primitus Perusinos, Romanos postmodum, deinde fere Italiæ populos universos." Guil. Ventura (*Fragmenta de Gestis Astensium*, in *Mon. Hist. Patr. SS.*, tom. iii, col. 701) calls the Flagellant pilgrimage " admirabilis Lombardorum commotio "; hermits came forth from their cells and summoned the cities to repent.

[2] G. Villani, viii, 122; xi, 23. The former were not received in Florence, the latter were welcomed all the more readily.

[3] Corio, fol. 281. Leonardo Aretino (*Hist. Flor.*, lib. xii, at the beginning) mentions a sudden revival called forth by the processions of the *dealbati* from the Alps to Lucca, Florence, and still farther.

[4] Pilgrimages to distant places had already become very rare. Those of the princes of the house of Este to Jerusalem, St Jago, and Vienna are enumerated in Murat., xxiv, col. 182, 187, 190, 279. For that of Rinaldo Albizzi to the Holy Land see Machiavelli, *Stor. Fiorent.*, lib. v. Here too the desire for fame is sometimes the motive. The chronicler Giov. Cavalcanti (*Ist. Fiorentine*, 1838, ii, 478, ed. Polidori) says of Leonardo Fescobaldi, who wanted to go with a companion (about 1400) to the Holy Sepulchre: " Stimarono di eternarsi nella mente degli uomini futuri."

[5] Bursellis, *Annal. Bonon.*, in Murat., xxiii, col. 890.

[6] Allegretto, in Murat., xxiii, col. 855 *sqq.* The report had got about that it had rained blood outside the gate. All rushed forth, yet " gli uomini di giudizio non lo credono."

[7] Burigozzo, *Archiv. Stor.*, iii, 486. For the misery which then prevailed in Lombardy Galeazzo Capello (*De Rebus nuper in Italia Gestis*) is the best authority. Milan suffered hardly less than Rome di in the sack of 1527.

the people, Fra Tommaso Nieto, was himself a Spaniard. The Host was borne along in a novel fashion, amid barefooted crowds of old and young. It was placed on a decorated bier, which rested on the shoulders of four priests in linen garments—an imitation of the Ark of the Covenant[1] which the Children of Israel once carried round the walls of Jericho. Thus did the afflicted people of Milan remind their ancient God of His old covenant with man; and when

FIG. 227. THE MADONNA OF THE CLOAK
Plaster cast by Bernardo Rossellino (?)
Arezzo, Palazzo dei Tribunali

the procession again entered the cathedral, and it seemed as if the vast building must fall in with the agonized cry of "*Misericordia!*" many who stood there may have believed that the Almighty would indeed subvert the laws of nature and of history, and send down upon them a miraculous deliverance.

There was one Government in Italy, that of Duke Ercole I of Ferrara,[2] which assumed the direction of public feeling, and compelled the popular revivals to move in regular channels. At the time when Savonarola was powerful in Florence, and the movement which he began spread far and wide among the population of Central Italy, the people of Ferrara voluntarily entered on a general fast (at the beginning of 1496). A Lazarist announced from the pulpit the approach of a season of war and famine such as the world had never seen; but the Madonna had assured some pious people[3] that these evils might

---

[1] It was also called "l' arca del testimonio," and people told how it was "conzado [constructed] con gran misterio."   [2] *Diario Ferrarese*, in Murat., xxiv, col. 317, 322, 323, 326, 386, 401.

[3] "Ad uno santo homo o santa donna," says the chronicle. Married men were forbidden to keep concubines.

471

be avoided by fasting. Upon this, the Court itself had no choice but to fast, but it took the conduct of the public devotions into its own hands. On Easter Day, April 3, a proclamation on morals and religion was published, forbidding blasphemy, prohibiting games, sodomy, concubinage, the letting of houses to prostitutes or panders, and the opening of all shops on feast-days, excepting those of the bakers and greengrocers. The Jews and Moors, who had taken refuge from the Spaniards at Ferrara, were now compelled again to wear the yellow O upon the breast. Contraveners were threatened not only with the punishments already provided by law, but also " with such severer penalties as the Duke might think good to inflict," of which one-fourth in case of a pecuniary fine was to be paid to the Duke, and the other three-fourths were to go to some public institution. After this the Duke and the Court went several days in succession to hear sermons in church, and on April 10 all the Jews in Ferrara were compelled to do the same.[1] On May 3 the director of police—that Zampante who has been already alluded to (pp. 70–71)—sent the crier to announce that whoever had given money to the police-officers in order not to be informed against as a blasphemer might, if he came forward, have it back with a further indemnification. These wicked officers, he said, had extorted as much as two or three ducats from innocent persons by threatening to lodge an information against them. They had then mutually informed against one another, and so had all found their way into prison. But as the money had been paid precisely in order not to have to do with Zampante it is probable that his proclamation induced few people to come forward. In 1500, after the fall of Lodovico il Moro, when a similar outbreak of popular feeling took place, Ercole [2] ordered a series of nine processions, in which there were four thousand children dressed in white, bearing the standard of Jesus. He himself rode on horseback, as he could not walk without difficulty. An edict was afterward published of the same kind as that of 1496. It is well known how many churches and monasteries were built by this ruler. He even sent for a live saint, the Suor Colomba,[3] shortly before he married his son Alfonso to Lucrezia Borgia (1502). A special messenger [4] fetched the saint with fifteen other nuns from Viterbo, and the Duke himself conducted her on her arrival at Ferrara into a convent prepared for her reception. We shall probably do him no injustice if we attribute all these measures very largely to political calculation. To the conception of government formed by the house of Este, as indicated above (pp. 66 sqq.), this employment of religion for the ends of statecraft belongs by a kind of logical necessity.

---

[1] The sermon was especially addressed to them; after it a Jew was baptized, " ma non di quelli," adds the annalist, " che erano stati a udire la predica."

[2] " Per buono rispetto a lui noto e perchè sempre è buono a star bene con Iddio," says the annalist. After describing the arrangements he adds resignedly: " La cagione perchè sia fatto et si habbia a fare non s' intende, basta che ogni bene è bene."

[3] It cannot have been Suor Colomba, since she had died on May 20, 1501. It was probably Lucia da Narni.—L. G.]

[4] He is called " Messo del Cancellieri del Duca." The whole thing was evidently intended to appear the work of the Court only, and not of any ecclesiastical authority.

CHAPTER III

RELIGION AND THE SPIRIT OF THE RENAISSANCE

BUT in order to reach a definite conclusion with regard to the religious sense of the men of this period we must adopt a different method. From their intellectual attitude in general we can infer their relation both to the divine idea and to the existing religion of their age.

These modern men, the representatives of the culture of Italy, were born with the same religious instincts as other medieval Europeans. But their powerful individuality made them in religion, as in other matters, altogether subjective, and the intense charm which the discovery of the inner and outer universe exercised upon them rendered them markedly worldly. In the rest of Europe religion remained, till a much later period, something given from without, and in practical life egoism and sensuality alternated with devotion and repentance. The latter had no spiritual competitors, as in Italy, or only to a far smaller extent.

Further, the close and frequent relations of Italy with Byzantium and the Mohammedan peoples had produced a dispassionate tolerance which weakened the ethnographical conception of a privileged Christendom. And when classical antiquity with its men and institutions became an ideal of life, as well as the greatest of historical memories, ancient speculation and scepticism obtained in many cases a complete mastery over the minds of Italians.

Since, again, the Italians were the first modern people of Europe who gave themselves boldly to speculations on freedom and necessity, and since they did so under violent and lawless political circumstances, in which evil seemed often to win a splendid and lasting victory, their belief in God began to waver, and their view of the government of the world became fatalistic. And when their passionate natures refused to rest in the sense of uncertainty they made a shift to help themselves out with ancient Oriental or medieval superstition. They took to astrology and magic.

Finally these intellectual giants, these representatives of the Renaissance, show, in respect to religion, a quality which is common in youthful natures. Distinguishing keenly between good and evil, they yet are conscious of no sin. Every disturbance of their inward harmony they feel themselves able to make good out of the plastic resources of their own nature, and therefore they feel no repentance. The need of salvation thus becomes felt more and more dimly, while the ambitions and the intellectual activity of the present either shut out altogether every thought of a world to come, or else cause it to assume a poetic instead of a dogmatic form.

When we look on all this as pervaded and often perverted by the all-powerful Italian imagination we obtain a picture of that time which is certainly more in accordance with truth than are vague declamations against modern paganism. And closer investigation often reveals to us that underneath this outward shell much genuine religion could still survive.

The fuller discussion of these points must be limited to a few of the most essential explanations.

That religion should again become an affair of the individual and of his own personal feeling was inevitable when the Church became corrupt in doctrine and tyrannous in practice, and is a proof that the European mind was still alive. It is true that this showed itself in many different ways. While the mystical and ascetical sects of the North lost no time in creating new outward forms for their new modes of thought and feeling, each individual in Italy went his own way, and thousands wandered on the sea of life without any religious guidance whatever. All the more must we admire those who attained and held fast to a personal religion. They were not to blame for being unable to have any part or lot in the old Church, as she then was; nor would it be reasonable to expect that they should all of them go through that mighty spiritual labour which was appointed to the German Reformers. The form and aim of this personal faith, as it showed itself in the better minds, will be set forth at the close of our work.

The worldliness, through which the Renaissance seems to offer so striking a contrast to the Middle Ages, owed its first origin to the flood of new thoughts, purposes, and views which transformed the medieval conception of nature and man. This spirit is not in itself more hostile to religion than that ' culture ' which now holds its place, but which can give us only a feeble notion of the universal ferment which the discovery of a new world of greatness then called forth. This worldliness was not frivolous, but earnest, and was ennobled by art and poetry. It is a lofty necessity of the modern spirit that this attitude, once gained, can never again be lost, that an irresistible impulse forces us to the investigation of men and things, and that we must hold this inquiry to be our proper end and work.[1] How soon and by what paths this search will lead us back to God, and in what ways the religious temper of the individual will be affected by it, are questions which cannot be met by any general answer. The Middle Ages, which spared themselves the trouble of induction and free inquiry, can have no right to impose upon us their dogmatical verdict in a matter of such vast importance.

To the study of man, among many other causes, was due the tolerance and indifference with which the Mohammedan religion was regarded. The knowledge and admiration of the remarkable civilization which Islam, particularly before the Mongol inundation, had attained was peculiar to Italy from the time

[1] See the quotations from Pico's *Discourse on the Dignity of Man* above, pp. 351, 352.

of the Crusades. This sympathy was fostered by the half-Mohammedan Government of some Italian princes, by dislike and even contempt for the existing Church, and by constant commercial intercourse with the harbours of the Eastern and Southern Mediterranean.[1] It can be shown that in the thirteenth century the Italians recognized a Mohammedan ideal of nobleness, dignity, and pride, which they loved to connect with the person of a sultan. A Mameluke sultan is commonly meant; if any name is mentioned it is the name of Saladin.[2] Even the Osmanli Turks, whose destructive tendencies were no secret, gave the Italians, as we have shown above (pp. 110 *sqq*.), only half a fright, and a peaceable accord with them was looked upon as no impossibility. Along with this tolerance, however, appeared the bitterest religious opposition to Mohammedanism; the clergy, says Filelfo, should come forward against it, since it prevailed over a great part of the world and was more dangerous to Christendom than Judaism was;[3] along with the readiness to compromise with the Turks appeared the passionate desire for a war against them which possessed Pius II during the whole of his pontificate, and which many of the humanists expressed in highflown declamations.

The truest and most characteristic expression of this religious indifference is the famous story of the *Three Rings*, which Lessing has put into the mouth of his Nathan, after it had been already told centuries earlier, though with some reserve, in the *Hundred Old Tales* (*Nov*. 72 or 73) and more boldly in Boccaccio.[4] In what language and in what corner of the Mediterranean it was first told can never be known; most likely the original was much more plainspoken than the two Italian adaptations. The religious postulate on which it rests—namely, deism—will be discussed later on in its wider significance for this period. The same idea is repeated, though in a clumsy caricature, in the famous proverb of the " three who have deceived the world—that is, Moses, Christ, and Mohammed."[5] If the Emperor Frederick II, in whom this saying is said to have originated, really thought so he probably expressed himself with more wit. Ideas of the same kind were also current in Islam.

[1] Not to speak of the fact that a similar tolerance or indifference was not uncommon among the Arabians themselves.

[2] So in the *Decamerone*. Sultans without name in Massuccio, *Nov*. 46, 48, 49: one called " Rè di Fes," another " Rè di Tunisi." In the *Commento di Dante*, i, 293, Boccaccio praises the Saladin, and in the *Dittamondo* of Fazio degli Uberti, ii, 25, we read, " il buono Saladin." For the Venetian alliance with the Sultan of Egypt in 1202 see G. Hanotaux in the *Revue Historique*, iv, pp. 74–102 (1877). There were naturally also many attacks on Mohammedanism. For the Turkish woman baptized first in Venice and again in Rome see Cecchetti, i, 487.

[3] *Philelphi Epistolæ*, fol. 90*b sqq*. (Venet., 1502).

[4] *Decamerone*, i, *Nov*. 3. Boccaccio is the first to name the Christian religion, which the others do not. For an old French authority of the thirteenth century see Tobler, *Li di dou Vrai Aniel* (Leipzig, 1871). For the Hebrew story of Abr. Abulafia (b. 1241 in Spain, came to Italy about 1290, in the hope of converting the Pope to Judaism), in which two servants claim each to hold the jewel buried for the son, see Steinschneider, *Polem. und Apol. Lit. der Arab. Sprache*, pp. 319 and 360. From these and other sources we conclude that the story originally was less definite than as we now have it (in Abulafia, for example, it is used polemically against the Christians), and that the doctrine of the equality of the three religions is a later addition. *Cf*. Reuter, *Gesch. der Relig. Aufklärung im M. A.*, iii, 302 *sqq*., 390 (Berlin, 1877).

[5] *De Tribus Impostoribus*, the name of a work attributed to Frederick II among many other people, and which by no means answers the expectations raised by the title. Latest edition by Weller, Heilbronn, 1876. The nationality of the author and the date of composition are both disputed. See Reuter, *op. cit.*, ii, 273–302.

At the height of the Renaissance, toward the close of the fifteenth century, Luigi Pulci offers us an example of the same mode of thought in the *Morgante Maggiore*. The imaginary world of which his story treats is divided, as in all heroic poems of romance, into a Christian and a Mohammedan camp. In accordance with the medieval temper, the victory of the Christian and the final reconciliation among the combatants was attended by the baptism of the defeated Islamites, and the *improvisatori*, who preceded Pulci in the treatment of these subjects, must have made free use of this stock incident. It was Pulci's object to parody his predecessors, particularly the worst among them, and this he does by those appeals to God, Christ, and the Madonna with which each canto begins; and still more clearly by the sudden conversions and baptisms, the utter senselessness of which must have struck every reader or hearer. This ridicule leads him, further, to the confession of his faith in the relative goodness of all religions,[1] which faith, notwithstanding his professions of orthodoxy,[2] rests on an essentially theistic basis. In another point too he departs widely from medieval conceptions. The alternatives in past centuries were Christian, or else pagan and Mohammedan; orthodox believer or heretic. Pulci draws a picture of the giant Margutte,[3] who, disregarding each and every religion, jovially confesses to every form of vice and sensuality, and reserves to himself only the merit of having never broken faith. Perhaps the poet intended to make something of this—in his way—honest monster, possibly to have led him into virtuous paths by Morgante, but he soon got tired of his own creation, and in the next canto brought him to a comic end.[4] Margutte had been brought forward as a proof of Pulci's frivolity; but he is needed to complete the picture of the poetry of the fifteenth century. It was natural that it should somewhere present in grotesque proportions the figure of an untamed egoism, insensible to all established rule, and yet with a remnant of honourable feeling left. In other poems sentiments are put into the mouths of giants, fiends, infidels, and Mohammedans which no Christian knight would venture to utter.

Antiquity exercised an influence of another kind than that of Islam, and this not through its religion, which was but too much like the Catholicism of this period, but through its philosophy. Ancient literature, now worshipped as something incomparable, is full of the victory of philosophy over religious tradition. An endless number of systems and fragments of systems were suddenly presented to the Italian mind, not as curiosities or even as heresies, but almost with the authority of dogmas, which had now to be reconciled rather than discriminated. In nearly all these various opinions and doctrines a certain kind of belief in God was implied; but taken altogether they formed a marked contrast to the Christian faith in a divine government of the world. And there

---

[1] In the mouth, nevertheless, of the fiend Astarotte, canto xxv, str. 231 *sqq.* *Cf.* str. 141 *sqq.*
[2] Canto xxviii, str. 38 *sqq.*
[3] Canto xviii, str. 112 to the end.
[4] Pulci touches, though hastily, on a similar conception in his Prince Chiaristante (canto xxi, str. 101 *sqq.*, 121 *sqq.*, 145 *sqq.*, 163 *sqq.*), who believes nothing and causes himself and his wife to be worshipped. We are reminded of Sigismondo Malatesta (p. 235).

was one central question, which medieval theology had striven in vain to solve, and which now urgently demanded an answer from the wisdom of the ancients —namely, the relation of Providence to the freedom or necessity of the human will. To write the history of this question even superficially from the fourteenth century onward would require a whole volume. A few hints must suffice here.

If we take Dante and his contemporaries as evidence we shall find that ancient philosophy first came into contact with Italian life in the form which offered the most marked contrast to Christianity—that is to say, Epicureanism. The writings of Epicurus were no longer preserved, and even at the close of the classical age a more or less one-sided conception of his philosophy had been formed. Nevertheless, that phase of Epicureanism which can be studied in Lucretius,[1] and especially in Cicero, is quite sufficient to make men familiar with a godless universe. To what extent his teaching was actually understood, and whether the name of the problematic Greek sage was not rather a catchword for the multitude, it is hard to say. It is probable that the Dominican Inquisition used it against men who could not be reached by a more definite accusation. In the case of sceptics born before the time was ripe, whom it was yet hard to convict of positive heretical utterances, a moderate degree of luxurious living may have sufficed to provoke the charge. The word is used in this conventional sense by Giovanni Villani [2] when he explains the Florentine fires of 1115 and 1117 as a divine judgment on heresies, among others, "on the luxurious and gluttonous sect of Epicureans." The same writer says of Manfred: "His life was Epicurean, since he believed neither in God, nor in the saints, but only in bodily pleasure."

Dante speaks still more clearly in the ninth and tenth cantos of the *Inferno*. That terrible fiery field covered with half-opened tombs, from which issued cries of hopeless agony, was peopled by the two great classes of those whom the Church had vanquished or expelled in the thirteenth century. The one were heretics who opposed the Church by deliberately spreading false doctrine; the other were Epicureans, and their sin against the Church lay in their general disposition, which was summed up in the belief that the soul dies with the body.[3] The Church was well aware that this one doctrine, if it gained ground, must be more ruinous to her authority than all the teachings of the Manichæans and Paterini, since it took away all reason for her interference in the affairs of men after death. That the means which she used in her struggles were precisely what had driven the most gifted natures to unbelief and despair was what she naturally would not herself admit.

[1] His work was first made known by Poggio.

[2] Giov. Villani, iv, 29; vi, 46. The name occurs as early as 1150 in Northern countries, but only in the conventional sense. It is defined by William of Malmesbury (iii, 237, ed. London, 1840): "Epicureorum . . . qui opinantur animam corpore solutam in ærem evanescere, in auras effluere."

[3] See the argument in the third book of Lucretius. The name of Epicurean was afterward used as synonymous with freethinker. Lorenzo Valla (*Opp.*, 795 *sqq.*) speaks as follows of Epicurus: "Quis eo parcior, quis contentior, quis modestior, et quidem in nullo philosophorum omnium minus invenio fuisse vitiorum, plurimique honesti viri cum Græcorum, tum Romanorum, Epicurei fuerunt." Valla was defending himself to Eugenius IV against the attacks of Fra Antonio da Bitonto and others.

Dante's loathing of Epicurus, or of what he took to be his doctrine, was certainly sincere. The poet of the life to come could not but detest the denier of immortality; and a world neither made nor ruled by God, no less than the vulgar objects of earthly life which the system appeared to countenance, could not but be intensely repugnant to a nature like his. But if we look closer we find that certain doctrines of the ancients made even on him an impression which forced the Biblical doctrine of the divine government into the background, unless, indeed, it was his own reflection, the influence of opinions then prevalent, or loathing for the injustice that seemed to rule this world, which made him give up the belief in a special Providence.[1] His God leaves all the details of the world's government to a deputy, Fortune, whose sole work it is to change and change again all earthly things, and who can disregard the wailings of men in unalterable beatitude.[2] Nevertheless, Dante does not for a moment loose his hold on the moral responsibility of man; he believes in free will.

The belief in the freedom of the will, in the popular sense of the words, has always prevailed in Western countries. At all times men have been held responsible for their actions, as though this freedom were a matter of course. The case is otherwise with the religious and philosophical doctrine, which labours under the difficulty of harmonizing the nature of the will with the laws of the universe at large. We have here to do with a question of more or less, which every moral estimate must take into account. Dante is not wholly free from those astrological superstitions which illumined the horizon of his time with deceptive light, but they do not hinder him from rising to a worthy conception of human nature. " The stars," he makes his Marco Lombardo say,[3] " give the first impulse to your actions," but

> Light has been given you for good and evil
> And free volition; which, if some fatigue
> In the first battles with the heavens it suffers,
> Afterward conquers all, if well 'tis nurtured.

Others might seek the necessity which annulled human freedom in another power than the stars, but the question was henceforth an open and inevitable one. So far as it was a question for the schools or the pursuit of isolated thinkers its treatment belongs to the historian of philosophy. But inasmuch as it entered into the consciousness of a wider public it is necessary for us to say a few words respecting it.

The fourteenth century was chiefly stimulated by the writings of Cicero, who, though in fact an eclectic, yet, by his habit of setting forth the opinions of different schools without coming to a decision between them, exercised the influence of a sceptic. Next in importance came Seneca, and the few works of Aristotle which had been translated into Latin. The immediate fruit of these

---

[1] *Inferno*, vii, 67–69.

[2 This interpretation by Burckhardt of Dante's Fortune is strongly contested. *Cf.* F. d' Ovidio, *Dante e la Magia* in the *Nuova Antologia*, third series, vol. 41, pp. 193–226; also Doren, *Die Fortuna im Mittelalter und in der Renaiss., Vorträge der Bibl. Warburg*, 1922–23, i, pp. 98 *sqq.*—W. G.]

[3] *Purgatorio*, xvi, 73. *Cf.* the theory of the influence of the planets in the *Convivio*. Even the fiend Astarotte in Pulci (*Morgante*, xxv, str. 150) attests the freedom of the human will and the justice of God.

studies was the capacity to reflect on great subjects, if not in direct opposition to the authority of the Church, at all events independently of it.[1]

In the course of the fifteenth century the works of antiquity were discovered and diffused with extraordinary rapidity. All the writings of the Greek philosophers which we ourselves possess were now, at least in the form of Latin translations, in everybody's hands. It is a curious fact that some of the most zealous apostles of this new culture were men of the strictest piety, or even ascetics (p. 273). Fra Ambrogio Camaldolese, as a spiritual dignitary chiefly occupied with ecclesiastical affairs, and as a literary man with the translation of the Greek Fathers of the Church, could not repress the humanistic impulse, and at the request of Cosimo de' Medici undertook to translate Diogenes Laertius into Latin.[2] His contemporaries, Niccolò Niccoli, Giannozzo Manetti, Donato Acciajuoli, and Pope Nicholas V,[3] united to a many-sided humanism profound Biblical scholarship and deep piety. In Vittorino da Feltre the same temper has been already noticed (pp. 220 *sqq.*). The same Matthew Vegio who added a thirteenth book to the *Æneid* had an enthusiasm for the memory of St Augustine and his mother Monica which cannot have been without a deeper influence upon him. The result of all these tendencies was that the Platonic Academy at Florence deliberately chose for its object the reconciliation of the spirit of antiquity with that of Christianity. It was a remarkable oasis in the humanism of the period.[4]

This humanism was, in fact, pagan, and became more and more so as its sphere widened in the fifteenth century. Its representatives, whom we have already described as the advance guard of an unbridled individualism, display as a rule such a character that even their religion, which is sometimes professed very definitely, becomes a matter of indifference to us. They easily got the name of atheists if they showed themselves indifferent to religion, and spoke freely against the Church; but not one of them ever professed, or dared to profess, a formal philosophical atheism.[5] If they sought for any leading principle it must have been a kind of superficial rationalism—a careless inference from the many and contradictory opinions of antiquity with which they busied themselves, and from the discredit into which the Church and her doctrines had fallen. This was the sort of reasoning which was near bringing Galeottus Martius[6] to the stake, had not his former pupil, Pope Sixtus IV, perhaps at

---

[1 This is, however, more especially true with reference to the authority of the Bible and the Church Fathers.—L. G.]

[2] *Cf.* Voigt, *Wiederbelebung*, 165–170. [It seems, however, more probable that he began his translation on his own initiative. *Cf.* Luiso, *Riv. delle Bibliot.*, vols. 8–10.—W. G.]

[3] Vespas. Fiorent., pp. 26, 320, 435, 626, 651; Murat., xx, col. 532.

[4] In Platina's introduction to his life of Christ the religious influence of the Renaissance is curiously exemplified (*Vita Paparum*, at the beginning); Christ, he says, fully attained the fourfold Platonic *nobilitas* according to his *genus*: " quem enim ex gentilibus habemus qui gloria et nomine cum David et Salomone, quique sapientia et doctrina cum Christo ipso conferri merito debeat et possit? " Judaism, like classical antiquity, was also explained on a Christian hypothesis. Pico and Pietro Galatino endeavoured to show that Christian doctrine was foreshadowed in the Talmud and other Jewish writings.

[5] On Pomponazzo see the special works; among others, Ritter, *Geschichte der Philosophie*, Bd. ix.

[6] Paul. Jovius, *Elog. Lit.*, p. 90. Galeottus Martius was, however, compelled to recant publicly. His letter to Lorenzo (May 17, 1478) begging him to intercede with the Pope, " satis enim pœnarum dedi," is given by Malagola, *Codro Urceo*, p. 433.

the request of Lorenzo de' Medici, saved him from the hands of the Inquisition. Galeotto had ventured to write that the man who walked uprightly, and acted according to the natural law born within him, would go to heaven, whatever nation he belonged to.

Let us take, by way of example, the religious attitude of one of the smaller men in the great army. Codrus Urceus [1] was first the tutor of the last Ordelaffo, Prince of Forlì, and afterward for many years professor at Bologna. Against the Church and the monks his language is as abusive as that of the rest. His tone in general is reckless to the last degree, and he constantly introduces himself in all his local history and gossip. But he knows how to speak to edification of the true God-man, Jesus Christ, and to commend himself by letter to the prayers of a saintly priest.[2] On one occasion, after enumerating the follies of the pagan religions, he thus goes on: " Our theologians, too, fight and quarrel *de lana caprina*, about the Immaculate Conception, Antichrist, Sacraments, Predestination, and other things, which were better let alone than talked of publicly." Once, when he was not at home, his room and manuscripts were burnt. When he heard the news he stood opposite a figure of the Madonna in the street and cried to it: " Listen to what I tell you; I am not mad, I am saying what I mean. If I ever call upon you in the hour of my death, you need not hear me or take me among your own, for I will go and spend eternity with the devil." [3] After which speech he found it desirable to spend six months in retirement at the house of a wood-cutter. With all this he was so superstitious that prodigies and omens gave him incessant frights, leaving him no belief to spare for the immortality of the soul. When his hearers questioned him on the matter he answered that no one knew what became of a man, of his soul or his body, after death, and the talk about another life was only fit to frighten old women. But when he came to die he commended in his will his soul or his spirit [4] to Almighty God, exhorted his weeping pupils to fear the Lord, and especially to believe in immortality and future retribution, and received the Sacrament with much fervour. We have no guarantee that more famous men in the same calling, however significant their opinions may be, were in practical life any more consistent. It is probable that most of them wavered inwardly between incredulity and a remnant of the faith in which they were brought up, and outwardly held for prudential reasons to the Church.

Through the connexion of rationalism with the newly born science of historical investigation, some timid attempts at Biblical criticism may here and

---

[1] *Codri Urcei Opera*, with his life by Bart. Bianchini; and in his philological lectures, pp. 65, 151, 278, etc.

[2] On one occasion he says, *In Laudem Christi*:

" Phœbum alii vates musasque Jovemque sequuntur,
    At mihi pro vero nomine Christus erit."

He also (fol. x*b*) attacks the Bohemians. Huss and Jerome of Prague are defended by Poggio in his famous letter to Leonardo Aretino, and placed on a level with Mucius Scævola and Socrates.

[3] "Audi virgo ea quæ tibi mentis compos et ex animo dicam. Si forte cum ad ultimum vitæ finem pervenero supplex accedam ad te spem oratum, ne me audias neve inter tuos accipias oro; cum infernis diis in æternum vitam degere decrevi."

[4] "Animum meum seu animam"—a distinction by which philology used then to perplex theology.

there have been made. A saying of Pius II [1] has been recorded, which seems intended to prepare the way for such criticism: " Even if Christianity were not confirmed by miracles, it ought still to be accepted on account of its morality." When Lorenzo Valla calls Moses and the Evangelists historians he does not seek to diminish their dignity and reputation, but is nevertheless conscious that in these words lies as decided a contradiction to the traditional view taken by the Church as in the denial that the Apostles' Creed was the work of all the Apostles, or that the letter of Abgarus to Christ was genuine.[2] The legends of the Church, in so far as they contained arbitrary versions of the Biblical miracles, were freely ridiculed,[3] and this reacted on the religious sense of the people. Where Judaizing heretics are mentioned we must understand chiefly those who denied the divinity of Christ, which was probably the offence for which Giorgio da Novara was burnt at Bologna about 1500.[4] But again at Bologna in 1497 the Dominican Inquisitor was forced to let the physician Gabrielle da Salò, who had powerful patrons, escape with a simple expression of penitence,[5] although he was in the habit of maintaining that Christ was not God, but son of Joseph and Mary, and conceived in the usual way; that by His cunning He had deceived the world to its ruin; that He may have died on the Cross on account of crimes which He had committed; that His religion would soon come to an end; that His Body was not really contained in the Sacrament, and that He performed His miracles not through any divine power, but through the influence of the heavenly bodies. This latter statement is most characteristic of the time—Faith is gone, but magic still holds its ground.[6]

A worse fate befell a canon of Bergamo, Zanino de Solcia, a few years earlier (1459), who had asserted that Christ did not suffer from love to man, but under the influence of the stars, and who advanced other curious scientific and moral ideas. He was forced to abjure his errors, and paid for them by perpetual imprisonment.[7]

With respect to the moral government of the world, the humanists seldom get beyond a cold and resigned consideration of the prevalent violence and misrule. In this mood the many works *On Fate*, or whatever name they bear, are written. They tell of the turning of the wheel of Fortune, and of the instability of earthly, especially political, things. Providence is only brought

---

[1] Platina, *Vitæ Pontiff.*, p. 311: " Christianam fidem si miraculis non esset confirmata, honestate sua recipi debuisse." It may be questioned whether all that Platina attributes to the Pope is, in fact, authentic.

[2] Preface to the *Historia Ferdinandi I* (*Hist. Ztschr.*, Bd. xxxiii, p. 61) and *Antid. in Pogg.*, lib. iv, *Opp.*, pp. 256 sqq. Pontanus (*De Sermone*, i, 18) says that Valla did not hesitate " dicere profiterique palam habere se quoque in Christum spicula." Pontanus, however, was a friend of Valla's enemies at Naples.

[3] Especially when the monks improvised them in the pulpit. But the old and recognized miracles did not remain unassailed. Firenzuola (*Opere*, vol. ii, p. 208, in the tenth novel) ridicules the Franciscans of Novara, who wanted to spend money which they had embezzled in adding a chapel to their church, " dove fusse dipinta quella bella storia, quando S. Francesco predicava agli uccelli nel deserto; e quando ei fece la santa zuppa, e che l' agnolo Gabriello gli portò i zoccoli."

[4] Some facts about him are to be found in Bapt. Mantuan., *De Patientia*, lib. iii, cap. 13.

[5] Bursellis, *Annal. Bonon.*, in Murat., xxiii, col. 915.

[6] How far these blasphemous utterances sometimes went has been shown by Gieseler (*Kirchengeschichte*, ii, iv, § 154, Anm.), who quotes several striking instances.

[7] Voigt, *Enea Silvio*, iii, 581. It is not known what happened to the Bishop Petro of Aranda, who (1500) denied the divinity of Christ and the existence of Hell and Purgatory, and denounced indulgences as a device of the Popes invented for their private advantage. For him see *Burchardi Diarium*, pp. 63 sqq. (ed. Leibnitz).

481

in because the writers would still be ashamed of undisguised fatalism, of the avowal of their ignorance, or of useless complaints. Gioviano Pontano [1] ingeniously illustrates the nature of that mysterious something which men call Fortune by a hundred incidents, most of which belonged to his own experience. The subject is treated more humorously by Æneas Sylvius, in the form of a vision seen in a dream. [2] The aim of Poggio, on the other hand, in a work written in his old age, [3] is to represent the world as a vale of tears, and to fix the happiness of various classes as low as possible. This tone became the prevalent one in the future. Distinguished men drew up a debit and credit of the happiness and unhappiness of their lives, and generally found that the latter outweighed the former. The fate of Italy and the Italians, so far as it could be told in 1510, has been described with dignity and an almost elegiac pathos by Tristano Caracciolo. [4] Applying this general tone of feeling to the humanists themselves, Pierio Valeriano afterward composed his famous treatise (pp. 275–276). Some of these themes, such as the fortunes of Leo, were most suggestive. All the good that can be said of him politically has been briefly and admirably summed up by Francesco Vettori; the picture of Leo's pleasures is given by Paolo Giovio and in the anonymous biography; [5] and the shadows which attended his prosperity are drawn with inexorable truth by the same Pierio Valeriano.

We cannot, on the other hand, read without a kind of awe how men sometimes boasted of their fortune in public inscriptions. Giovanni II Bentivoglio, ruler of Bologna, ventured to carve in stone on the newly built tower by his palace that his merit and his fortune had given him richly of all that could be desired [6]—and this a few years before his expulsion. The ancients, when they spoke in this tone, had nevertheless a sense of the envy of the gods. In Italy it was probably the *condottieri* (p. 40) who first ventured to boast so loudly of their fortune.

But the way in which resuscitated antiquity affected religion most powerfully was not through any doctrines or philosophical system, but through a general tendency which it fostered. The men, and in some respects the institutions, of antiquity were preferred to those of the Middle Ages, and in the eager attempt to imitate and reproduce them religion was left to take care of itself. All was absorbed in the admiration for historical greatness (Part II, Chapter III, and above, *passim*). To this the philologians added many special follies of their own, by which they became the mark for general attention. How far

---

[1] Jov. Pontan., *De Fortuna, Opp.*, i, 792–921. Cf. *Opp.*, ii, 286.

[2] Æneas Sylvius, *Opera*, p. 611.   [3] Poggius, *De Miseriis Humanæ Conditionis*.

[4] Caracciolo, *De Varietate Fortunæ*, in Murat., xxii, one of the most valuable writings of a period rich in such works. On Fortune in public processions see p. 417.

[5] *Leonis X Vita Anonyma*, in Roscoe, ed. Bossi, xii, p. 153.

[6] Bursellis, *Annal. Bonon.*, in Murat., xxiii, col. 909: "Monimentum hoc conditum a Joanne Bentivolo secundo patriæ rectore, cui virtus et fortuna cuncta quæ optari possunt bona affatim præstiterunt." It is still not quite certain whether this inscription was outside, and visible to everybody, or, like another mentioned just before, hidden on one of the foundation-stones. In the latter case a fresh idea is involved. By this secret inscription, which perhaps only the chronicler knew of, Fortune is to be magically bound to the building.

[According to the words of the chronicle, the inscription cannot have stood on the walls of the newly built tower. The exact spot is uncertain.—L. G.]

Paul II was justified in calling his abbreviators and their friends to account for their paganism is certainly a matter of great doubt, as his biographer and chief victim, Platina (pp. 236, 326), has shown a masterly skill in explaining his vindictiveness on other grounds, and especially in making him cut a ludicrous figure. The charges of infidelity, paganism,[1] denial of immortality, and so forth were not made against the accused till the charge of high treason had broken down. Paul, indeed, if we are correctly informed about him, was by no means the man to judge of intellectual things. He knew little Latin, and spoke Italian at consistories and in diplomatic negotiations. It was he who exhorted the Romans to teach their children nothing beyond reading and writing. His priestly narrowness of view reminds us of Savonarola (pp. 460–461), with the difference that Paul might fairly have been told that he and his like were in great part to blame if culture made men hostile to religion. It cannot, nevertheless, be doubted that he felt a real anxiety about the pagan tendencies which surrounded him. And what, in truth, may not the humanists have allowed themselves at the Court of the profligate pagan Sigismondo Malatesta? How far these men, destitute for the most part of fixed principle, ventured to go depended assuredly on the sort of influences they were exposed to. Nor could they treat of Christianity without paganizing it (Part III, Chapter X). It is curious, for instance, to notice how far Gioviano Pontano carried this confusion. He speaks of a saint not only as *divus*, but as *deus*; the angels he holds to be identical with the genii of antiquity;[2] and his notion of immortality reminds us of the old kingdom of the Shades. This spirit occasionally appears in the most extravagant shapes. In 1526, when Siena was attacked by the exiled party,[3] the worthy canon Tizio, who tells us the story himself, rose from his bed on July 22, called to mind what is written in the third book of Macrobius,[4] celebrated Mass, and then pronounced against the enemy the curse with which his author had supplied him, only altering " Tellus mater teque Juppiter obtestor " into " Tellus teque Christe Deus obtestor." After he had done this for three days the enemy retreated. On the one side, these things strike us as an affair of mere style and fashion; on the other, as a symptom of religious decadence.

[1] " Quod nimium gentilitatis amatores essemus." Paganism, at least in externals, certainly went rather far. Inscriptions lately found in the catacombs show that the members of the academy described themselves as *sacerdotes*, and called Pomponius Lætus *pontifex maximus*; the latter once addressed Platina as *pater sanctissimus*. Gregorovius, vii, 578.

[2] While the plastic arts at all events distinguished between angels and *putti*, and used the former for all serious purposes. In the *Annal. Estens.*, in Murat., xx, col. 468, the *amorino* is naïvely called *instar Cupidinis angelus. Cf.* the speech made before Leo X (1521), in which the passage occurs: " Quare et te non jam Juppiter, sed Virgo Capitolina Dei parens quæ hujus urbis et collis reliquis præsides, Romamque et Capitolium tutaris." Gregorovius, viii, 294.

[3] Della Valle, *Lettere Sanesi*, iii, 18.

[4] Macrob., *Saturnal.*, iii, 9. Doubtless the canon did not omit the gestures there prescribed. *Cf.* Gregorovius, viii, 294, for Bembo. For the paganism thus prevalent in Rome see also Ranke, *Päpste*, i, 73 *sqq. Cf.* also Gregorovius, viii, 268.

CHAPTER IV

MIXTURE OF ANCIENT AND MODERN SUPERSTITION

BUT in another way, and that dogmatically, antiquity exercised a perilous influence. It imparted to the Renaissance its own forms of superstition. Some fragments of this had survived in Italy all through the Middle Ages, and the resuscitation of the whole was thereby made so much the more easy. The part played by the imagination in the process need not be dwelt upon. This only could have silenced the critical intellect of the Italians.

The belief in a divine government of the world was in many minds destroyed by the spectacle of so much injustice and misery. Others, like Dante, surrendered at all events this life to the caprices of chance, and if they nevertheless retained a sturdy faith it was because they held that the higher destiny of man would be accomplished in the life to come. But when the belief in immortality began to waver then fatalism got the upper hand, or sometimes the latter came first and had the former as its consequence.

The gap thus opened was in the first place filled by the astrology of antiquity, or even of the Arabians. From the relations of the planets among themselves and to the signs of the Zodiac future events and the course of whole lives were inferred, and the most weighty decisions were taken in consequence. In many cases the line of action thus adopted at the suggestion of the stars may not have been more immoral than that which would otherwise have been followed. But too often the decision must have been made at the cost of honour and conscience. It is profoundly instructive to observe how powerless culture and enlightenment were against this delusion, since the latter had its support in the ardent imagination of the people, in the passionate wish to penetrate and determine the future. Antiquity, too, was on the side of astrology.

At the beginning of the thirteenth century this superstition suddenly appeared in the foreground of Italian life. The Emperor Frederick II always travelled with his astrologer Theodorus; and Ezzelino da Romano [1] with a large, well-paid Court of such people, among them the famous Guido Bonatto and the long-bearded Saracen, Paul of Bagdad. In all important undertakings they fixed for him the day and the hour, and the gigantic atrocities of which he was guilty may have been in part practical inferences from their prophecies.

---

[1] *Monachus Paduan.*, lib. ii, in Urstisius, *Scriptores*, i, pp. 598, 599, 602, 607. The last Visconti (p. 53) had also a number of these men in his service (*cf.* Decembrio, in Murat., xx, col. 1017); he undertook nothing without their advice. Among them was a Jew named Helias. Gasparino da Barzizzi once addressed him: " Magna vi astrorum fortuna tuas res reget " (G. B., *Opera*, ed. Furietto, p. 38).

Soon all scruples about consulting the stars ceased. Not only princes, but free cities [1] had their regular astrologers, and at the universities,[2] from the fourteenth to the sixteenth century, professors of this pseudo-science were appointed, and lectured side by side with the astronomers. It was well known that Augustine and other fathers of the Church had combated astrology, but their old-fashioned notions were dismissed with easy contempt.[3] The Popes [4] commonly made no secret of their star-gazing, though Pius II, who also despised magic, omens, and the interpretation of dreams, is an honourable exception.[5] Julius II, on the other hand, had the day for his coronation and the day for his return from Bologna calculated by the astrologers.[6] Even Leo X seems to have thought the flourishing condition of astrology a credit to his pontificate,[7] and Paul III never held a consistory till the star-gazers had fixed the hour.[8]

It may fairly be assumed that the better natures did not allow their actions to be determined by the stars beyond a certain point, and that there was a limit where conscience and religion made them pause. In fact, not only did pious and excellent people share the delusion, but they actually came forward to profess it publicly. One of these was Maestro Pagolo of Florence,[9] in whom we can detect the same desire to turn astrology to moral account which meets us in the late Roman Firmicus Maternus.[10] His life was that of a saintly ascetic. He ate almost nothing, despised all temporal goods, and only collected books. A skilled physician, he practised only among his friends, and made it a condition of his treatment that they should confess their sins. He frequented the small but famous circle which assembled in the monastery of the Angeli around Fra Ambrogio Camaldolese (p. 479). He also saw much of Cosimo the Elder, especially in his last years; for Cosimo accepted and used astrology, though probably only for objects of lesser importance. As a rule, however, Pagolo interpreted the stars only to his most confidential friends. But even without this severity of morals the astrologers might be highly respected and show

[1] For example, Florence, where Bonatto filled the office for a long period. See too Matteo Villani, xi, 3, where the city astrologer is evidently meant.

[2] Libri, *Histoire des Sciences Mathématiques*, ii, 52, 193. At Bologna this professorship is said to have existed in 1125. *Cf.* the list of professors at Pavia, in Corio, fol. 290. For the professorship at the Sapienza under Leo X see Roscoe, *Leo X*, ed. Bossi, v, p. 283. The following towns were centres of astrology—Milan and its university at Pavia, Bologna, and Mantua.

[3] J. A. Campanus lays stress on the value and importance of astrology, and concludes with the words: "Quamquam Augustinus sanctissimus ille vir quidem ac doctissimus, sed fortassis ad fidem religionemque propensior negat quicquam vel boni vel mali astrorum necessitate contingere." "Oratio initio studii Perugiæ habita"—cf. *Opera* (Rome, 1495).

[4] About 1260 Pope Alexander IV compelled a cardinal (and shamefaced astrologer) Bianco to bring out a number of political prophecies. Giov. Villani, vi, 81.

[5] *De Dictis*, etc., *Alfonsi, Opera*, p. 493. He held it to be "pulchrius quam utile." Platina, *Vitæ Pontiff.*, p. 310. For Sixtus IV *cf.* Jac. Volaterranus, in Murat., xxiii, col. 173, 186. He caused the hours for audiences, receptions, and the like, to be fixed by the *planetarii*. In the *Europa*, c. 49, Pius II mentions that Baptista Blasius, an astronomer from Cremona, had prophesied the misfortunes of Fr. Foscaro *tanquam prævidisset*.

[6] Brosch, *Julius II*, pp. 97 and 323 (Gotha, 1878).

[7] P. Valeriano, *De Infel. Lit.* (pp. 318–324), speaks of Fr. Friuli, who wrote on Leo's horoscope, and "abditissima quæque anteactæ, ætatis et uni ipsi cognita principi explicuerat quæque incumberent quæque futura essent ad unguem ut eventus postmodum comprobavit, in singulos fere dies prædixerat."

[8] Ranke, *Päpste*, i, 247.

[9] Vespas. Fiorent., p. 660 (*cf.* 341). *Ibid.*, p. 121, another Pagolo is mentioned as Court mathematician and astrologer of Federigo of Montefeltro. Curiously enough he was a German.

[10] Firmicus Maternus, *Matheseos Libri VIII*, at the end of the second book.

themselves everywhere. There were also far more of them in Italy than in other European countries, where they appeared only at the great Courts, and there not always. All the great householders in Italy, when the fashion was once established, kept an astrologer, who, it must be added, was not always sure of his dinner.[1] Through the literature of this science, which was widely diffused even before the invention of printing, a dilettantism also grew up which as far as possible followed in the steps of the masters. The worst class of astrologers were those who used the stars either as an aid or a cloak to magical arts.

Yet, apart from the latter, astrology is a miserable feature in the life of that time. What a figure do all these highly gifted, many-sided, original characters play when the blind passion for knowing and determining the future dethrones their powerful will and resolution! Now and then, when the stars send them too cruel a message, they manage to brace themselves up, act for themselves, and say boldly, " Vir sapiens dominabitur astris "—" the wise man is master of the stars " [2]—and then again relapse into the old delusion.

In all the better families the horoscope of the children was drawn as a matter of course, and it sometimes happened that for half a lifetime men were haunted by the idle expectation of events which never occurred. The stars [3] were questioned whenever a great man had to come to any important decision, and even consulted as to the hour at which any undertaking was to be begun. The journeys of princes, the reception of foreign ambassadors,[4] the laying of the foundation-stone of public buildings, depended on the answer. A striking instance of the latter occurs in the life of the aforenamed Guido Bonatto, who by his personal activity and by his great systematic work on the subject [5] deserves to be called the restorer of astrology in the thirteenth century. In order to put an end to the struggle of the Guelphs and Ghibellines at Forlì he persuaded the inhabitants to rebuild the city walls and to begin the works under a constellation

[1] In Bandello, iii, *Nov.* 60, the astrologer of Alessandro Bentivoglio in Milan confessed himself a poor devil before the whole company.

[2] It was in such a moment of resolution that Lodovico il Moro had the cross with this inscription made, which is now in the minster at Chur. Sixtus IV too once said that he would try if the proverb was true. On this saying of the astrologer Ptolemæus, which B. Fazio took to be Virgilian, see Laur. Valla, *Opera*, p. 461.

[3] The father of Piero Capponi, himself an astrologer, put his son into trade lest he should get the dangerous wound in the head which threatened him (*Vita di P. Capponi*, *Archiv. Stor.*, iv, ii, p. 15). For an instance in the life of Cardanus see above, p. 330. The physician and astrologer Pierleoni of Spoleto believed that he would be drowned, avoided in consequence all watery places, and refused brilliant positions offered him at Venice and Padua (Paul. Jovius, *Elog. Liter.*, pp. 67 *sqq.*). Finally he threw himself into the water, in despair at the charge brought against him of complicity in Lorenzo's death, and was actually drowned. Hier. Aliottus had been told to be careful in his sixty-second year, as his life would then be in danger. He lived with great circumspection, kept clear of the doctors, and the year passed safely (H. A., *Opuscula*, ii, 72; Arezzo, 1769). Marsilio Ficino, who despised astrology (*Opp.*, p. 772) was written to by a friend (*Epist.*, lib. 17): " Præterea me memini a duobus vestrorum astrologis audivisse, te ex quadam siderum positione antiquas revocaturum philosophorum sententias."

[4] For instances in the life of Lodovico il Moro see Senarega, in Murat., xxiv, col. 518, 524; Benedictus, in Eccard, ii, col. 1623. And yet his father, the great Francesco Sforza, had despised astrology, and his grandfather Giacomo had not at any rate followed its warnings. Corio, fol. 321, 413.

[5] For the facts here quoted see *Ann. Foroliv.*, in Murat., xxii, col. 233 sqq. (*cf.* col. 150). Leon Battista Alberti endeavoured to give a spiritual meaning to the ceremony of laying the foundation. *Opere Volgari*, tom. iv, p. 314 (or *De Re Ædific.*, lib. i). For Bonatto see Filippo Villani, *Vite* and *Della Vita e delle Opere di Guido Bonati, Astrologo e Astronomo del Secolo Decimoterzo, raccolte da R. Boncompagni* (Rome, 1851). Bonatto's great work, *De Astronomia*, lib. x, has been often printed.

FIG. 228. THE TRIUMPH OF MINERVA, THE SIGN OF THE RAM, AND
SCENES FROM LIFE AT THE COURT OF BORSO D'ESTE

Allegorical and astrological fresco in the Palazzo Schifanoja, Ferrara

Photo Alinari

indicated by himself. If, then, two men, one from each party, at the same moment put a stone into the foundation there would henceforth and for ever be no more party divisions in Forlì. A Guelph and a Ghibelline were selected for this office; the solemn moment arrived, each held the stone in his hands, the workmen stood ready with their implements, Bonatto gave the signal, and the Ghibelline threw down his stone on to the foundation. But the Guelph hesitated, and at last refused to do anything at all, on the ground that Bonatto himself had the reputation of a Ghibelline and might be devising some mysterious mischief against the Guelphs. Upon which the astrologer addressed him: "God damn thee and the Guelph party, with your distrustful malice. This constellation will not appear above our city for five hundred years to come." In fact, God soon afterward did destroy the Guelphs of Forlì, but now, writes the chronicler about 1480, the two parties are thoroughly reconciled, and their very names are heard no longer.[1]

Nothing that depended upon the stars was more important than decisions in time of war. The same Bonatto procured a series of victories for the great Ghibelline leader Guido da Montefeltro, by telling him the propitious hour for marching.[2] When Montefeltro was no longer accompanied by him [3] he lost the courage to maintain his despotism, and entered a Minorite monastery, where he lived as a monk for many years, till his death. In the war with Pisa in 1362 the Florentines commissioned their astrologer to fix the hour for the march,[4] and almost came too late through suddenly receiving orders to take a circuitous route through the city. On former occasions they had marched out by the Via di Borgo S. Apostolo, and the campaign had been unsuccessful. It was clear that there was some bad omen connected with the exit through this street against Pisa, and consequently the army was now led out by the Porta Rossa. But as the tents stretched out there to dry had not been taken away, the flags—another bad omen—had to be lowered. The influence of astrology in war was confirmed by the fact that nearly all the *condottieri* believed in it. Jacopo Caldora was cheerful in the most serious illness, knowing that he was fated to fall in battle, which, in fact, happened.[5] Bartolommeo Alviano was convinced that his wounds in the head were as much a gift of the stars as his military command.[6] Niccolò Orsini Pitigliano asked the physicist and

---

[1] In the horoscopes of the second foundation of Florence (Giov. Villani, iii, 1, under Charles the Great) and of the first of Venice (see above, p. 82) an old tradition is perhaps mingled with the poetry of the Middle Ages.

[2] For one of these victories see the remarkable passage quoted from Bonatto in Steinschneider, in the *Ztschr. d. D. Morg. Ges.*, xxv, p. 416. On Bonatto *cf. ibid.*, xviii, 120 *sqq.*

[3] *Ann. Foroliv.*, pp. 235–238; Filippo Villani, *Vite*; Machiavelli, *Stor. Fiorent.*, lib. i. When constellations which augured victory appeared Bonatto ascended with his book and astrolabe to the tower of S. Mercuriale above the *piazza*, and when the right moment came gave the signal for the great bell to be rung. Yet it was admitted that he was often wide of the mark, and foresaw neither his own death nor the fate of Montefeltro. Not far from Cesena he was killed by robbers, on his way back to Forlì from Paris and from Italian universities where he had been lecturing. As a weather prophet he was once overmatched and made game of by a countryman.

[4] Matteo Villani, xi, 3; see above, p. 484.

[5] Jov. Pontan., *De Fortitudine*, lib. i. See p. 486, note 4, for the honourable exception made by the first Sforza.

[6] Paul. Jovius, *Elog.*, under "Livianus," p. 219.

astrologer Alessandro Benedetto [1] to fix a favourable hour for the conclusion of his bargain with Venice (1495). When the Florentines on June 1, 1498, solemnly invested their new *condottiere* Paolo Vitelli with his office the marshal's staff which they handed him was, at his own wish, decorated with pictures of the constellations. [2] There were, nevertheless, generals like Alfonso the Great of Naples who did not allow their march to be settled by the prophets. [3]

FIG. 229. AN ASTROLOGER CASTING A BOY'S HOROSCOPE
After Giorgione
Dresden, Art Gallery
Photo Allgemeine Verlagsanstalt, Munich

Sometimes it is not easy to make out whether in important political events the stars were questioned beforehand, or whether the astrologers were simply impelled afterward by curiosity to find out the constellation which decided the result. When Giangaleazzo Visconti (p. 32) by a master-stroke of policy took prisoner his uncle Bernabò, with the latter's family (1385), we are told by a contemporary that Jupiter, Saturn, and Mars stood in the house of the Twins, [4] but we cannot say if the deed was resolved on in consequence. It is also

[1] Who tells the story himself. Benedictus, in Eccard, ii, col. 1617.
[2] In this sense we must understand the words of Jac. Nardi, *Vita d' Ant. Giacomini*, p. 66. The same pictures were common on clothes and household utensils. At the reception of Lucrezia Borgia in Ferrara the mule of the Duchess of Urbino wore trappings of black velvet with astrological figures in gold. *Archiv. Stor.*, App. II, p. 305.
[3] Æneas Sylvius, in the passage quoted above, p. 485; cf. *Opp.*, 481.
[4] Azario, in Corio, fol. 258.

489

probable that the advice of the astrologers was often determined by political calculation not less than by the course of the planets.[1]

All Europe through the latter part of the Middle Ages had allowed itself to be terrified by predictions of plagues, wars, floods, and earthquakes, and in this respect Italy was by no means behind other countries. The unlucky year 1494, which for ever opened the gates of Italy to the stranger, was undeniably ushered in by many prophecies of misfortune [2]—only we cannot say whether such prophecies were not ready for each and every year.

This mode of thought was extended with thorough consistency into regions where we should hardly expect to meet with it. If the whole outward and spiritual life of the individual is determined by the facts of his birth the same law also governs groups of individuals and historical products—that is to say, nations and religions; and as the constellation of these things changes so do the things themselves. The idea that each religion has its day first came into Italian culture in connexion with these astrological beliefs, chiefly from Jewish and Arabian sources.[3] The conjunction of Jupiter with Saturn brought forth, we are told,[4] the faith of Israel; that of Jupiter with Mars, the Chaldean; with the Sun, the Egyptian; with Venus, the Mohammedan; with Mercury, the Christian; and the conjunction of Jupiter with the Moon will one day bring forth the religion of Antichrist. Cecco d'Ascoli had already blasphemously calculated the nativity of Christ, and deduced from it His death upon the Cross. For this he was burnt at the stake in 1327, at Florence.[5] Doctrines of this sort ended by simply darkening men's whole perceptions of spiritual things.

So much more worthy, then, of recognition is the warfare which the clear Italian spirit waged against this army of delusions. Notwithstanding the great monumental glorification of astrology, as in the frescoes in the Salone at Padua,[6] and those in Borso's summer palace (Schifanoia) at Ferrara, notwithstanding the shameless praises of even such a man as the elder Beroaldus,[7] there was no want of thoughtful and independent minds to protest against it. Here, too, the way had been prepared by antiquity, but it was their own common sense and observation which taught them what to say. Petrarch's attitude toward the astrologers, whom he knew by personal intercourse, is one of bitter

[1] Considerations of this kind probably influenced the Turkish astrologers who after the battle of Nicopolis advised the Sultan Bajazet I to consent to the ransom of John of Burgundy, since "for his sake much Christian blood would be shed." It was not difficult to foresee the further course of the French civil war. *Magn. Chron. Belgicum*, p. 358; Juvénal des Ursins, *ad a.* 1396.

[2] Benedictus, in Eccard, ii, col. 1579. It was said of King Ferrante in 1493 that he would lose his throne "sine cruore sed sola fama"—which actually happened.

[3] *Cf.* Steinschneider, *Apokalypsen mit polemischer Tendenz, D. M. G. Z.*, xxviii, 627 *sqq.*; xxix, 261.

[4] Bapt. Mantuan., *De Patientia*, lib. iii, cap. 12.

[5] Giov. Villani, x, 39, 40. Other reasons also existed—for example, the jealousy of his colleagues. Bonatto had taught the same, and had explained the miracle of Divine Love in St Francis as the effect of the planet Mars. *Cf.* Jo. Picus, *Adversus Astrologos*, ii, 5.

[6] They were painted by Miretto at the beginning of the fifteenth century. According to Scardeonius they were destined "ad indicandum nascentium naturas per gradus et numeros"—a more popular way of teaching than we can now well imagine. It was astrology "à la portée de tout le monde."

[7] He says (*Orationes*, fol. 35, *In Nuptias*) of astrology: "hæc efficit ut homines parum a Diis distare videantur"! Another enthusiast of the same time is Jo. Garzonius, *De Dignitate Urbis Bononiæ*, in Murat., xxi, col. 1163.

contempt;[1] and no one saw through their system of lies more clearly than he. The novels, from the time when they first began to appear—from the time of the *Cento Novelle Antiche*—are almost always hostile to the astrologers.[2] The Florentine chroniclers bravely keep themselves free from the delusions which, as part of historical tradition, they are compelled to record. Giovanni Villani says more than once,[3] " No constellation can subjugate either the free will of man, or the counsels of God."

Matteo Villani[4] declares astrology to be a vice which the Florentines had inherited, along with other superstitions, from their pagan ancestors, the Romans. The question, however, did not remain one for mere literary discussion, but the parties for and against disputed publicly. After the terrible floods of 1333, and again in 1345, astrologers and theologians discussed with great minuteness the influence of the stars, the Will of God, and the justice of His punishments.[5] These struggles never ceased throughout the whole time of the Renaissance,[6] and we may conclude that the protesters were in earnest, since it was easier for them to recommend themselves to the great by defending, than by opposing, astrology.

FIG. 230. WOODCUT FROM SAVONAROLA'S TRACT AGAINST ASTROLOGERS (FLORENCE, 1490)
Photo Rosenthal, Munich

In the circle of Lorenzo the Magnificent, among his most distinguished Platonists, opinions were divided on this question. That Marsilio Ficino defended astrology, and drew the horoscope of the children of the house, promising the little Giovanni, afterward Leo X, that he would one day be

---

[1] Petrarch, *Epist. Seniles*, iii, 1 (p. 765), and elsewhere. The letter in question was written to Boccaccio. On Petrarch's polemic against the astrologers see Geiger, *Petrarca*, pp. 87–91 and 267, n. 11. [Petrarch, although he railed against astrology, yet called Mayno de' Mayneri, the " great astrologer," his good friend, and prided himself on the prophecy made in his youth, that something great would come of him (*Epist. Sen.*, iii; *cf.* Rajna, *Giorn. Stor.*, x, 101 *sqq.*).—L. G.]

[2] Franco Sacchetti (*Nov.* 151) ridicules their claims to wisdom.

[3] Gio. Villani, iii, x, 39. Elsewhere he appears as a devout believer in astrology, x, 120; xii, 40.

[4] In the passage xi, 3.

[5] Gio. Villani, xi, 2; xii, 4.

[6] The author of the *Annales Placentini* (in Murat., xx, col. 931), the same Alberto da Rivalta mentioned at p. 246, took part in this controversy. The passage is in other respects remarkable, since it contains the popular opinion with regard to the nine known comets, their colour, origin, and significance. *Cf.* Gio. Villani, xi, 67. He speaks of a comet as the herald of great and generally disastrous events.

Pope,[1] as Giovio would have us believe, is an invention—but other academicians accepted astrology. Pico della Mirandola,[2] on the other hand, made an epoch in the subject by his famous refutation. He detects in this belief the root of all impiety and immorality. If the astrologer, he maintains, believes in anything at all he must worship not God, but the planets, from which all good and evil are derived. All other superstitions find a ready instrument in astrology, which serves as handmaid to geomancy, chiromancy, and magic of every kind. As to morality, he maintains that nothing can more foster evil than the opinion that heaven itself is the cause of it, in which case the faith in eternal happiness and punishment must also disappear. Pico even took the trouble to check off the astrologers inductively, and found that in the course of a month three-fourths of their weather prophecies turned out false. But his main achievement was to set forth, in the fourth book, a positive Christian doctrine of the freedom of the will and the government of the universe, which seems to have made a greater impression on the educated classes throughout Italy than all the revivalist preachers put together. The latter, in fact, often failed to reach these classes.

The first result of his book was that the astrologers ceased to publish their doctrines,[3] and those who had already printed them were more or less ashamed of what they had done. Gioviano Pontano, for example, in his book on Fate (p. 482), had recognized the science, and in a great work of his own,[4] the several parts of which were dedicated to his highly placed friends and fellow-believers, Aldo Manucci, P. Bembo, and Sannazaro, had expounded the whole theory of it in the style of the old Firmicus, ascribing to the stars the growth of every bodily and spiritual quality. He now in his dialogue *Ægidius* surrendered, if not astrology, at least certain astrologers, and sounded the praises of free will, by which man is enabled to know God.[5] Astrology remained more or less in fashion, but seems not to have governed human life in the way it formerly had done. The art of painting, which in the fifteenth century had done its best to foster the delusion, now expressed the altered tone of thought. Raphael, in the cupola of the Cappella Chigi,[6] represents the gods of the different planets and the starry firmament, watched, however, and guided by beautiful angel-figures, and receiving from above the blessing of the Eternal Father. There was also another cause which now began to tell against astrology in Italy. The Spaniards took no interest in it, not even the generals, and those who wished

---

[1] Paul. Jovius, *Vita Leonis* X, lib. iii, where it appears that Leo himself was a believer at least in premonitions and the like; see above, p. 485. [Geiger declares this report of Paul. Jovius to be a fiction.—W. G.]

[2] Jo. Picus Mirand., *Adversus Astrologos*, lib. xii (1495).

[3] According to Paul. Jovius (*Elog. Lit.*, pp. 76 *sqq.*, under Jo. Picus) the result he achieved was "ut subtilium disciplinarum professores a scribendo deterruisse videatur."

[4] *De Rebus Cælestibus*, lib. xiv (*Opp.*, iii, 1963-2591). In the twelfth book, dedicated to Paolo Cortese, he will not admit the latter's refutation of astrology. *Ægidius, Opp.*, ii, 1455-1514. Pontano had dedicated his little work *De Luna* (*Opp.*, iii, 2592) to the same hermit Egidio (of Viterbo?).

[5] For the latter passage see p. 1486. The difference between Pontano and Pico is thus put by Franc. Pudericus, one of the interlocutors in the dialogue (p. 1496): "Pontanus non ut Johannes Picus in disciplinam ipsam armis equisque, quod dicitur, irrumpit, cum illam tueatur, ut cognitu maxime dignam ac pene divinam, sed astrologos quosdam, ut parum cautos minimeque prudentes insectetur et rideat."

[6] In S. Maria del Popolo at Rome. The angels remind us of Dante's theory at the beginning of the *Convivio*.

to gain their favour [1] declared open war against the half-heretical, half-Mohammedan science. It is true that Guicciardini [2] writes in 1529: "How happy are the astrologers, who are believed if they tell one truth to a hundred lies, while other people lose all credit if they tell one lie to a hundred truths." But the contempt for astrology did not necessarily lead to a return to the belief in Providence. It could as easily lead to an indefinite fatalism.

FIG. 231. CUPOLA MOSAIC OF THE CHIGI CHAPEL
By Raphael
Rome, S. Maria del Popolo
Photo Seemann, Leipzig

In this respect, as in others, Italy was unable to make its own way healthily through the ferment of the Renaissance, because the foreign invasion and the Counter-Reformation came upon it in the middle. Without such interfering causes its own strength would have enabled it thoroughly to get rid of these fantastic illusions. Those who hold that the onslaught of the strangers and the Catholic reactions were necessities for which the Italian people was itself solely responsible will look on the spiritual bankruptcy which they produced

---

[1] This was the case with Antonio Galateo, who, in a letter to Ferdinand the Catholic (Mai, *Spicileg. Rom.*, vol. viii, p. 226, *ad a.* 1510), disclaims astrology with violence, and in another letter to the Count of Potenza (*ibid.*, p. 539) infers from the stars that the Turks would attack Rhodes the same year.

[2] Ricordi, *loc. cit.*, n. 57.

as a just retribution. But it is a pity that the rest of Europe had indirectly to pay so large a part of the penalty.

The belief in omens seems a much more innocent matter than astrology. The Middle Ages had everywhere inherited them in abundance from the various pagan religions; and Italy did not differ in this respect from other countries. What is characteristic of Italy is the support lent by humanism to the popular superstition. The pagan inheritance was here backed up by a pagan literary development.

The popular superstition of the Italians rested largely on premonitions and inferences drawn from ominous occurrences,[1] with which a good deal of magic, mostly of an innocent sort, was connected. There was, however, no lack of learned humanists who boldly ridiculed these delusions, and to whose attacks we partly owe the knowledge of them. Gioviano Pontano, the author of the great astrological work already mentioned (p. 492), enumerates with pity in his *Charon* a long string of Neapolitan superstitions—the grief of the women when a fowl or a goose caught the pip; the deep anxiety of the nobility if a hunting falcon did not come home, or if a horse sprained his foot; the magical formulæ of the Apulian peasants, recited on three Saturday evenings, when mad dogs were at large. The animal kingdom, as in antiquity, was regarded as specially significant in this respect, and the behaviour of the lions, leopards, and other beasts kept by the State (pp. 287 *sqq.*) gave the people all the more food for reflection, because they had come to be considered as living symbols of the State. During the siege of Florence, in 1529, an eagle which had been shot at fled into the city, and the Signoria gave the bearer four ducats, because the omen was good.[2] Certain times and places were favourable or unfavourable, or even decisive one way or the other, for certain actions. The Florentines, so Varchi tells us, held Saturday to be the fateful day on which all important events, good as well as bad, commonly happened. Their prejudice against marching out to war through a particular street has been already mentioned (p. 488). At Perugia one of the gates, the Porta Eburnea, was thought lucky, and the Baglioni always went out to fight through it.[3] Meteors and the appearance of the heavens were as significant in Italy as elsewhere in the Middle Ages, and the popular imagination saw warring armies in an unusual formation of clouds, and heard the clash of their collision high in the air.[4] The superstition became a more serious matter when it attached itself to sacred things, when figures of the Virgin wept or moved the eyes,[5] or when public calamities were associated with some alleged act of impiety, for which the people demanded

---

[1] Many instances of such superstitions in the case of the last Visconti are mentioned by Decembrio (in Murat., xx, col. 1016 *sqq.*). Odaxius says in his speech at the burial of Guidobaldo (*Bembi Opera*, i, 598 *sqq.*) that the gods had announced his approaching death by thunderbolts, earthquakes, and other signs and wonders.

[2] Varchi, *Stor. Fiorent.*, lib. iv (p. 174); prophecies and premonitions were then as rife in Florence as at Jerusalem during the siege. *Cf. ibid.*, iii, 143, 195; iv, 43, 177.

[3] Matarazzo, *Archiv. Stor.*, xvi, ii, p. 208.

[4] Prato, *Archiv. Stor.*, iii, 324, for the year 1514.

[5] For the Madonna dell' Arbore in the cathedral at Milan, and what she did in 1515, see Prato, *loc. cit.*, p. 327. He also records the discovery of a dead dragon as broad as a horse in the excavations for a mortuary chapel near S. Nazaro. The head was taken to the Palace of the Trivulzi, for whom the chapel was built.

expiation. In 1478, when Piacenza was visited with a violent and prolonged rainfall, it was said that there would be no dry weather till a certain usurer, who had been lately buried at S. Francesco, had ceased to rest in consecrated

FIG. 232. THE MADONNA RESCUING A CHILD FROM THE POWER OF A DEVIL
By Niccolò Alunno
Rome, Galleria Colonna
Photo Alinari

earth. As the bishop was not obliging enough to have the corpse dug up, the young fellows of the town took it by force, dragged it round the streets amid frightful confusion, offered it to be insulted and maltreated by former creditors, and at last threw it into the Po.[1] Even Politian accepted this point

---

[1] "Et fuit mirabile quod illico pluvia cessavit." *Diar. Parmense*, in Murat., xxii, col. 280. The author shares the popular hatred of the usurers. *Cf.* col. 371.

of view in speaking of Giacomo Pazzi, one of the leaders of the conspiracy of 1478 in Florence which is called after his name. When he was put to death he devoted his soul to Satan with fearful words. Here, too, rain followed and threatened to ruin the harvest; here, too, a party of men, mostly peasants, dug up the body in the church, and immediately the clouds departed and the sun shone—"so gracious was fortune to the opinion of the people," adds the great scholar.[1] The corpse was first cast into unhallowed ground, the next day again dug up, and after a horrible procession through the city thrown into the Arno.

These facts and the like bear a popular character, and might have occurred in the tenth just as well as in the sixteenth century. But now comes the literary influence of antiquity. We know positively that the humanists were peculiarly susceptible to prodigies and auguries, and instances of this have been already quoted. If further evidence were needed it would be found in Poggio. The same radical thinker who denied the rights of noble birth and the inequality of men (see above, pp. 354 *sqq.*) not only believed in all the medieval stories of ghosts and devils (fol. 167, 179), but also in prodigies after the ancient pattern, like those said to have occurred on the last visit of Eugenius IV to Florence.[2]

> Near Como there was seen one evening four thousand dogs, who took the road to Germany; these were followed by a great herd of cattle, and these by an army on foot and horseback, some with no heads and some with almost invisible heads, and then a gigantic horseman with another herd of cattle behind him.

Poggio also believes in a battle of magpies and jackdaws (fol. 180). He even relates, perhaps without being aware of it, a well-preserved piece of ancient mythology. On the Dalmatian coast a Triton had appeared, bearded and horned, a genuine sea-satyr, ending in fins and a tail; he carried away women and children from the shore, till five stout-hearted washerwomen killed him with sticks and stones.[3] A wooden model of the monster which was exhibited at Ferrara makes the whole story credible to Poggio. Though there were no more oracles and it was no longer possible to take counsel of the gods, yet it became again the fashion to open Virgil at hazard and take the passage hit upon as an omen[4] (*Sortes Virgilanæ*). Nor can the belief in dæmons current in the later period of antiquity have been without influence on the Renaissance. The work of Jamblichus or Abammon on the mysteries of the Egyptians, which may have contributed to this result, was printed in a Latin translation at the end of the fifteenth century. The Platonic Academy at Florence was not free from

---

[1] *Conjurationis Pactianæ Commentarius*, in the appendices to Roscoe's *Lorenzo*. Politian was in general an opponent of astrology. The saints were naturally able to cause the rain to cease. *Cf.* Æneas Sylvius in his life of Bernardino da Siena (*De Vir. Ill.*, p. 25): "jussit in virtute Jesu nubem abire, quo facto solutis absque pluvia nubibus, prior serenitas rediit."

[2] Poggio, *Facetiæ*, fol. 167, 174, 179, 180. Æneas Sylvius (*De Europa*, c. 53, 54, *Opera*, pp. 451, 455) mentions prodigies which may have really happened, such as combats between animals and strange appearances in the sky, and mentions them chiefly as curiosities, even when adding the results attributed to them. Similarly Antonio Ferrari (il Galateo), *De Situ Iapygiæ*, p. 121, with the explanation: "Et hæ, ut puto, species erant earum rerum quæ longe aberant atque ab eo loco in quo species visæ sunt minime poterant."

[3] Poggio, *Facetiæ*, fol. 160. *Cf.* Pausanias, ix, 20.

[4] Varchi, iii, 195. Two suspected persons decided on flight in 1529, because they opened the *Æneid* at Book III, 44. *Cf.* Rabelais, *Pantagruel*, iii, 10.

hese and other neoplatonic dreams of the Roman decadence. A few words must be given here to the belief in dæmons and to the magic which was connected with this belief.

The popular faith in what is called the spirit-world was nearly the same in Italy as elsewhere in Europe.[1] In Italy, as elsewhere, there were ghosts—

FIG. 233. ST MARK STILLING THE STORM
By a Venetian master
Venice, Accademia

that is, reappearances of deceased persons; and if the view taken of them differed in any respect from that which prevailed in the North the difference betrayed itself only in the ancient name *ombra*. Nowadays if such a shade presents itself a couple of Masses are said for its repose. That the spirits of bad men appear in a dreadful shape is a matter of course, but along with this we find the notion that the ghosts of the departed are universally malicious. The dead, says the

---

[1] The imaginations of the scholars, such as the *splendor* and the *spiritus* of Cardanus and the *dæmon familiaris* of his father, may be taken for what they are worth. *Cf.* Cardanus, *De Propria Vita*, cap. 4, 38, 47. He was himself an opponent of magic (cap. 39). For the prodigies and ghosts he met with see cap. 37 and 41. For the terror of ghosts felt by the last Visconti see Decembrio, in Murat., xx, col. 1016.

priest in Bandello,[1] kill the little children. It seems as if a certain shade was here thought of as separate from the soul, since the latter suffers in Purgatory, and when it appears does nothing but wail and pray. To lay the ghost the tomb was opened, the corpse pulled to pieces, the heart burned, and the ashes scattered to the four winds.[2] At other times what appears is not the ghost of a man, but of an event—of a past condition of things. So the neighbours explained the diabolical appearances in the old palace of the Visconti near S. Giovanni in Conca, at Milan, since here it was that Bernabò Visconti had caused countless victims of his tyranny to be tortured and strangled, and no wonder if there were strange things to be seen.[3] One evening a swarm of poor people with candles in their hands appeared to a dishonest guardian of the poor at Perugia, and danced round about him; a great figure spoke in threatening tones on their behalf—it was St Alò, the patron saint of the poor-house.[4] These modes of belief were so much a matter of course that the poets could make use of them as something which every reader would understand. The appearance of the slain Lodovico Pico under the walls of the besieged Mirandola is finely represented by Castiglione.[5] It is true that poetry made the freest use of these conceptions when the poet himself had outgrown them.

Italy, too, shared the belief in dæmons with the other nations of the Middle Ages. Men were convinced that God sometimes allowed bad spirits of every class to exercise a destructive influence on parts of the world and of human life. The only reservation made was that the man to whom the Evil One came as a tempter could use his free will to resist.[6] In Italy the dæmonic influence, especially as shown in natural events, easily assumed a character of poetical greatness. In the night before the great inundation of the Val d'Arno in 1333 a pious hermit above Vallombrosa heard a diabolical tumult in his cell, crossed himself, stepped to the door, and saw a crowd of black and terrible knights gallop by in armour. When conjured to stand one of them said: "We go to drown the city of Florence on account of its sins, if God will let us."[7] With

---

[1] "Molte fiate i morti guastano le creature." Bandello, ii, *Nov.* 1. We read (Galateo, p. 177) that the *animæ* of wicked men rise from the grave, appear to their friends and acquaintances, "animalibus vexi, pueros sugere ac necare, deinde in sepulcra reverti."

[2] Galateo, *loc. cit.* We also read (p. 119) of the Fata Morgana and other similar appearances.

[3] Bandello, iii, *Nov.* 20. It is true that the ghost was only a lover wishing to frighten the occupier of the palace, who was also the husband of the beloved lady. The lover and his accomplices dressed themselves up as devils; one of them, who could imitate the cry of different animals, had been sent for from a distance.

[4] Graziani, *Archiv. Stor.*, xvi, i, p. 640, *ad a.* 1467. The guardian died of fright.

[5] *Balth. Castilionii Carmina*, ed. P. A. Serassi, ii, pp. 294 *sqq.*; Prosopopeja Lud. Pici.

[6] Alexandri ab Alexandro, *Dierum Genialium*, lib. vi (Colon., 1539), is an authority of the first rank for these subjects, the more so as the author, a friend of Pontanus and a member of his academy, asserts that what he records either happened to himself or was communicated to him by thoroughly trustworthy witnesses. Lib. vi, cap. 19: two evil men and a monk are attacked by devils, whom they recognize by the shape of their feet, and put to flight, partly by force and partly by the sign of the Cross. Lib. vi, cap. 21: a servant, cast into prison by a cruel prince on account of a small offence, calls upon the devil, is miraculously brought out of the prison and back again, visits meanwhile the nether world, shows the prince his hand scorched by the flames of hell, tells him on behalf of a departed spirit certain secrets which had been communicated to the latter, exhorts him to lay aside his cruelty, and dies soon after from the effects of the fright. Lib. ii, c. 19; iii, 15; v, 23: ghosts of departed friends, of St Cataldus, and of unknown beings in Rome, Arezzo, and Naples. Lib. ii, 22; iii, 8: appearances of mermen and mermaids at Naples, in Spain, and in the Peloponnesus; in the latter case guaranteed by Theodore Gaza and George of Trebizond.

[7] Gio. Villani, xi, 2. He had it from the Abbot of Vallombrosa, to whom the hermit had communicated it.

this the nearly contemporary vision at Venice (1340) may be compared, out of which a great master of the Venetian school, probably Giorgione, made the marvellous picture of a galley full of dæmons, which speeds with the swiftness of a bird over the stormy lagoon to destroy the sinful island-city, till the three saints, who have stepped unobserved into a poor boatman's skiff, exorcized the fiends and sent them and their vessel to the bottom of the waters.[1]

To this belief the illusion was now added that by means of magical arts it was possible to enter into relations with the Evil Ones, and use their help to further the purposes of greed, ambition, and sensuality. Many persons were probably accused of doing so before the time when it was actually attempted by many; but when the so-called magicians and witches began to be burned the deliberate practice of the black art became more frequent. With the smoke of the fires in which the suspected victims were sacrificed were spread the narcotic fumes by which numbers of ruined characters were drugged into magic; and with them many calculating impostors became associated.

The primitive and popular form in which the superstition had probably lived on uninterruptedly from the time of the Romans [2] was the art of the witch (strega). The witch, so long as she limited herself to mere divination,[3] might be innocent enough, were it not that the transition from prophecy to active help could easily, though often imperceptibly, be a fatal downward step. She was credited in such a case not only with the power of exciting love or hatred between man and woman, but also with purely destructive and malignant arts, and was especially charged with the sickness of little children, even when the malady obviously came from the neglect and stupidity of the parents. It is still questionable how far she was supposed to act by mere magical ceremonies and formulæ, or by a conscious alliance with the fiends, apart from the poisons and drugs which she administered with a full knowledge of their effect.

The more innocent form of the superstition, in which the mendicant friar could venture to appear as the competitor of the witch, is shown in the case of the witch of Gaeta, whom we read of in Pontano.[4] His traveller Suppatius reaches her dwelling while she is giving audience to a girl and a servant-maid, who come to her with a black hen, nine eggs laid on a Friday, a duck, and some white thread—for it is the third day since the new moon. They are then sent away, and bidden to come again at twilight. It is to be hoped that nothing worse than divination is intended. The mistress of the servant-maid is pregnant

---

[1] Another view of the dæmons was given by Gemisthos Pletho, whose great philosophical work οἱ νόμοι, of which only fragments are now left (ed. Alexander, Paris, 1858), was probably known more fully to the Italians of the fifteenth century, either by means of copies or of tradition, and exercised undoubtedly a great influence on the philosophical, political, and religious culture of the time. According to him the dæmons, who belong to the third order of the gods, are preserved from all error, and are capable of following in the steps of the gods who stand above them; they are spirits who bring to men the good things " which come down from Zeus through the other gods in order; they purify and watch over man, they raise and strengthen his heart." Cf. Fritz Schultze, Gesch. der Philosophie der Renaissance (Jena, 1874).

[2] Yet but little remained of the wonders attributed to her. For probably the last metamorphosis of a man into an ass, in the eleventh century under Leo IX, see William of Malmesbury, ii, 171.

[3] This was probably the case with the possessed woman, who in 1513 at Ferrara and elsewhere was consulted by distinguished Lombards as to future events. Her name was Rodogina. See Rabelais, Pantagruel, iv, 58.

[4] Jov. Pontan., Antonius.

by a monk; the girl's lover has proved untrue and has gone into a monastery. The witch complains:

> "Since my husband's death I support myself in this way, and should make a good thing of it, since the Gaetan women have plenty of faith, were it not that the monks baulk me of my gains by explaining dreams, appeasing the anger of the saints for money, promising husbands to the girls, men-children to the pregnant women, offspring to the barren, and besides all this visiting the women at night when their husbands are away fishing, in accordance with the assignations made in daytime at church."

Suppatius warns her against the envy of the monastery, but she has no fear, since the guardian of it is an old acquaintance of hers.[1]

But the superstition further gave rise to a worse sort of witches—namely, those who deprived men of their health and life. In these cases the mischief, when not sufficiently accounted for by the evil eye and the like, was naturally attributed to the aid of powerful spirits. The punishment, as we have seen in the case of Finicella (p. 454), was the stake; and yet a compromise with fanaticism was sometimes practicable. According to the laws of Perugia, for example, a witch could settle the affair by paying down four hundred pounds.[2] The matter was not then treated with the seriousness and consistency of later times. In the territories of the Church, at Norcia (Nursia), the home of St Benedict, in the upper Apennines, there was a perfect nest of witches and sorcerers, and no secret was made of it. It is spoken of in one of the most remarkable letters of Æneas Sylvius,[3] belonging to his earlier period. He writes to his brother:

> The bearer of this came to me to ask if I knew of a Mount of Venus in Italy, for in such a place magical arts were taught, and his master, a Saxon and a great astronomer,[4] was anxious to learn them. I told him that I knew of a Porto Venere not far from Carrara, on the rocky coast of Liguria, where I spent three nights on the way to Basel; I also found that there was a mountain called Eryx in Sicily, which was dedicated to Venus, but I did not know whether magic was taught there. But it came into my mind while talking that in Umbria, in the old Duchy [Spoleto], near the town of Nursia, there is a cave beneath a steep rock, in which water flows. There, as I remember to have heard, are witches [striges], dæmons, and nightly shades, and he that has the courage can see and speak to ghosts [spiritus], and learn magical arts.[5] I have not seen it, nor taken any trouble about it, for that which is learned with sin is better not learned at all.

He nevertheless names his informant, and begs his brother to take the bearer of the letter to him, should he be still alive. Æneas goes far enough here in

---

[1] How widespread the belief in witches then was is shown by the fact that in 1483 Politian gave a *prælectio* "in priora Aristotelis Analytica cui titulus Lamia" (Italian trans. by Isidore del Lungo, Florence, 1864). *Cf.* Reumont, *Lorenzo dei Medici*, ii, 75–77. Fiesole, according to this, was, in a certain sense, a witches' nest.

[2] Graziani, *Archiv. Stor.*, xvi, i, p. 565, *ad a.* 1445, speaking of a witch at Nocera who offered only half the sum, and was accordingly burnt. The law was aimed at such persons as "facciono le fature overo venefitie overo encantatione d' immunde spirite a nuocere," *loc. cit.*, note 1, 2.

[3] Lib. i, *Ep.* 46, *Opera*, pp. 531 *sqq.* For *umbra*, p. 532, read *Umbria*, and for *lacum* read *locum*.

[4] He calls him later on: "Medicus Ducis Saxoniæ, homo tum dives tum potens."

[5] In the fourteenth century there existed a kind of hell-gate near Ansedonia, in Tuscany. It was a cave, with footprints of men and animals in the sand, which whenever they were effaced reappeared the next day. Uberti, *Il Dittamondo*, lib. iii, cap. 9.

his politeness to a man of position, but personally he was not only freer from superstition than his contemporaries (pp. 466, 485), but he also stood a test on the subject which not every educated man of our own day could endure. At the time of the Council of Basel, when he lay sick of the fever for seventy-five days at Milan, he could never be persuaded to listen to the magic-doctors, though a man was brought to his bedside who a short time before had marvellously cured two thousand soldiers of fever in the camp of Piccinino. While still an invalid, Æneas rode over the mountains to Basel, and got well on the journey.[1]

We learn something more about the neighbourhood of Norcia through the necromancer who tried to get Benvenuto Cellini into his power. A new book of magic was to be consecrated,[2] and the best place for the ceremony was among the mountains in that district. The master of the magician had once, it is true, done the same thing near the Abbey of Farfa, but had there found difficulties which did not present themselves at Norcia; further, the peasants in the latter neighbourhood were trustworthy people who had practice in the matter, and who could afford considerable help in case of need. The expedition did not take place, else Benvenuto would probably have been able to tell us something of the impostor's assistants. The whole neighbourhood was then proverbial. Aretino says somewhere of an enchanted well, " there dwell the sisters of the sibyl of Norcia and the aunt of the Fata Morgana." And about the same time Trissino could still celebrate the place in his great epic [3] with all the resources of poetry and allegory as the home of authentic prophecy.

After the famous Bull of Innocent VIII (1484) [4] witchcraft and the persecution of witches grew into a great and revolting system. The chief representatives of this system of persecution were German Dominicans; and Germany and, curiously enough, those parts of Italy nearest Germany were the countries most afflicted by this plague. The Bulls and injunctions of the Popes themselves [5] refer, for example, to the Dominican province of Lombardy, to Cremona, to the dioceses of Brescia and Bergamo. We learn from Sprenger's famous theoretico-practical guide, the *Malleus Maleficarum*, that forty-one witches were burnt at Como in the first year after the publication of the Bull; crowds of Italian women took refuge in the territory of the Archduke Sigismund, where they believed themselves to be still safe. Witchcraft ended by taking

[1] *Pii II Comment.*, lib. i, p. 10.

[2] Benv. Cellini, lib. i, cap. 65.

[3] *L'Italia Liberata da' Goti*, canto xiv. It may be questioned whether Trissino himself believed in the possibility of his description, or whether he was not rather romancing. The same doubt is permissible in the case of his probable model, Lucan (Book VI), who represents the Thessalian witch conjuring up a corpse before Sextus Pompeius.

[4] *Septimo Decretal.*, lib. v, tit. xii. It begins: " Summis desiderantes affectibus," etc. [Pastor (iii, pp. 250 sqq.) denies after careful consideration that Innocent introduced the persecution of witches with the Bull.—W. G.] I may here remark that a full consideration of the subject has convinced me that there are in this case no grounds for believing in a survival of pagan beliefs. To satisfy ourselves that the imagination of the mendicant friars is solely responsible for this delusion we have only to study, in the memoirs of Jacques du Clerc, the so-called trial of the Waldenses of Arras in 1459. A century's prosecutions and persecutions brought the popular imagination into such a state that witchcraft was accepted as a matter of course and reproduced itself naturally.

[5] Of Alexander VI, Leo X, Adrian VI.

firm root in a few unlucky Alpine valleys, especially in the Val Camonica;[1] the system of persecution had succeeded in permanently infecting with the delusion those populations which were in any way predisposed for it. This essentially German form of witchcraft is what we should think of when reading the stories and novels of Milan or Bologna.[2] That it did not make further progress in Italy is probably due to the fact that elsewhere a highly developed *stregheria* was already in existence, resting on a different set of ideas. The Italian witch practised a trade, and needed for it money and, above all, sense. We find nothing about her of the hysterical dreams of the Northern witch, of marvellous journeys through the air, of Incubus and Succubus; the business of the *strega* was to provide for other people's pleasure. If she was credited with the power of assuming different shapes, or of transporting herself suddenly to distant places, she was so far content to accept this reputation, as her influence was thereby increased; on the other hand, it was perilous for her when the fear of her malice and vengeance, and especially of her power for enchanting children, cattle, and crops, became general. Inquisitors and magistrates were then thoroughly in accord with popular wishes if they burnt her.

By far the most important field for the activity of the *strega* lay, as has been said, in love affairs, and included the stirring up of love and of hatred, the producing of abortion, the pretended murder of the unfaithful man or woman by magical arts, and even the manufacture of poisons.[3] Owing to the unwillingness of many persons to have to do with these women, a class of occasional practitioners arose who secretly learned from them some one or other of their arts, and then used this knowledge on their own account. The Roman prostitutes, for example, tried to enhance their personal attractions by charms of another description, in the style of Horatian Canidia. Aretino[4] may not only have known, but have also told the truth about them in this particular. He gives a list of the loathsome messes which were to be found in their boxes—hair, skulls, ribs, teeth, dead men's eyes, human skin, the navels of little children, the soles of shoes and pieces of clothing from tombs. They even went themselves to the graveyard and fetched bits of rotten flesh, which they slily gave their lovers to eat—with more that is still worse. Pieces of the hair and nails of the lover were boiled in oil stolen from the ever-burning lamps in the church.

[1] Proverbial as the country of witches—for example, *Orlandino*, i, 12.

[2] For example, Bandello, iii, *Nov.* 29 and 52; Prato, *Archiv. Stor.*, iii, 409. Bursellis, *Annal. Bonon.*, in Murat., xxiii, col. 897, mentions the condemnation of a prior in 1468, who kept a ghostly brothel: " cives Bononienses coire faciebat cum dæmonibus in specie puellarum." He offered sacrifices to the dæmons. See for a parallel case Procop., *Hist. Arcana*, c. 12, where a real brothel is frequented by a dæmon, who turns the other visitors out of doors. The Galateo (p. 116) confirms the existence of the belief in witches: " volare per longinquas regiones, choreas per paludes dicere et dæmonibus congredi, ingredi, et egredi per clausa ostia et foramina."

[3] For the loathsome apparatus of the witches' kitchens see *Macaroneide*, *Phant.* xvi and xxi, where the whole procedure is described.

[4] In the *Ragionamento del Zoppino*. He is of opinion that the courtesans learn their arts from certain Jewish women, who are in possession of *malie*. The following passage is very remarkable. Bembo says in the life of Guidobaldo (*Opera*, i, 614): " Guid. constat sive corporis et naturæ vitio, seu quod vulgo creditum est, actibus magicis ab Octaviano patruo propter regni cupiditatem impeditum, quarum omnino ille artium expeditissimus habebatur, nulla cum femina coire unquam in tota vita potuisse, nec unquam fuisse ad rem uxoriam idoneum."

The most innocuous of their charms was to make a heart of glowing ashes, and then to pierce it while singing:

> Prima che 'l fuoco spenghi,
> Fa ch' a mia porta venghi;
> Tal ti punga mio amore
> Quale io fo questo cuore.

There were other charms practised by moonshine, with drawings on the ground, and figures of wax or bronze, which doubtless represented the lover, and were treated according to circumstances.

These things were so customary that a woman who, without youth and beauty, nevertheless exercised a powerful charm on men, naturally became suspected of witchcraft. The mother of Sanga,[1] secretary to Clement VII, poisoned her son's mistress, who was a woman of this kind. Unfortunately the son died too, as well as a party of friends who had eaten of the poisoned salad.

Next comes, not as helper but as competitor to the witch, the magician or enchanter—*incantatore*—who was still more familiar with the most perilous business of the craft. Sometimes he was as much or more of an astrologer than of a magician; he probably often gave himself out as an astrologer in order not to be prosecuted as a magician, and a certain astrology was essential in order to find out the favourable hour for a magical process.[2] But since many spirits are good[3] or indifferent, the magician could sometimes maintain a very tolerable reputation, and Sixtus IV in 1474 had to proceed expressly against some Bolognese Carmelites,[4] who asserted in the pulpit that there was no harm in seeking information from the dæmons. Very many people believed in the possibility of the thing itself; an indirect proof of this lies in the fact that the most pious men believed that by prayer they could obtain visions of good spirits. Savonarola's mind was filled with these things; the Florentine Platonists speak of a mystic union with God; and Marcellus Palingenius (p. 266) gives us to understand clearly enough that he had to do with consecrated spirits.[5] The same writer is convinced of the existence of a whole hierarchy of bad dæmons, who have their seat from the moon downward, and are ever on the watch to do some mischief to nature and human life.[6] He even tells of his own personal acquaintance with some of them, and as the scope of the present work does not allow of a systematic exposition of the then prevalent belief in spirits the narrative of Palingenius may be given as one instance out of many.[7]

At S. Silvestro, on Soracte, he had been receiving instruction from a pious hermit on the nothingness of earthly things and the worthlessness of human life; and when the night drew near he set out on his way back to Rome. On

---

[1] Varchi, *Stor. Fiorent.*, ii, p. 153.

[2] Curious information is given by Landi, in the *Commentario*, fol. 36a and 37a, about two magicians, a Sicilian and a Jew; we read of magical mirrors, of a death's-head speaking, and of birds stopped short in their flight.

[3] Stress is laid on this reservation. Corn. Agrippa, *De Occulta Philosophia*, cap. 39.

[4] *Septimo Decretal.*, *loc. cit.*

[5] *Zodiacus Vitæ*, xii, 363–539 (*cf.* x, 393 *sqq.*).

[6] *Ibid.*, ix, 291 *sqq.*

[7] *Ibid.*, ix, 770 *sqq.*

the road, in the full light of the moon, he was joined by three men, one of whom called him by name, and asked him whence he came. Palingenius made answer: "From the wise man on the mountain." "O fool," replied the stranger, "dost thou in truth believe that anyone on earth is wise? Only higher beings [*divi*] have wisdom, and such are we three, although we wear the shapes of men. I am named Saracil, and these two Sathiel and Jana. Our kingdom lies near the moon, where dwell that multitude of intermediate beings who have sway over earth and sea." Palingenius then asked, not without an inward tremor, what they were going to do at Rome. The answer was: "One of our comrades, Ammon, is kept in servitude by the magic arts of a youth from Narni, one of the attendants of Cardinal Orsini; for mark it, O men, there is proof of your own immortality therein, that you can control one of us; I myself, shut up in crystal, was once forced to serve a German, till a bearded monk set me free. This is the service which we wish to render at Rome to our friend, and we shall also take the opportunity of sending one or two distinguished Romans to the nether world." At these words a light breeze arose, and Sathiel said: "Listen, our messenger is coming back from Rome, and this wind announces him." And then another being appeared, whom they greeted joyfully, and whom they questioned about Rome. His utterances are strongly anti-Papal: Clement VII was again allied with the Spaniards and hoped to root out Luther's doctrines, not with arguments, but by the Spanish sword. This is wholly in the interest of the dæmons, whom the impending bloodshed would enable to carry away the souls of thousands into hell. At the close of this conversation, in which Rome with all its guilt is represented as wholly given over to the Evil One, the apparitions vanish, and leave the poet sorrowfully to pursue his way alone.[1]

Those who would form a conception of the extent of the belief in those relations to the dæmons which could be openly avowed in spite of the penalties attaching to witchcraft may be referred to the much-read work of Agrippa of Nettesheim on *Secret Philosophy*. He seems originally to have written it before he was in Italy,[2] but in the dedication to Trithemius he mentions Italian authorities among others, if only by way of disparagement. In the case of equivocal persons like Agrippa, or of the knaves and fools into whom the majority of the rest may be divided, there is little that is interesting in the system they profess, with its formulæ, fumigations, ointments, and the rest of it.[3] But this system was filled with quotations from the superstitions of antiquity, the influence of which on the life and passions of Italians is at times most remarkable and fruitful. We might think that a great mind must be thoroughly ruined before it surrendered itself to such influences; but the violence of hope and

---

[1] The mythical type of the magician among the poets of the time was Malagigi. Speaking of him, Pulci (*Morgante*, canto xxiv, 106 *sqq.*) gives his theoretical view of the limits of dæmonic and magic influence. It is hard to say how far he was in earnest. *Cf.* canto xxi.

[2] Polydorus Virgilius was an Italian by birth, but his work *De Prodigiis* treats chiefly of superstition in England, where his life was passed. Speaking of the prescience of the dæmons, he makes a curious reference to the sack of Rome in 1527.

[3] Yet murder is hardly ever the end, and never, perhaps, the means. A monster like Gilles de Retz (about 1440), who sacrificed more than a hundred children to the dæmons, has scarcely a distant counterpart in Italy.

desire led even vigorous and original men of all classes to have recourse to the magician, and the belief that the thing was feasible at all weakened to some extent the faith, even of those who kept at a distance, in the moral order of the world. At the cost of a little money and danger it seemed possible to defy with impunity the universal reason and morality of mankind, and to spare one-self the intermediate steps which otherwise lie between a man and his lawful or unlawful ends.

Let us here glance for a moment at an older and now decaying form of superstition. From the darkest period of the Middle Ages, or even from the days of antiquity, many cities of Italy had kept the remembrance of the con-nexion of their fate with certain buildings, statues, or other material objects. The ancients had left records of consecrating priests or *telestæ*, who were present at the solemn foundation of cities, and magically guaranteed their prosperity by erecting certain monuments or by burying certain objects (*telesmata*). Tradi-tions of this sort were more likely than anything else to live on in the form of popular, unwritten legend; but in the course of centuries the priest naturally became transformed into the magician, since the religious side of his function was no longer understood. In some of his Virgilian miracles at Naples[1] the ancient remembrance of one of these *telestæ* is clearly preserved, his name being in course of time supplanted by that of Virgil. The enclosing of the mysterious picture of the city in a vessel is neither more nor less than a genuine, ancient *telesma*; and Virgil, the founder of Naples, is only the officiating priest, who took part in the ceremony, presented in another dress. The popular imagina-tion went on working at these themes till Virgil became responsible also for the brazen horse, for the heads at the Nolan Gate, for the brazen fly over another gate, and even for the Grotto of Posilippo—all of them things which in one respect or other served to put a magical constraint upon Fate, and the first two of which seemed to determine the whole fortune of the city. Medieval Rome also preserved confused recollections of the same kind. At the church of S. Ambrogio at Milan there was an ancient marble Hercules; so long, it was said, as this stood in its place, so long would the Empire last. That of the Germans is probably meant, as the coronation of their Emperors at Milan took place in this church.[2] The Florentines[3] were convinced that the temple of Mars, afterward transformed into the Baptistery, would stand to the end of time, according to the constellation under which it had been built; they had, as Christians, removed from it the marble equestrian statue; but since the de-struction of the latter would have brought some great calamity on the city—also according to a constellation—they set it upon a tower by the Arno. When Totila conquered Florence the statue fell into the river, and was not fished out again till Charles the Great refounded the city. It was then placed on a pillar

---

[1] See the treatise of Roth, *Ueber den Zauberer Virgilius*, in Pfeiffer's *Germania*, iv, and Comparetti's *Virgil in the Middle Ages*. That Virgil began to take the place of the older *telestæ* may be explained partly by the fact that the frequent visits made to his grave even in the time of the Empire struck the popular imagination.

[2] Uberti, *Dittamondo*, lib. iii, cap. 4.

[3] For what follows see Gio. Villani, i, 42, 60; ii, 1; iii, 1; v, 38; xi, 1. He himself does not believe such godless superstitions. *Cf.* Dante, *Inferno*, xiii, 146.

at the entrance to the Ponte Vecchio, and on this spot Buondelmonte was slain in 1215. The origin of the great feud between Guelph and Ghibelline was thus associated with the dreaded idol. During the inundation of 1333 the statue vanished for ever.[1]

But the same *telesma* reappears elsewhere. Guido Bonatto, already mentioned, at the refounding of the walls of Forlì was not satisfied with requiring certain symbolic acts of reconciliation from the two parties (p. 488). By burying a bronze or stone equestrian statue,[2] which he had produced by astrological or magical arts, he believed that he had defended the city from ruin, and even from capture and plunder. When Cardinal Albornoz (p. 120) was Governor of Romagna some sixty years later the statue was accidentally dug up and then shown to the people, probably by the order of the Cardinal, that it might be known by what means the cruel Montefeltro had defended himself against the Roman Church. And again, half a century later, when an attempt to surprise Forlì had failed, men began to talk afresh of the virtue of the statue, which had perhaps been saved and reburied. It was the last time that they could do so; for a year later Forlì was really taken. The foundation of buildings all through the fifteenth century was associated not only with astrology (p. 486) but also with magic. The large number of gold and silver medals which Paul II buried in the foundations of buildings[3] was noticed, and Platina was by no means displeased to recognize an old pagan *telesma* in the fact. Neither Paul nor his biographer were in any way conscious of the medieval religious significance of such an offering.[4]

But this official magic, which in many cases rests only on hearsay, was comparatively unimportant by the side of the secret arts practised for personal ends.

The form which these most often took in daily life is shown by Ariosto in his comedy of the necromancers.[5] His hero is one of the many Jewish exiles from Spain, although he also gives himself out for a Greek, an Egyptian, and an African, and is constantly changing his name and costume. He pretends that his incantations can darken the day and lighten the darkness, that he can move the earth, make himself invisible, and change men into beasts; but these vaunts are only an advertisement. His true object is to make his account out of unhappy and troubled marriages, and the traces which he leaves behind him in his course are like the slime of a snail, or often like the ruin wrought by a hailstorm. To attain his ends he can persuade people that the box in which a lover is hidden is full of ghosts, or that he can make a corpse talk. It is at all events a good sign that poets and novelists could reckon on popular

---

[1] According to a fragment given in Baluz., *Miscell.*, ix, 119, the Perugians had a quarrel in ancient times with the Ravennates, " et milites marmoreum qui juxta Ravennam se continue volvebat ad solem usurpaverunt et ad eorum civitatem virtuosissime transtulerunt." For the Florentine legends mentioned here see Davidsohn, *Gesch. v. Florenz.*, i, App., p. 122, and Villari, *I Prieni Due Secole*, i, pp. 63 *sqq.*

[2] The local belief on the matter is given in *Annal. Foroliv.*, in Murat., xxii, col. 207, 238; more fully in Fil. Villani, *Vite*, p. 43.

[3] Platina, *Vitæ Pontiff.*, p. 320: " Veteres potius hac in re quam Petrum, Anacletum, et Linum imitatus."

[4] Which it is easy to recognize, for example, in Sugerius, *De Consecratione Ecclesiæ* (Duchesne, *Scriptores*, iv, 355), and in *Chron. Petershusanum*, i, 13 and 16.

[5] *Cf.* the *Calandra* of Bibbiena.

applause in holding up this class of men to ridicule. Bandello not only treats the sorcery of a Lombard monk as a miserable, and in its consequences terrible, piece of knavery,[1] but he also describes with unaffected indignation[2] the disasters which never cease to pursue the credulous fool.

> A man hopes with *Solomon's Key* and other magical books to find the treasures hidden in the bosom of the earth, to force his lady to do his will, to find out the secrets of princes, and to transport himself in the twinkling of an eye from Milan to Rome. The more often he is deceived, the more steadfastly he believes. . . . Do you remember the time, Signor Carlo, when a friend of ours, in order to win the favour of his beloved, filled his room with skulls and bones like a churchyard?

The most loathsome tasks were prescribed—to draw three teeth from a corpse or a nail from its finger, and the like; and while the hocus-pocus of the incantation was going on the unhappy participants sometimes died of terror.

Benvenuto Cellini did not die during the well-known incantation (1532) in the Coliseum at Rome,[3] although both he and his companions witnessed no ordinary horrors; the Sicilian priest, who probably expected to find him a useful coadjutor in the future, paid him the compliment as they went home of saying that he had never met a man of so sturdy a courage. Every reader will make his own reflections on the proceedings themselves. The narcotic fumes and the fact that the imaginations of the spectators were predisposed for all possible terrors are the chief points to be noticed, and explain why the lad who formed one of the party, and on whom they made most impression, saw much more than the others. But it may be inferred that Benvenuto himself was the one whom it was wished to impress, since the dangerous beginning of the incantation can have had no other aim than to arouse curiosity. For Benvenuto had to think before the fair Angelica occurred to him; and the magician told him afterward that love-making was folly compared with the finding of treasures. Further, it must not be forgotten that it flattered his vanity to be able to say, " The dæmons have kept their word, and Angelica came into my hands, as they promised, just a month later " (cap. 68). Even on the supposition that Benvenuto gradually lied himself into believing the whole story it would still be permanently valuable as evidence of the mode of thought then prevalent.

As a rule, however, the Italian artists, even " the odd, capricious, and eccentric " among them, had little to do with magic. One of them in his anatomical studies may have cut himself a jacket out of the skin of a corpse, but at the advice of his confessor he put it again into the grave.[4] Indeed, the frequent study of anatomy probably did more than anything else to destroy the belief in the magical influence of various parts of the body, while at the same

---

[1] Bandello, iii, *Nov.* 52. Fr. Filelfo (*Epist. Venet.*, lib. 34, fol. 240 *sqq.*) attacks necromancy fiercely. He is tolerably free from superstition (*Sat.*, iv, 4), but believes in the *mali effectus* of a comet (*Epist.*, fol. 246*b*).

[2] Bandello, iii, *Nov.* 29. The magician exacts a promise of secrecy strengthened by solemn oaths, in this case by an oath at the high altar of S. Petronio at Bologna, at a time when no one else was in the church. There is a good deal of magic in the *Macaroneide, Phant.* xviii.

[3] Benv. Cellini, i, cap. 64.

[4] Vasari, viii, 143, *Vita di Andrea da Fiesole*. It was Silvio Cosini, who also " went after magical formulæ and other follies."

time the incessant observation and representation of the human form made the artist familiar with a magic of a wholly different sort.

In general, notwithstanding the instances which have been quoted, magic seems to have been markedly on the decline at the beginning of the sixteenth century—that is to say, at a time when it first began to flourish vigorously out of Italy; and thus the tours of Italian sorcerers and astrologers in the North seem not to have begun till their credit at home was thoroughly impaired. In the fourteenth century it was thought necessary to watch carefully the lake on Mount Pilatus, near Scariotto, to hinder the magicians from there consecrating their books.[1] In the fifteenth century we find, for example, that the offer was made to produce a storm of rain in order to frighten away a besieging army; and even then the commander of the besieged town—Nicolò Vitelli in Città di Castello—had the good sense to dismiss the sorcerers as godless persons.[2] In the sixteenth century no more instances of this official kind appear, although in private life the magicians were still active. To this time belongs the classic figure of German sorcery, Dr Johann Faust; the Italian ideal, on the other hand, Guido Bonatto, dates back to the thirteenth century.

It must nevertheless be added that the decrease of the belief in magic was not necessarily accompanied by an increase of the belief in a moral order, but that in many cases, like the decaying faith in astrology, the delusion left behind it nothing but a stupid fatalism.

One or two minor forms of this superstition, pyromancy, chiromancy,[3] and others, which obtained some credit as the belief in sorcery and astrology was declining, may be here passed over, and even the pseudo-science of physiognomy has by no means the interest which the name might lead us to expect. For it did not appear as the sister and ally of art and psychology, but as a new form of fatalistic superstition, and, what it may have been among the Arabians, as the rival of astrology. The author of a physiognomical treatise, Bartolommeo Cocle, who styled himself a " metoposcopist,"[4] and whose science, according to Giovio, seemed like one of the most respectable of the free arts, was not content with the prophecies which he made to the many clever people who daily consulted him, but wrote also a most serious " catalogue of such whom great dangers of life were awaiting." Giovio, although grown old in the free thought of Rome—" in hac luce romana "—is of opinion that the predictions contained therein had only too much truth in them.[5] We learn

---

[1] Uberti, *Dittamondo*, iii, cap. 1. In the March of Ancona he visits Scariotto, the supposed birthplace of Judas, and observes: " I must not here pass over Mount Pilatus, with its lake, where throughout the summer the guards are changed regularly. For he who understands magic comes up hither to have his books consecrated, whereupon, as the people of the place say, a great storm arises." (The consecration of books, as has been remarked, p. 501, is a special ceremony, distinct from the rest.) In the sixteenth century the ascent of Pilatus near Lucerne was forbidden " by lib und guot," as Diebold Schilling records. It was believed that in the lake on the mountain lay a ghost, which was the spirit of Pilate. When people ascended the mountain or threw anything into the lake fearful storms sprang up.

[2] *De Obsedione Tiphernatium*, 1474 (*Rer. Ital. Script. ex Florent. Codicibus*, tom. ii).

[3] This superstition, which was widely spread among the soldiery (about 1520), is ridiculed by Limerno Pitocco in the *Orlandino*, v, 60.

[4] Paul. Jovius, *Elog. Lit.*, p. 106, under " Cocles," Barthol. Coclitis, *Chiromantia et Physiognomia Anaphrasis* (Bologna, 1523). Most important is Cardanus in his *Metoposcopia*, lib. 13.

[5] It is the enthusiastic collector of portraits who is speaking here.

from the same source how the people aimed at in these and similar prophecies took vengeance on the seer. Giovanni Bentivoglio caused Lucas Gauricus to be five times swung to and fro against the wall, on a rope hanging from a lofty winding staircase, because Lucas had foretold to him the loss of his authority.[1] Ermes Bentivoglio sent an assassin after Cocle, because the unlucky "metoposcopist" had unwillingly prophesied to him that he would die an exile in battle. The murderer seems to have derided the dying man in his last moments, saying that the prophet had foretold to him that he would shortly commit an infamous murder. The reviver of chiromancy, Antioco Tiberto of Cesena,[2] came by an equally miserable end at the hands of Pandolfo Malatesta of Rimini, to whom he had prophesied the worst that a tyrant can imagine—namely, death in exile and in the most grievous poverty. Tiberto was a man of intelligence, who was supposed to give his answers less according to any methodical chiromancy than by means of his shrewd knowledge of mankind; and his high culture won for him the respect of those scholars who thought little of his divination.[3]

Alchemy, in conclusion, which is not mentioned in antiquity till quite late under Diocletian, played only a very subordinate part at the best period of the Renaissance.[4] Italy went through the disease earlier, when Petrarch in the fourteenth century confessed, in his polemic against it, that gold-making was a general practice.[5] Since then that particular kind of faith, devotion, and isolation which the practice of alchemy required became more and more rare in Italy, just when Italian and other adepts began to make their full profit out of the great lords in the North.[6] Under Leo X the few Italians who busied themselves with it were called *ingenia curiosa*,[7] and Aurelio Augurelli, who dedicated to Leo X, the great despiser of gold, his didactic poem on the making of the metal is said to have received in return a beautiful but empty purse. The mystic science which besides gold sought for the omnipotent philosopher's stone is a late Northern growth, which had its rise in the theories of Paracelsus and others.

[1] From the stars, since Gauricus did not know physiognomy. For his own fate he had to refer to the prophecies of Cocle, since his father had omitted to draw his horoscope. [In fact, the punishment Gauricus suffered was less severe than that described in the text. *Cf.* Ronchini, *Atti e Memorie, Napoli*, vii. Also certain writings by Gabotto 1892 and Percopo 1895.—L. G.]

[2] Paul. Jovius, *loc. cit.*, pp. 100 *sqq.*, under Tibertus.

[3] The most essential facts as to these side-branches of divination are given by Corn. Agrippa, *De Occulta Philosophia*, cap. 57.

[4] Libri, *Histoire des Sciences Mathématiques*, ii, 122.

[5] "Novi nihil narro, mos est publicus" (*Remed. utr. Fort.*, p. 93), one of the lively passages of this book, written "ab irato."

[6] Chief passage in Trithem., *Ann. Hirsaug.*, ii, 286 *sqq.*

[7] "Neque enim desunt," Paul. Jovius, *Elog. Lit.*, p. 150, under "Pomp. Gauricus"; *cf. ibid.*, p. 130, under "Aurel. Augurellus," *Macaroneide, Phant.* xii.

CHAPTER V

GENERAL DISINTEGRATION OF BELIEF

ITH these superstitions, as with ancient modes of thought generally, the decline in the belief of immortality stands in the closest connexion.[1] This question has the widest and deepest relations with the whole development of the modern spirit.

One great source of doubt in immortality was the inward wish to be under no obligations to the hated Church. We have seen that the Church branded those who thus felt as Epicureans (pp. 477 *sqq.*). In the hour of death many doubtless called for the Sacraments, but multitudes during their whole lives, and especially during their most vigorous years, lived and acted on the negative supposition. That unbelief on this particular point must often have led to a general scepticism is evident of itself, and is attested by abundant historical proof. These are the men of whom Ariosto says: " Their faith goes no higher than the roof." [2] In Italy, and especially in Florence, it was possible to live as an open and notorious unbeliever if a man only refrained from direct acts of hostility against the Church.[3] The confessor, for instance, who was sent to prepare a political offender for death began by inquiring whether the prisoner was a believer, " for there was a false report that he had no belief at all." [4]

The unhappy transgressor here referred to—the same Pietro Paolo Boscoli who has been already mentioned (p. 80)—who in 1513 took part in an attempt against the newly restored family of the Medici, is a faithful mirror of the religious confusion then prevalent. Beginning as a partisan of Savonarola, he became afterward possessed with an enthusiasm for the ancient ideals of liberty, and for paganism in general; but when he was in prison his early friends regained the control of his mind and secured for him what they considered a pious ending. The tender witness and narrator of his last hours is one of the artistic family of the Della Robbia, the learned philologist Luca. " Ah," sighs Boscoli, " get Brutus out of my head for me, that I may go my way as

---

[1] In writing a history of Italian unbelief it would be necessary to refer to the so-called Averrhoism which was prevalent in Italy and especially in Venice about the middle of the fourteenth century. It was opposed by Boccaccio and Petrarch in various letters, and by the latter in his work *De Sui Ipsius et Aliorum Ignorantia.* Although Petrarch's opposition may have been increased by misunderstanding and exaggeration, he was nevertheless fully convinced that the Averrhoists ridiculed and rejected the Christian religion.

[2] Ariosto, *Sonetto*, 34: " Non credere sopra il tetto." The poet uses the words of an official who had decided against him in a matter of property.

[3] We may here again refer to Gemisthos Plethon, whose disregard of Christianity had an important influence on the Italians, and particularly on the Florentines of that period.

[4] *Narrazione del Caso del Boscoli, Archiv. Stor.*, i, 273 *sqq.* The standing phrase was " non aver fede "; *cf.* Vasari, vii, 122, *Vita di Piero di Cosimo.*

a Christian." "If you will," answers Luca, "the thing is not difficult; for you know that these deeds of the Romans are not handed down to us as they were, but idealized [*con arte accresciute*]." The penitent now forces his understanding to believe, and bewails his inability to believe voluntarily. If he could only live for a month with pious monks he would truly become spiritually minded. It comes out that these partisans of Savonarola know their Bible very imperfectly; Boscoli can only say the *Paternoster* and *Ave Maria*, and earnestly begs Luca to exhort his friends to study the sacred writings, for only what a man has learned in life does he possess in death. Luca then reads and explains to him the story of the Passion according to the Gospel of St Matthew; the poor listener, strange to say, can perceive clearly the Godhead of Christ, but is perplexed at His manhood; he wishes to get as firm a hold of it "as if Christ came to meet him out of a wood." His friend thereupon exhorts him to be humble, since this was only a doubt sent him by the devil. Soon after it occurs to the penitent that he has not fulfilled a vow made in his youth to go on pilgrimage to the Impruneta; his friend promises to do it in his stead. Meantime the confessor—a monk, as was desired, from Savonarola's monastery—arrives, and, after giving him the explanation quoted above of the opinion of St Thomas Aquinas on tyrannicide, exhorts him to bear death manfully. Boscoli makes answer: "Father, waste no time on this; the philosophers have taught it me already; help me to bear death out of love to Christ." What follows—the communion, the leave-taking, and the execution—is very touchingly described. One point deserves special mention. When Boscoli laid his head on the block he begged the executioner to delay the stroke for a moment:

> During the whole time since the announcement of the sentence he had been striving after a close union with God, without attaining it as he wished, and now in this supreme moment he thought that by a strong effort he could give himself wholly to God.

It is clearly some half-understood expression of Savonarola that was troubling him.

If we had more confessions of this character the spiritual picture of the time would be the richer by many important features which no poem or treatise has preserved for us. We should see more clearly how strong the inborn religious instinct was, how subjective and how variable the relation of the individual to religion, and what powerful enemies and competitors religion had. That men whose inward condition is of this nature are not the men to found a new Church is evident; but the history of the Western spirit would be imperfect without a view of that fermenting period among the Italians, while other nations, who have had no share in the evolution of thought, may be passed over without loss. But we must return to the question of immortality.

If unbelief in this respect made such progress among the more highly cultivated natures the reason lay partly in the fact that the great earthly task of discovering the world and representing it in word and form absorbed most of the higher spiritual faculties. We have already spoken (p. 473) of the inevitable worldliness of the Renaissance. But this investigation and this art were necessarily accompanied by a general spirit of doubt and inquiry. If this spirit shows itself but little in literature, if we find, for example, only isolated instances of the beginnings of Biblical criticism (p. 449), we are not therefore to infer that it had no existence. The sound of it was overpowered only by the need of representation and creation in all departments—that is, by the artistic instinct; and it was further checked, whenever it tried to express itself theoretically, by the already existing despotism of the Church. This spirit of doubt must, for reasons too obvious to need discussion, have inevitably and chiefly busied itself with the question of the state of man after death.

And here came in the influence of antiquity, and worked in a twofold fashion on the argument. In the first place men set themselves to master the psychology of the ancients, and tortured the letter of Aristotle for a decisive answer. In one of the Lucianic dialogues of the time [1] Charon tells Mercury how he questioned Aristotle on his belief in immortality when the philosopher crossed in the Stygian boat; but the prudent sage, although dead in the body and nevertheless living on, declined to compromise himself by a definite answer—and centuries later how was it likely to fare with the interpretation of his writings? All the more eagerly did men dispute about his opinion and that of others on the true nature of the soul, its origin, its pre-existence, its unity in all men, its absolute eternity, even its transformations; and there were men who treated of these things in the pulpit.[2] The dispute was warmly carried on even in the fifteenth century; some proved that Aristotle taught the doctrine of an immortal soul;[3] others complained of the hardness of men's hearts, who would not believe that there was a soul at all till they saw it sitting down on a chair before them;[4] Filelfo in his funeral oration on Francesco Sforza brings forward a long list of opinions of ancient and even of Arabian philosophers in favour of immortality, and closes the mixture, which covers a folio page and a half of print,[5] with the words: "Besides all this we have the Old and New Testaments, which are above all truth." Then came the Florentine Platonists with their master's doctrine of the soul, supplemented at times, as in the case of Pico, by Christian teaching. But the opposite opinion prevailed in the instructed world. At the beginning of the sixteenth century the stumbling-block which it put in the way of the Church was so serious that Leo X set forth a Constitution [6] at the Lateran Council in 1513 in defence of the immortality and individuality of the soul, the latter against those who asserted that there was but one soul in all men. A few years later appeared the work of Pomponazzo, in which the impossibility of a philosophical proof of immortality is maintained; and the contest was now waged incessantly with replies and apologies, till it was silenced by the Catholic reaction. The pre-existence of the soul in God, conceived more or less in accordance with Plato's

---

[1] Jov. Pontan., *Charon, Opp.*, ii, 1128-1195. [2] *Faustini Terdocei Triumphus Stultitiæ*, lib. ii.
[3] For example, Borbone Morosini about 1460; *cf.* Sansovino, *Venezia*, lib. xiii, p. 243. He wrote " de immortalite animæ ad mentem Aristotelis." Pomponius Lætus, as a means of effecting his release from prison, pointed to the fact that he had written an epistle on the immortality of the soul. See the remarkable defence in Gregorovius, vii, 580 *sqq.* See, on the other hand, Pulci's ridicule of this belief in a sonnet, quoted by Galeotti, *Archiv. Stor. Ital.*, postscript, ix, 49 *sqq.*   [4] Vespas. Fiorent., p. 260.
[5] *Orationes Philelphi*, fol. 18.   [6] *Septimo Decretal.*, lib. v, tit. iii, cap. 8.

theory of ideas, long remained a common belief, and proved of service even to the poets.[1] The consequences which followed from it as to the mode of the soul's continued existence after death were not more closely conside...

There was a second way in which the influence of antiquity made itsel... chiefly by means of that remarkable fragment of the sixth book of Cic... *Republic* known by the name of " Scipio's Dream." Without the commen... of Macrobius it would probably have perished like the rest of the second... of the work; it was now diffused in countless manuscript copies,[2] and, after... discovery of typography, in a printed form, and edited afresh by various co... mentators. It is the description of a transfigured hereafter for great me... pervaded by the harmony of the spheres. This pagan heaven, for which man... other testimonies were gradually extracted from the writings of the ancients... came step by step to supplant the Christian heaven in proportion as the ideal... of fame and historical greatness threw into the shade the ideal of the Christian... life, without, nevertheless, the public feeling being thereby offended, as it was... by the doctrine of personal annihilation after death. Even Petrarch founds his hope chiefly on this dream of Scipio, on the declarations found in other Ciceronian works, and on Plato's *Phædo*, without making any mention of the Bible.[3] " Why," he asks elsewhere, " should not I as a Catholic share a hope which was demonstrably cherished by the heathen? " Soon afterward Coluccio Salutati wrote his *Labours of Hercules* (still existing in manuscript), in which it is proved at the end that the valorous man, who has well endured the great labours of earthly life, is justly entitled to a dwelling among the stars.[4] If Dante still firmly maintained that the great pagans, whom he would have gladly welcomed in Paradise, nevertheless must not come beyond the Limbo at the entrance to Hell,[5] the poetry of a later time accepted joyfully the new liberal ideas of a future life. Cosimo the Elder, according to Bernardo Pulci's poem on his death, was received in Heaven by Cicero, who had also been called the " father of his country," by the Fabii, by Curius, Fabricius, and many others; with them he would adorn the choir where only blameless spirits sing.[6]

But in the old writers there was another and less pleasing picture of the world to come—the shadowy realms of Homer and of those poets who had not sweetened and humanized the conception. This made an impression on certain temperaments. Gioviano Pontano somewhere attributes to Sannazaro the story of a vision which he beheld one morning early, while half awake.[7] He seemed to see a departed friend, Ferrandus Januarius, with whom he had often

---

[1] Ariosto, *Orlando*, vii, 61. Ridiculed in *Orlandino*, iv, 67 and 68. Cariteo, a member of the Neapolitan Academy of Pontanus, uses the idea of the pre-existence of the soul in order to glorify the house of Aragon. Roscoe, *Leo X*, ed. Bossi, ii, 288.

[2] Orelli, *ad* Cic., *De Republ.*, lib. vi. *Cf.* Lucan, *Pharsalia*, ix, at the beginning.

[3] Petrarch, *Epist. Fam.*, iv, 3; iv, 6.

[4] Fil. Villani, *Vite*, p. 15. This remarkable passage is as follows: " Che agli uomini fortissimi poichè hanno vinto le mostruose fatiche della terra, debitamente sieno date le stelle."

[5] *Inferno*, iv, 24 *sqq.* Cf. *Purgatorio*, vii, 28; xxii, 100.

[6] This pagan heaven is referred to in the epitaph on the artist Niccolò dell' Arca:

" Nunc te Praxiteles, Phidias, Polycletus adorant
Miranturque tuas, o Nicolæ, manus."

In Bursellis, *Ann. Bonon.*, in Murat., xxiii, col. 912.

[7] In his late work *Actius*.

discoursed on the immortality of the soul, and whom he now asked whether it was true that the pains of hell were really dreadful and eternal. The shadow gave an answer like that of Achilles when Odysseus questioned him. " So much I tell and aver to thee, that we who are parted from earthly life have the strongest desire to return to it again." He then saluted his friend and disappeared.

It cannot but be recognized that such views of the state of man after death partly presuppose and partly promote the dissolution of the most essential dogmas of Christianity. The notion of sin and salvation must have almost entirely evaporated. We must not be misled by the effects of the great preachers of repentance or by the epidemic revivals which have been described above (Part VI, Chapter II). For even granting that the individually developed classes had shared in them like the rest, the cause of their participation was rather the need of emotional excitement, the rebound of passionate natures, the horror felt at great national calamities, the cry to heaven for help. The awakening of the conscience had by no means necessarily the sense of sin and the felt need of salvation as its consequence, and even a very severe outward penance did not perforce involve any repentance in the Christian meaning of the word. When the powerful natures of the Renaissance tell us that their principle is to repent of nothing [1] they may have in their minds only matters that are morally indifferent, faults of unreason or imprudence; but in the nature of the case this contempt for repentance must extend to the sphere of morals, because its origin —namely, the consciousness of individual force—is common to both sides of human nature. The passive and contemplative form of Christianity, with its constant reference to a higher world beyond the grave, could no longer control these men. Machiavelli ventured still farther, and maintained that it could not be serviceable to the State and to the maintenance of public freedom.[2]

The form assumed by the strong religious instinct which, notwithstanding all, survived in many natures was theism or deism, as we may please to call it. The latter name may be applied to that mode of thought which simply wiped away the Christian element out of religion, without either seeking or finding any other substitute for the feelings to rest upon. Theism may be considered that definite heightened devotion to the one Supreme Being which the Middle Ages were not acquainted with. This mode of faith does not exclude Christianity, and can either ally itself with the Christian doctrines of sin, redemption, and immortality, or else exist and flourish without them.

Sometimes this belief presents itself with childish naïveté and even with a half-pagan air, God appearing as the almighty fulfiller of human wishes. Agnolo Pandolfini [3] tells us how after his wedding he shut himself in with his wife, and knelt down before the family altar with the picture of the Madonna, and prayed not to her, but to God, that He would vouchsafe to them the right use of their property, a long life in joy and unity with each other, and many

[1] Cardanus, De Vita Propria, cap. 13: "Non pœnitere ullius rei quam voluntarie effecerim, etiam quæ male cessisset"; else I should be of all men the most miserable.

[2] Discorsi, ii, cap. 2.

[3] Del Governo della Famiglia, p. 114.

male descendants: "for myself I prayed for wealth, honour, and friends, for her blamelessness, honesty, and that she might be a good housekeeper." When the language used has a strong antique flavour it is not always easy to keep apart the pagan style and the theistic belief.[1]

This temper sometimes manifests itself in times of misfortune with a striking sincerity. Some addresses to God are left us from the latter period of Firenzuola, when for years he lay ill of fever, in which, though he expressly declares himself a believing Christian, he shows that his religious consciousness is essentially theistic.[2] His sufferings seem to him neither as the punishment of sin nor as preparation for a higher world; they are an affair between him and God only, Who has put the strong love of life between man and his despair. "I curse, but only curse nature, since Thy greatness forbids me to utter Thy name. . . . Give me death, Lord, I beseech Thee, give it me now!"

In these utterances and the like it would be vain to look for a conscious and consistent theism; the speakers partly believed themselves to be still Christians, and for various other reasons respected the existing doctrines of the Church. But at the time of the Reformation, when men were driven to come to a distinct conclusion on such points, this mode of thought came forward as a fuller consciousness; a number of the Italian Protestants came forward as Anti-Trinitarians and Socinians, and even as exiles in distant countries made the memorable attempt to found a Church on these principles. From the foregoing exposition it will be clear that apart from humanistic rationalism other spirits were at work in this field.

One chief centre of theistic modes of thought lay in the Platonic Academy at Florence, and especially in Lorenzo the Magnificent himself. The theoretical works and even the letters of these men show us only half their nature. It is true that Lorenzo, from his youth till he died, expressed himself dogmatically as a Christian,[3] and that Pico was drawn by Savonarola's influence to accept the point of view of a monkish ascetic.[4] But in the hymns of Lorenzo,[5] which we

---

[1] *Cf.* the short ode of M. Antonio Flaminio in the *Coryciana* (see p. 270):

> "Dii quibus tam Corycius venusta
> Signa, tam dives posuit sacellum,
> Ulla si vestros animos piorum
> Gratia tangit,
>
> Vos jocos risusque senis faceti
> Sospites servate diu: senectam
> Vos date et semper viridem et Falerno
> Usque madentem.
>
> At simul longo satiatus aevo
> Liquerit terras, dapibus Deorum
> Laetus intersit, potiore mutans
> Nectare Bacchum."

[2] Firenzuola, *Opere*, iv, pp. 147 *sqq.*

[3] Nic. Valori, *Vita di Lorenzo, passim.* For the advice to his son, Cardinal Giovanni, see Fabroni, *Laurentius*, note 178, and the appendices to Roscoe's *Lorenzo de' Medici.*

[4] *Jo. Pici Vita,* auct. Jo. Franc. Pico. For his *Deprecatio ad Deum* see *Deliciae Poetarum Italorum.*

[5] *Orazione,* Roscoe, *Leo X,* ed. Bossi, viii, 120 ("Magno Dio per la cui costante legge"); hymn ("oda il sacro inno tutta la natura") in Fabroni, *Laurentius,* Adnot. 9; *L'Altercazione,* in the *Poesie di Lor. Magn.,* i, 265. The other poems here named are quoted in the same collection. [Bonardi (*Giorn. Stor.,* xxxiii, pp. 77–82) has shown that at least three of these hymns are translations of older ones.—W. G.]

are tempted to regard as the highest product of the spirit of this school, an unreserved theism is set forth—a theism which strives to treat the world as a great moral and physical cosmos. While the men of the Middle Ages look on the world as a vale of tears, which Pope and Emperor are set to guard against the coming of Antichrist, while the fatalists of the Renaissance oscillate between seasons of overflowing energy and seasons of superstition or of stupid resignation, here in this circle of chosen spirits [1] the doctrine is upheld that the visible world was created by God in love, that it is the copy of a pattern pre-existing in Him, and that He will ever remain its eternal mover and restorer. The soul of man can by recognizing God draw Him into its narrow boundaries, but also by love to Him itself expand into the Infinite—and this is blessedness on earth.

Echoes of medieval mysticism here flow into one current with Platonic doctrines, and with a characteristically modern spirit. One of the most precious fruits of the knowledge of the world and of man here comes to maturity, on whose account alone the Italian Renaissance must be called the leader of modern ages.

[1] If Pulci in his *Morgante* is anywhere in earnest with religion, he is so in canto xvi, str. 6. This deistic utterance of the fair pagan Antea is perhaps the plainest expression of the mode of thought prevalent in Lorenzo's circle, to which tone the words of the dæmon Astarotte (quoted above, p. 476) form in a certain sense the complement.

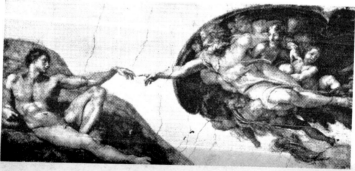

FIG. 234. THE CREATION OF ADAM
By Michelangelo
Rome, Sixtine Chapel

INDEX TO VOLUME II

INDEX

INDEX

INDEX

INDEX

INDEX